FAMILY THERAPY REVIEW

This unique text uses one common case to demonstrate the applications of a wide range of family therapy models. Readers will find it useful when studying for the national family therapy licensing exam, which requires that exam takers be able to apply these models to case vignettes. The authors, all of whom are practicing family therapists, apply their chosen model of family therapy to a single, hypothetical case to highlight what each model looks like in practice. Beginning therapists will find the exposure to new ideas about therapy useful and will be better able to establish which approaches they want to explore in more depth. Experienced therapists and supervisors will find it useful to understand what "those other family therapists" are doing and to meet the challenge of supervising those from different perspectives. *Family Therapy Review* is the practical tool therapists need to make sense of the field and meet the varied challenges their clients present.

Anne Rambo, Ph.D., has taught in Nova Southeastern University's family therapy program for over 20 years and has supervised hundreds of students who are now licensed marriage and family therapists (MFTs). She has a strong interest in training and supervision.

Charles West, Ph.D., is administrative faculty in the marriage and family therapy program at Northcentral University. He is a past president of the Association of Marital and Family Therapy Regulatory Boards and has extensive clinical and supervision experience.

AnnaLynn Schooley, Ph.D., has taught for many years for Capella University, the home of the nation's largest marriage and family therapy program. She has been an agency clinical director as well as an academic and private practitioner, specializing in supervision for licensure.

Tommie V. Boyd, Ph.D., is the chair of the family therapy department at Nova Southeastern University and on faculty. She also has over 30 years of clinical and supervision experience and is the recipient of an American Association for Marriage and Family Therapy (AAMFT) Leadership Award.

FAMILY THERAPY REVIEW

Contrasting Contemporary Models

Edited by Anne Rambo, Charles West,
AnnaLynn Schooley, and Tommie V. Boyd

Routledge
Taylor & Francis Group

NEW YORK AND LONDON

First published 2013
by Routledge
711 Third Avenue, New York, NY 10017

Simultaneously published in the UK
by Routledge
27 Church Road, Hove, East Sussex BN3 2FA

Routledge is an imprint of the Taylor & Francis Group, an informa business

Library of Congress Cataloging in Publication Data
Family therapy review : contrasting contemporary models / edited by
Anne Rambo ... [et al.].
p. cm.
Includes bibliographical references and index.
ISBN 978-0-415-80662-6 (hardback) —
ISBN 978-0-415-80663-3 (paperback)
1. Family psychotherapy—Case studies.   2. Psychotherapist and patient—Case studies.
I. Rambo, Anne Hearon.

RC488.5.F3492   2012

616.89'156—dc23   2012007313

ISBN: 978-0-415-80662-6 (hbk)
ISBN: 978-0-415-80663-3 (pbk)
ISBN: 978-0-203-10319-7 (ebk)

Typeset in Bembo
by Apex CoVantage, LLC

To our students, who are the future of family therapy; and with grateful appreciation to our spouses, Irving, Diana, Melody, and Bill.

CONTENTS

EDITOR AND CONTRIBUTOR BIOGRAPHIES

Editors' Note: All of the authors who contributed to this book actually practice the model or approach about which they write. We tried to select those with extensive clinical as well as supervisory and training experience.

Christine Ajayi, Ph.D.—Dr. Ajayi has served as the director of counseling services at New Mount Zion AME Church in Tallahassee, Florida, and is currently visiting professor at Nova Southeastern University. She is involved with the Program for Strengthening African American Marriages (ProSAAM) project and has helped to publish some of the program's findings. She has received extensive training on issues of cultural competence as a SAMHSA/AAMFT Minority Fellow and a Florida Education Fund McKnight Doctoral Fellow.

Harlene Anderson, Ph.D.—Dr. Anderson is a founding member of *Access-Success,* the Houston Galveston Institute, and the Taos Institute. She has written widely on collaborative approaches, including the books *Conversation, Language and Possibilities, Appreciative Organizations,* and *Collaborative Therapy: Relationships and Conversations That Make a Difference.* She is the recipient of the 2000 American Association for Marriage and Family Therapy Outstanding Contributions to Marriage and Family Therapy Award and the 2008 American Academy of Family Therapy Award for Distinguished Contribution to Family Therapy Theory and Practice.

Brent J. Atkinson, Ph.D.—Dr. Atkinson is principal architect of pragmatic experiential therapy, an approach that translates new knowledge about how the brain processes emotion into practical methods for improving relationships and increasing personal success. He is a widely known teacher, researcher, and therapist. Dr. Atkinson is director of postgraduate training at the Couples Clinic & Research Institute in Geneva, Illinois.

Brent Bradley, Ph.D.—Dr. Bradley is associate professor and director of the graduate family therapy program at the University of Houston–Clear Lake. Dr. Bradley is renowned for his research, writing, and experiential manner of training therapists for working deeply with emotion. He has widely published on emotionally focused therapy (EFT) and is coauthor and coeditor of the newly published *Emotionally Focused Couple Therapy Case Book: New Directions in Treating Couples.*

Monte Bobele, Ph.D.—Dr. Bobele is a professor of psychology at Our Lady of the Lake University in San Antonio and a faculty member of the Houston Galveston Institute. His many publications in the area of brief therapy include his recent book, *When One Hour Is All You Have: Effective Therapy for Walk-In Clients,* and numerous case studies including the classic *Interactional Treatment of Intractable Hiccups.* He is the recipient of a Fulbright Specialist award for his work in Mexico.

Virginia Boney, Ph.D.—Dr. Boney is the director of the Relationship Center of Jacksonville, Florida, and in addition to her private practice, she publishes and presents widely on couples therapy issues. She also teaches couples counseling at the University of North Florida. Dr. Boney is one of only two certified Gottman couples therapists in the southeast United States and is also trained in emotion focused couples therapy.

Charmaine Borda, Ph.D.—Dr. Borda is director at the Blue Couch, Inc., and an adjunct faculty at Nova Southeastern University. She has trained family therapy students together with Dr. Salvador Minuchin since 2008. Her areas of specialization are sexual abuse and trauma. She has worked closely with the Florida Department of Children and Families and other child-welfare organizations in Broward County, advocating for over a decade on behalf of abused, abandoned, neglected, and maltreated youths.

Tommie V. Boyd, Ph.D.—Dr. Boyd is chair of the family therapy department and an associate professor at Nova Southeastern University. She has published and presented widely in the areas of medical family therapy and training and supervision. Her recent research includes grant-funded projects on family therapy with Parkinson's patients and their caregivers, returning veterans, and patients with autism spectrum disorders. She is a past president of the Florida Association for Marriage and Family Therapy (FAMFT) and has been active at the state and national level in legislative and parity issues for medical family therapists. She is a recipient of the AAMFT Leadership Award.

Christopher Burnett, Psy.D.—Dr. Burnett is a professor of family therapy at Nova Southeastern University. His area of specialty is Bowen Systems Theory. He was a featured presenter at the 2001, 2005, and 2007 AAMFT Advanced

Clinical Training Institutes and has worked for over 15 years as an independent human systems consultant in both the corporate and not-for-profit sectors. His clients have ranged from multimillion-dollar public corporations to institutions of higher education, county government, and United Way–supported community organizations.

Ronald J. Chenail, Ph.D.—Dr. Chenail is vice president for institutional effectiveness and professor of family therapy at Nova Southeastern University. He is the founding editor of the *Qualitative Report* and its sister publication, the *Weekly Qualitative Report,* as well as a past editor of the *Journal of Marital and Family Therapy.* His books include *Medical Discourse and Systemic Frames of Comprehension, Practicing Therapy: Exercises for Growing Therapists* (with Anne Rambo and Anthony Heath), *The Talk of the Clinic: Explorations in the Analysis of Medical and Therapeutic Discourse* (with Bud Morris), and *Qualitative Research Proposals and Reports: A Guide* (with Patricia Munhall).

Jacqueline Clarke, M.A.—Ms. Clarke holds an M.A. in counseling psychology from the Caribbean Graduate School of Theology in Kingston, Jamaica. She has been an instructor at the Jamaica Theological Seminary and a psychotherapist in the Cayman Islands. Her current research involves couples with differing faith backgrounds.

Pat Cole, Ph.D.—Dr. Cole is an associate professor of family therapy and family business at Nova Southeastern University. She directed the Family Business Institute and was cochair of the 2010 Family Enterprise Research Conference in Cancun, Mexico. She has published widely in the area of family relationships and family businesses, including her groundbreaking research with Dr. Kit Johnson on previously married couples who successfully continue to run businesses following their divorce.

Melissa Elliott, M.S.N.—Ms. Elliott is a family therapist and clinical nurse specialist at the University of Virginia Psychiatric Inpatient Unit. She has published and presented widely in the areas of medical family therapy and religious/spiritual issues in psychotherapy. She is coauthor of *Encountering the Sacred in Psychotherapy* and author of "Opening Therapy to Conversations with a Personal God" in *Spiritual Resources in Family Therapy* (ed. Froma Walsh).

Carmel Flaskas, M.A. Hons., HonD.—Dr. Flaskas is an associate professor in social work at the University of New South Wales, Sydney, where she convenes the master of couple and family therapy program. She has published widely on psychoanalytic ideas in the systemic context and on knowledge in family therapy. Dr. Flaskas has been awarded an honorary doctorate by the Tavistock Clinic in conjunction with the University of East London for her contributions to systemic psychotherapy and the ANZJFT (*Australian and New Zealand Journal of Family Therapy*) award for Distinguished Contributions to Australian Family Therapy.

Douglas Flemons, Ph.D.—Dr. Flemons is a professor of family therapy at Nova Southeastern University (NSU) and codirector of the NSU Office of Suicide and Violence Prevention. He is the author of three books—*Of One Mind, Writing Between the Lines,* and *Completing Distinctions*—and coauthor of a fourth, the forthcoming *Therapeutic Suicide Assessment.* He has published and presented widely in the areas of hypnotherapy, psychotherapy, Eastern philosophy, and suicide prevention. Dr. Flemons and his wife, Dr. Shelley Green, coedited *Quickies: The Handbook of Brief Sex Therapy* and serve as codirectors of Context Consultants in East Fort Lauderdale, Florida, where Dr. Flemons has a practice specializing in hypnotherapy and brief therapy.

Shelley Green, Ph.D.—Dr. Green, a professor of family therapy at Nova Southeastern University (NSU), has published and presented widely in the areas of AIDS/HIV, sexuality, clinical supervision, and qualitative research. Dr. Green and her husband, Dr. Douglas Flemons, coedited *Quickies: The Handbook of Brief Sex Therapy* and serve as codirectors of Context Consultants, a private practice in East Fort Lauderdale, Florida, where Dr. Green specializes in working with clients' sexual issues. Dr. Green also serves as training director for Stable Foundations, which, in collaboration with the family therapy program at NSU, offers equine-assisted family therapy on a 15-acre ranch near the NSU campus.

Mary Hale-Haniff, Ph.D.—Dr. Hale-Haniff has an extensive private practice. She has presented nationally and internationally on helping families and organizations change and has worked with Virginia Satir on explicating holistic aspects of Satir's way of knowing. She is a past president of the Florida Association for Marriage and Family Therapy and is active nationally on professional boards.

Tyon L. Hall, M.S.—Ms. Hall works with the Veterans Administration as a readjustment counseling therapist. She is an experienced couples therapist and is currently researching couples therapy with military families. She is president and CEO of the Abdon Group, a private practice.

Terry D. Hargrave, Ph.D.—Dr. Hargrave is a professor of marriage and family therapy at Fuller Theological Seminary and is president and in practice at Amarillo Family Institute. He has authored numerous professional articles and 11 books, including *Restoration Therapy: Understanding and Guiding Healing in Marriage and Family Therapy* (coauthored with Franz Pfitzer) and *The Essential Humility of Marriage: Honoring the Third Identity in Couple Therapy.* He has been selected as a national conference plenary speaker and as a master's series therapist by the American Association for Marriage and Family Therapy.

Randy J. Heller, Ph.D.—In addition to being a family therapist, Dr. Heller is a certified Supreme Court family mediator, certified hypnotherapist, and founder of the Family Network. She has received specialized training in collaborative family law.

Through the Family Network, she practices with family law attorneys and neutral financial professionals as part of a team to facilitate the peaceful resolution of issues related to marital dissolution. She is a Florida- and AAMFT-approved supervisor.

James Hibel, Ph.D.–Dr. Hibel is the senior associate dean for institutional enhancement in the division of applied interdisciplinary studies at Nova Southeastern University. He has been in private practice as a family therapist, in Palm Beach Gardens, Florida, since 1980. He has published and presented widely on narrative practices, assessing outcomes in clinical training programs, and supervision issues.

Edith Huntley, Ph.D.–Dr. Huntley is in private practice and has published and presented on self of therapist issues. She is currently at work on a book about the influence of Virginia Satir in the field of family therapy. She is the former mental health director of Bay Point Schools, a group of residential treatment facilities.

James Keim, M.S.W.—Mr. Keim was the director of training for Jay Haley and Cloe Madanes at the Family Therapy Institute of Washington. He is coauthor of the book *The Violence of Men* with Cloe Madanes and Dinah Smelser and a contributor to many other books on psychotherapy. He is a founder of the Children's Organization of Southeast Asia, which provides shelter, safety, and a positive future to girls and young women who are at risk or victims of trafficking, sexual exploitation, and abuse.

Mathis Kennington, M.MFT.—Mr. Kennington was a 2010 AAMFT minority fellow. He has conducted collaborative research with the Virginia Department of Corrections on the relationship of incarcerated parents with their children. He has published and presented in the areas of social justice and diversity.

Trahern LaFavor, M.S.—Mr. LaFavor works in the MST program for Henderson Behavioral Health Center. At the 2008 MST International Conference, Mr. LaFavor was awarded the Sustained Excellence Award for his superior therapeutic outcomes. Mr. LaFavor is also active in faith-based work and is completing his doctoral degree.

Sue Levin, Ph.D.—Dr. Levin is executive director of the Houston Galveston Institute (HGI), an associate of the Taos Institute, and faculty at Our Lady of the Lake University. She has published and presented widely on collaborative approaches and has led HGI's outreach work to the community after hurricanes Katrina, Rita, and Ike. She is the recipient of an Outstanding Contribution Award by the Taos Institute.

Howard A. Liddle, Ed.D., ABPP—Dr. Liddle is professor in the departments of epidemiology and public health, psychology, and counseling psychology and director of the Center for Treatment Research on Adolescent Substance Abuse at the University of Miami. He is the author of numerous articles and books on multidimensional family therapy (MDFT) and other works including *Family*

Psychology: Science-Based Interventions and *Handbook of Family Therapy Training and Supervision*. His many awards include the Hazelden Foundation Dan Anderson Research Award and the American Family Therapy Academy (AFTA) Distinguished Contribution to Research Award.

Marion Lindblad-Goldberg, Ph.D.—Dr. Lindblad-Goldberg is clinical professor of psychology in the University of Pennsylvania School of Medicine in Philadelphia. She is also director of the Philadelphia Child and Family Therapy Training Center. Her numerous books include *Creating Competence from Chaos: A Comprehensive Guide to Home Based Services,* with Martha Morrison Dore and Lenora Stern, which became the foundation for the Family Based Mental Health Services Program implemented throughout the state of Pennsylvania.

Sylvia London, M.A.—Ms. London is a founding member and faculty at Grupo Campos Eliseos, an independent institute in Mexico City interested in the application of postmodern and social-constructionist ideas in multiple settings. She teaches, trains, and consults to a number of universities and institutions around the world. She is faculty at the Houston Galveston Institute, where she codirects the International Certificate in Collaborative Practices, and is an associate at the Taos Institute.

Stephen Madigan, Ph.D.—Dr. Madigan is the director of the Vancouver School for Narrative Therapy in Vancouver, Canada. He was recently awarded the American Family Therapy Association Distinguished Contributions to Innovative Practice Award and is the author of numerous books and articles, including the American Psychological Association's recently published book entitled *Narrative Therapy: Theory and Practice* and its accompanying six-part video series—*Narrative Therapy Through Time*. Dr. Madigan teaches narrative therapy workshops worldwide and hosts the annual International Therapeutic Conversations conference.

Martha Gonzalez Marquez, Ph.D.—Dr. Marquez spent six years on the faculty of the Gainesville Family Institute, a postgraduate training program in Gainesville, Florida, specializing in the oppression sensitive model of family therapy developed by doctors Andrés Nazario, Jr., Herb Steier, and Gina Early. She is now associate chair of the family therapy program at Nova Southeastern University. While presenting and publishing on the cultural awareness model developed through her research, Dr. Marquez also maintains an active private practice specializing in work with culturally diverse couples.

Kim Mason, M.S.W.—Ms. Mason is an FFT (functional family therapy) national supervisor and clinical coordinator for the Florida Redirection Project. Her work prior to coming to FFT included work with youth in crisis, residential services for girls who had been sexually abused, development of afterschool programs, development and facilitation of therapeutic groups for adolescent girls, and hospice-based work. She was a keynote speaker at the 2010 Evidence Based Practice Symposium.

Linda Metcalf, Ph.D.—Dr. Metcalf is a professor at Texas Wesleyan University in the department of education, where she is the coordinator of school counseling. She is a national and international presenter and the author of seven books on solution-focused therapy as well as the editor of *Marriage and Family Therapy: A Practice-Oriented Approach,* which she wrote with 19 of her graduate students. She is the current president of the American Association for Marriage and Family Therapy.

Tomomi Mikawa, M.A.—Ms. Mikawa is an associate faculty at Now I See a Person Institute and is a California marriage and family therapist registered intern, supervised by Dr. Susan E. Swim.

John K. Miller, Ph.D.—Dr. Miller is an associate professor at Nova Southeastern University and director of the Sino-American Family Therapy Institute. In 2009–2010, Dr. Miller won a Fulbright Senior Research Scholar award from the U.S. Department of State to live and conduct research for a yearlong project in Beijing, China. He has been a visiting faculty lecturer to many of the top psychology programs in Asia including Beijing Normal University, Fuzhou University (Fuzhou, China), Tongji University (Shanghai), Chinese University of Hong Kong (CUHK), Royal University of Phnom Penh (Cambodia), and Shaanxi Normal University (X'ian, China) and is actively engaged in several family therapy training projects in China and Southeast Asia.

Joan A. Muir, Ph.D.—Dr. Muir is the associate director of the Brief Strategic Family Therapy Institute, at the Center for Family Studies at the University of Miami, and the training director for the Center for Family Studies. She has published and presented widely on the brief strategic family therapy model as well as on cultural adaptations for family interventions.

Andrés Nazario, Jr., Ph.D.—While director of the Gainesville Family Institute, a postgraduate training program in Gainesville, Florida, Dr. Nazario developed the oppression-sensitive model of family therapy with Herb Steier and Gina Early. The Florida Association for Marriage and Family Therapy's annual award for a family therapist making significant contributions to diversity issues is named in his honor the Andrés Nazario Diversity Award. In addition to publishing and presenting internationally, Dr. Nazario maintains an active private practice.

Angela Priest, M.A.—Ms. Priest received her master of arts degree in marriage and family therapy from Alliant International University. She received her training in postmodern, social-constructionist thought at Now I See a Person Institute, where her focus was providing collaborative, recovery-focused care across a multitude of client issues, including depression, anxiety, family and relational issues, and social welfare cases, among others. Her research interests include the effects of collaborative therapeutic processes on the therapeutic relationship and the efficacy of the therapeutic process.

Jodi Aronson Prohofsky, Ph.D.—Dr. Prohofsky is senior vice president for clinical and network operations at Magellan Health Services. She has held various senior executive roles in other health services and insurance-based companies over the past 20 years. She is a certified intrinsic coach and Six Sigma Yellow Belt, in addition to being a family therapist.

Anne Rambo, Ph.D.—Dr. Rambo is an associate professor of family therapy at Nova Southeastern University. She is the recipient of the 2002 Andrés Nazario Diversity Award for her work with at-risk and special needs children in public schools. Her previous books include *Practicing Therapy: Exercises for Growing Therapists* (with Anthony Heath and Ronald J. Chenail) and *"I Know My Child Can Do Better": A Frustrated Parent's Guide to Educational Options.*

Jeff Randall, Ph.D.—Dr. Randall is an assistant professor in the Family Services Research Center of the department of psychiatry and behavioral sciences at the Medical University of South Carolina. He is the project director of a National Institute on Drug Abuse and National Institute on Alcohol Abuse and Alcoholism (NIDA/NIAAA)–funded project entitled "A Randomized Clinical Trial of Juvenile Drug Court and Multisystemic Therapy (MST)." This project is in its fourth year of funding and has recently received three additional years of funding from the Center for Substance Abuse Treatment for the continuation of clinical services.

Wendel A. Ray, Ph.D.—Dr. Ray is a professor in the marriage and family therapy program at the University of Louisiana at Monroe and a senior research fellow and former director of the Mental Research Institute (MRI). He is the author of numerous articles and 10 books on brief therapy and the history of family therapy. He conducts training in brief therapy internationally.

Paul Rhodes, Ph.D.—Dr. Rhodes is senior lecturer at the Clinical Psychology Unit, University of Sydney. He was the editor of *Australian and New Zealand Journal of Family Therapy* (2007–2009), the recipient of the 2005 Quality Service Award from Children's Hospital at Westmead for development of the Eating Disorders Family-Based Treatment Team, and the 2003 National Research Prize of the Australasian Society for the Scientific Study of Intellectual Disability. The author of numerous articles, book chapters, and books, his most recent book is *A Practical Guide to Family Therapy: Structured Guidelines and Key Skills* (with Andrew Wallis).

Michael Robbins, Ph.D.—Dr. Robbins is a senior scientist at the Oregon Research Institute, director of research for Functional Family Therapy, Inc., and a voluntary faculty member of the department of epidemiology and public health at the University of Miami School of Medicine. He has published and presented widely on both functional family therapy and brief strategic family therapy and has been the principal investigator on federally funded grants. His most recent book is *The Handbook of Family Therapy* (coedited with T. L. Sexton and G. Weeks).

Ruban Roberts, M.S.W.—Mr. Roberts is a senior trainer with the Brief Strategic Family Therapy Institute at the Center for Family Studies at the University of Miami. He is also a senior research associate at the University of Miami. He presents nationally on the BSFT model and is a member of the Miami–Dade County Juvenile Justice Board.

Brian Rosenberg, Ph.D.—Dr. Rosenberg is director of training and development at MEDNAX National Medical Group. Previously, he was director of organizational effectiveness for Broward Health. He also teaches and practices family therapy.

Jose Szapocznik, Ph.D.—Dr. Szapocznik is the director of the Center for Family Studies and a professor of both psychiatry and psychology at the University of Miami. He is also the associate dean for community development and the chair of the department of epidemiology and public health at the University of Miami Miller School of Medicine. His many publications in the area of brief strategic family therapy have earned him the American Association for Marriage and Family Therapy Outstanding Research Publications Award (2003).

AnnaLynn Schooley, Ph.D.—Dr. Schooley is core faculty in the counselor education program at Capella University and conducts ongoing research into online education for marriage and family therapists. She presents and publishes on qualitative research, supervision and training issues, and work with GLBT families. She has an extensive private practice focusing on supervision for licensure and is both a past president and current president elect of the Florida Association for Marriage and Family Therapy, and she is active in licensing issues nationally.

Richard Schwartz, Ph.D.—Dr. Schwartz is coauthor (with Michael Nichols) of *Family Therapy: Concepts and Methods,* the most widely used family therapy text in the United States. In 2000 he founded the Center for Self Leadership, a private practice and training facility that focuses on internal family systems, the model he originated. His many books include *Internal Family Systems Therapy,* and he presents internationally on the model.

Lee Shilts, Ph.D.—Dr. Shilts is a professor of marriage and family therapy at Capella University. Dr. Shilts has published numerous articles on applications of solution-focused brief therapy and, in 2003 (with Insoo Kim Berg), developed an innovative program called Working on What Works (WoWW), utilizing solution-focused concepts within school classrooms, which is now in use nationwide. Dr. Shilts has an active private practice with Psychological Associates of Broward.

Susan E. Swim, Ph.D.—Dr. Swim has been on faculty at the Houston Galveston Institute since the early 1980s, specializing in teaching and supervision from a social constructionist viewpoint, and was a long-term faculty member of the department of counseling and family sciences at Loma Linda University as well. She publishes and presents widely on collaborative and reflecting team approaches. She is the founder of Now I See a Person, an equine-assisted psychotherapy practice.

Margarita Tarragona, Ph.D.—Dr. Tarragona is one of Mexico City's most well-known therapists and teachers. She is a cofounder of Grupo Campos Elíseos and is on the graduate faculty of the psychology department of the Universidad Iberoamericana. She is also faculty of the Houston Galveston Institute and a member of the board of directors of the International Positive Psychology Association (IPPA).

Maelouise Tennant, Ph.D.—Ms. Tennant comes to family therapy from an extensive background in business. She is presently conducting research on the survivors of Ponzi schemes, using a narrative solutions framework. She has trained for several years with Joe Eron of the Catskill Family Institute in the narrative solutions approach and is in private practice at the Jupiter Counseling Center.

Holly Waldroon, Ph.D.—Dr. Waldroon is a research scientist at the Oregon Research Institute and director of the Center for Family and Adolescent Research in Albuquerque. She is an author on many research publications involving functional family therapy, including a meta-analysis of outcomes since 1971. She has also assisted in several federally funded research projects involving FFT (functional family therapy).

Marlene F. Watson, Ph.D.—Dr. Watson is an associate professor and former chair of the couple and family therapy department at Drexel University. She is the first marriage and family therapist to be awarded the prestigious Robert Wood Johnson Health Policy Fellowship Award. Dr. Watson received the 2009 American Family Therapy Academy's Distinguished Contribution to Social Justice Award and was recognized by the *Utne Reader* as one of 10 "cultural healers" nationwide for her work with substance-dependent prison inmates and their families.

Yulia Watters, Ph.D.—Dr. Watters has worked in a wide variety of medical and hospice settings, including the NSU medical center in the Internal Medicine and Geriatric Clinics, Vitas Innovative Hospice Care, Golf Coast Jewish Community

Services (Extended Geriatric Residential Treatment Program), the Southwest Focal Point Senior Center Geriatric Clinic, and the Federal Guidance Center for Suicidology at the Moscow Research Institute of Psychiatry, Russia. Dr. Watters publishes and presents internationally on medical family therapy issues and specializes in grief and loss. She has an extensive private practice.

Charles West, Ph.D.—Dr. West is core faculty for the marriage and family therapy program of Northcentral University. He is also past president of the Association of Marital and Family Therapy Regulatory Boards (AMFTRB). He has published and presented widely in the areas of professional regulation, ethics, and supervision. Dr. West maintains an active practice in third-wave behavioral couples therapy.

Cathie J. Witty, Ph.D.—Dr. Witty is the director of the conflict and peace studies program at the University of North Carolina at Greensboro. In addition to her Ph.D. in anthropology and her MPA, she earned an additional M.A. in marriage and family therapy in 2001 and has maintained a clinical practice with HIV/AIDS clients and child abuse survivors. Dr. Witty also worked for two years in Kosovo with Doctors of the World, USA, engaged in community building and advocacy work with families and disabled children.

Dan Wulff, Ph.D.—Dr. Wulff is an associate professor in the faculty of social work at the University of Calgary, as well as a family therapist and supervisor at the Calgary Family Therapy Centre (with Karl Tomm). He is a board member of the Taos Institute and a coeditor of the *Qualitative Report* (with Ronald J. Chenail). He values the many training experiences he had with Carl Whitaker.

Miyoung Yoon Hammer, Ph.D.—Dr. Hammer is an assistant professor of family therapy at Fuller Theological Seminary. She previously served as an associate faculty member at the Chicago Center for Family Health, an affi liate of the University of Chicago. The majority of Yoon Hammer's clinical experience has been in medical settings, providing therapy for patients and their families at clinics, cancer centers, and hospitals.

Monica Zarate, M.S. Ed.—Ms. Zarate is a Brief Strategic Family Therapy Institute senior trainer for the Center for Family Studies of the University of Miami. She has presented nationally and internationally on brief strategic family therapy. She has published on the topic of change processes in Hispanic families.

INTRODUCTION: ABOUT THIS BOOK

This book is an introduction to the vibrant and challenging "family" of family therapy approaches. It is a starting point for comparisons, contrasts, and decisions. Readers may find it helpful when studying for the national licensing exam, which requires reviewing all the extant models of family therapy, although information about ethics, laws, and basic accepted practice should be reviewed as well. Beginning therapists may find it useful to introduce them to new ideas about therapy and help them establish which approaches they want to explore in more depth. Experienced therapists, and supervisors, may find it useful as they seek to understand what "those other family therapists" are doing and to meet the challenge of supervising those from different perspectives. For everyone, we hope it will be an entertaining and instructive snapshot of our fascinating field.

Most likely you are reading this book so you can compare and contrast models, and that is indeed the bulk of the book. Sections II and III of our book are organized around a single hypothetical case. Each author applies his or her chosen model of therapy to this same case (listed at after this introduction). The reader can therefore directly observe what each model would look like in practice. We use the word *model* advisedly. Many therapists now prefer the term *approach,* as *model* can seem too mechanistic, as if it were a blueprint to be followed rigidly. This is not our intent. For the most part, unless authors specifically and strenuously objected, we use the term *model* simply because it is in widespread use in the field and on the national licensing exam. Our intent in using the word *model* is simply to convey a general theoretical and practical framework that informs, but does not limit, a particular therapist's work with clients.

Each of our authors has considerable experience working with the model about which they write. We chose authors who have published and/or presented on the model in question and who practice it as their model of choice as well. Thus, these are snapshots of these models in actual pragmatic application.

We have grouped the various models into sections, depending upon a common theoretical base and common history. These are our own groupings, not those of the authors, and of course the same models could be grouped or combined in different ways. Our groupings are simply to stimulate conversation and to allow us to make the comparisons we wished to make. Each grouping of models is introduced with a brief note about their history, with recommendations for foundational (historically important and key) readings for those models. We end each grouping with comments comparing and contrasting within this group of models and between this group and all the other models. The aim of such comparison and contrast is to illuminate important similarities and differences. Unless otherwise noted, these introductions, comparisons, and contrasts are written by the editors. They do not represent absolute truth, but simply our thoughts, which we hope will encourage the reader to begin comparing and contrasting as well.

Also, in each section, we have included a brief update from a leading practitioner of the originating (oldest) model in that section, to give us a current snapshot of how the models in this group are being applied now. This is to inform us how MRI (Mental Research Institute), structural, and other originating models have changed over the years, what is happening now, and/or any interesting new applications, such as the application of narrative therapy to international conflict resolution. Our purpose is to point out that models are constantly evolving and growing; new ones come along, but the old ones continue. This is only one snapshot, by a practitioner of the models, rather than a complete report of all possible applications.

Before diving into this comparison and contrast in Sections II and III, however, we begin with Section I, which provides us with a little information about the field itself: what sets family therapy apart and what are the underlying theoretical concepts (Chapter 1); what are the skills common to all models of family therapy and what are the requirements for practice (Chapters 2 and 3). Also within Section I, we consider issues that all family therapists struggle with, regardless of model. These include diversity issues (Chapter 4), evidence and efficacy issues (Chapter 5), and issues of faith/spirituality (Chapter 6).

Then, in Section II, we move to the models of family therapy, and, in Section III, to a discussion of those models designed primarily for couples. As discussed in Chapter 49, family therapists practicing the models of family therapy covered in Chapters 7–48 generally see couples as well, but in addition, some models have developed that are designed to be unique to couples, and these are covered in Section III, along with a discussion of the distinction. This is an interesting and controversial issue in the field. We conclude our sections on family and couples therapy models (Sections 2 and 3) with a brief conclusion, giving some guidelines for choosing your particular model or models of choice.

Finally, in Section IV, we finish with short overviews of some of the more interesting recent applications of family therapy to alternative settings and unconventional populations (Chapters 58–66). This whirlwind tour of family therapy will serve, we hope, to whet your appetite for more prolonged study of our fascinating field. Additional reading is recommended online, for each model, and for the field as a whole; please check out this site (www.shss.nova.edu/familythera pyreview) for ongoing updates as well.

For additional reading that will be helpful to study for the licensure exam, and for general information:

Ethics and HIPAA Regulations

American Association for Marital and Family Therapy. (2007). *Legal guidelines for family therapists.* Washington, DC: Author.

American Association for Marital and Family Therapy. (2001). *User's guide to the AAMFT Code of Ethics.* Washington, DC: Author.

Bernstein, B., & Hartsell, T. (2008). *The portable ethicist for mental health professionals: An A–Z guide to responsible practice: with HIPAA update* (2nd ed.). New York, NY: John Wiley and Sons.

Woody, R., & Woody, J. (2001). *Ethics in marriage and family therapy.* Washington, DC: American Association for Marital and Family Therapy.

Overviews of the Field

Gehart, D., & Tuttle, A. (2002). *Theory-based treatment planning for marriage and family therapists.* St. Paul, MN: Brooks Cole.

Metcalf, L. (Ed.) (2011). *Marriage and family therapy: A practice-oriented approach.* New York, NY: Springer.

Nichols, M. (Ed.) (2010). *Family therapy: Concepts and methods.* Upper Saddle River, NJ: Prentice Hall.

Piercy, F., Sprenkle, D., Wetchler, J., & Associates (Eds.) (1996). *Family therapy sourcebook.* New York, NY: Guilford Press.

THE COMMON CASE AND QUESTIONS

The following is the hypothetical common case addressed by all our authors applying various models of family and couple therapy, along with the questions we asked all of them to address. This may be of use as you review the chapters in Sections II and III.

COMMON CASE: Mary and Fred are the parents of Johnny, age 15. Johnny states he hates school and often skips class to hang out with his friends, possibly engaging in high-risk behaviors. He is not passing his grade. Mary and Fred argue about how to handle this situation; Mary thinks perhaps Johnny would benefit from a more nurturing school environment; Fred thinks Johnny should be punished. Mary's mother, Bess, calls frequently to express her opinion, which is similar to Mary's. Mary is developing frequent headaches, which she attributes to stress around this issue.

ADDITION for couples-therapy-only authors: Mary and Fred present for couples therapy, stating they have lost interest in each other, as they have become so consumed with child and in-law issues. They wish to redevelop their intimacy.

QUESTIONS: 1. What additional information do you need before you could consider this case situation, if any? 2. Who would you want to see in therapy? Why? 3. List three questions you would ask at the first session. 4. How would the goal of therapy be established? 5. How would you see yourself, as the therapist, facilitating change for these clients and/or this family?

These were starting point questions, and each author was free to construct more information and discuss the case in their own terms as well.

Section I

ABOUT THE FIELD
OF FAMILY THERAPY

1

WHAT IS FAMILY THERAPY?

Underlying Premises

Anne Rambo and James Hibel

Family therapists do not necessarily see whole families; they may see individuals, couples, or groups. What makes family therapy a distinct profession is its relational focus. An example may help make this clear. Not too long ago, I (Rambo) was present in a meeting at a public school concerning a young girl who was being bullied by other children. The young girl was developmentally delayed and an easy target for the more narrow-minded of her peers. Their teasing and verbal abuse were making her quite miserable. I was the only family therapist present. To my consternation, conversation among the other professionals centered around what combination of medication, individual therapy, and education in coping skills would help this child be less miserable. I longed for the presence of another family therapist, one who utilized any family therapy approach whatsoever. Differences between models of family therapy are significant and result in widely varying types of intervention. But our similarities are as important as our differences. Any family therapist would have viewed this situation relationally and therefore broadened the discussion to include the harassing peers, the parents, the school administrators, and other elements of the system. Any other family therapist would have joined me in declining to act as if the problem belonged to the child alone.

This relational focus is what we all share. Differing approaches, however, draw to greater and lesser extents on particular relational theories. In this chapter, we will give a brief overview of these theories. This is by no means a complete discussion of these theories, each of which may require a lifetime of study to fully understand. Nor is it our purpose to definitively link particular family therapy approaches to particular foundational theories, though we will present some beginning thoughts on such connections in this chapter and later on in our compare and contrast chapters. These are our opinions as editors, and the reader may draw different conclusions. For now, it is sufficient to note that these relational theories inform to varying degrees all models in our field.

We begin with the oldest of the systemic theories we will consider, general systems theory. Ludwig von Bertanlanffy is generally considered the originator of general systems theory. Von Bertanlanffy was a biologist, and his ideas stem from the consideration of living systems. While he began work on the theory in the mid-1920s, he began publishing in the area in the 1930s. The ideas of general systems theory, now widely accepted in the field, include: the whole is greater than the sum of the parts; systems can usefully be viewed in terms of hierarchy, executive organization, and subsystems; and the system itself strives toward preservation, so that individual members of the system can be considered to act in the service of the system as well as in their own interests. These ideas have informed or influenced all models of family therapy but are most influential (in our view) on the psychoanalytic/experiential (IIA) and structural/strategic (IIC) models.

Next, we will consider a model developed in the 1930s and written about extensively in the 1940s, attachment theory. When John Bowlby asked to see his individual child client's mother, in the 1930s, and was reprimanded for doing so by his supervising analyst, Melanie Klein (Bowlby, 1982), it can be argued that his resistance to that reprimand then began his relational consideration of human development. His focus was on the mother/child unit as a relationship, rather than on the individual psyche of either one alone, and this relational focus was continued in the field of object relations. Attachment theory and object relations remain an influence on psychoanalytic/experiential models (IIA) and to a certain extent on structural/strategic models (IIC) as well. The influence of attachment theory may also be noted in many of the couples therapy models (Chapters 50 and 54).

Next we come to natural systems theory, which dates from the 1950s. Murray Bowen is considered the originator of natural systems theory. Bowen was a psychoanalytically trained psychiatrist who became a family therapist. Natural systems theory is biological in nature, as is general systems theory. Bowen proposes that all life proceeds from less differentiation toward more differentiation. This can be seen at the level of cells and at the level of nation states. Within the family, however, it is seen in the growth of the child from a symbiotic state to a more mature, differentiated relationship with the family of origin. Those models most influenced by natural systems theory are the intergenerational models (IIB).

Also in the 1950s, Gregory Bateson began his work applying the theory of cybernetics to human systems such as families. Cybernetics is the comparative study of intelligences, and Norbert Weiner, involved in the development of computers, is generally given the credit for inventing cybernetics. However, Bateson contributed his own unique perspective to these ideas, blending cybernetic ideas about communication and pattern with his background as an anthropologist. Bateson contributed the ideas of nonpathologizing, circular causality (that human interactions arise out of complex circular feedback loops, for which no one person is responsible), multiple realities (that everyone sees the world differently and that this should be respected), and an ecological sensitivity to intervention, leading those therapists who practice from a Batesonian perspective to avoid normative ideas about families and focus on minimalist interventions. From this perspective, human interactions are most usefully seen in terms of relationship, rather than power and control (Green, 2011). Brief therapy models (Chapter 33) are heavily influenced by Batesonian thought, but to a greater and lesser extent also influenced by the work of the hypnotherapist Milton Erickson (whose work is covered in a separate "models" chapter, as Ericksonian therapy became its own model—see Chapter 28). Bateson provided the focus on pattern and interaction and the resolution to intervene minimally; Erickson provided the tools for minimal but effective intervention. Narrative therapy models (IIE) are also influenced by Bateson, but in combination with Foucault. Finally, collaborative models (Chapter 39) also reflect Batesonian influence.

Michel Foucault was a French philosopher writing in the 1960s, but his ideas came to the family therapy field primarily through the influence of Michael White, an originating narrative family therapist. White took Foucault's ideas of privileged versus submerged voices, and socially constructed personal narratives, to craft a therapy that worked to liberate clients from socially imposed limits on their views of self. "Just therapy," another Australian model of family therapy, is similarly influenced in its stance toward issues of power and privilege and the therapist's responsibility to help liberate the client. These models originated in Australia and New Zealand but have now spread worldwide. Foucault and White have been an influence on the whole field, but most directly on narrative therapy models (IIE). The feminist critique of family therapy in the 1980s, most notable within the United States but also with an influence worldwide, has brought about an additional wave of questioning of power and privilege within relationships, especially along gender lines (Doherty & Baptiste, 1993). Like the influence of Foucault, feminist theory encourages the therapist to consider issues of power and privilege and actively intervene to address them. Feminist theory has influenced the entire field, across models (Doherty & Baptiste, 1993).

In the 1980s, advances in the field of biology (Mingers, 1991) led to renewed interest in constructivism, the idea that each individual transforms information from the environment in an active, meaning-creating manner. This was paralleled with a growing interest within the social sciences in deconstruction and poststructuralism, which had earlier influenced the humanities and the study of literature (Burr, 2003). This questioning of objective reality and of mechanistic models of human behavior is often called social constructionism (Burr, 2003; Hoyt, 1994). Postmodern thinking, the rejection of modernist norms and assumptions, is a key component. When translated into family therapy terms, social constructionist ideas lead to the rejection of norms and the inclusion of each client's individual reality. An active therapist imposing his or her value judgments and preferred reality on the client would be seen as antithetical to this theoretical position. Problems appear in and are dissolved by discourse, and the role of the therapist becomes simply to participate in this process. Two of the brief therapy models (MRI and solution-focused brief therapy [SFBT], see Chapters 29 and 30) are often seen as social constructionist (Hoyt, 1994). This has to do with their focus on the client's own reality and the rejection of culturally imposed norms, which resonates with the Batesonian foundation of these models as well. Milan in its classic form (discussed in Chapter 31) is not usually considered social constructionist, as the team took an authoritative, "expert" role, but current practitioners of the Milan model often utilize the paradox and counterparadox more playfully and see themselves as working in a social constructionist framework, as discussed by Paul Rhodes in his chapter for our book (Chapter 31). While considered social constructionist by some (Hoyt, 1994), MRI, like classic Milan, is seen by others as having too active and directive a therapist role to be considered truly postmodern; SFBT is excepted, even when MRI and Milan are not, because the SFBT therapist is only building on behaviors the client has already spontaneously experienced, not suggesting new ones (Anderson, 2011). Narrative family therapists (IIE) are generally considered social constructionists, in their focus on alternative stories and multiple, shifting discourses (Anderson, 2011). The collaborative models (Chapter 39) are generally considered to be the most singularly influenced by social constructionism, constructivist theory, and postmodern ideas in general (Anderson, 2011).

Of course, these varying theories do not exist in isolation, and they are combined and recombined over time, in varying ways, by different practitioners. They may be combined with nonsystemic theories as well, such as psychoeducational and cognitive behavioral theories. They may be and often are combined with each other. For example, the reader will note that several of our authors identify their approach as *post* something—post-Milan or post-psychoanalytic. This use of the prefix *post* is intended to convey the author's postmodern perspective—thus, the approach is offered not as the one right way or as a complete explanation of human behavior, but simply as one reality with which the author has a relationship. In recent years, the influence of social constructionism has even led therapists influenced by other theories to distance themselves from rigid adherence to a model. Similarly, the influence of Foucault, through narrative therapy, has led the entire field to be more conscious of diversity and political issues.

Pressure from funding agencies to develop a stronger evidence base for particular models of family therapy has, however, been a pull in the opposite direction, toward a more positivist, modernist approach. From the perspective of an insurance company or federal agency, there does need to be an objective truth that can be measured, and as clear and specific a model as possible, preferably in manualized form. This has led to a split in the field between models whose practitioners are more comfortable with objective research demonstrating their efficacy and models whose practitioners tend to rely more on individual client satisfaction and avoid experimental conditions, which they may view as not postmodern. An interesting exception is SFBT (Chapter 30), as the leadership of the solution-focused brief therapy association deliberately chose to pursue the process of becoming evidence based a few years back (www.sfbta.org), despite their postmodern/collaborative leanings. This has led to increased funding for solution-focused therapy, and there is now some movement within narrative family therapy (IIE) to follow suit (www.dulwichcentre.com.au/narrative-therapy-research.html). Structural/strategic family therapy (IIC), however, clearly has a significant head start on the compilation of such evidence, as do some models of couples therapy (Chapters 50–53).

So far we have been considering family therapy models based on foundational *systemic* theories. We also include in our book family psychoeducation, which applies to families' basic educational and skills training concepts, and cognitive behavioral approaches, which draw on social learning theory. These are individual rather than systemic theories, but they have vast application to families. Family psychoeducation has its own chapter. Cognitive behavioral approaches are covered in the couples therapy section, where they have had the most impact. It is worth noting, however, that many systemic family therapists include psychoeducational and cognitive behavioral interventions in their work with families, in addition to their other approaches. Couples therapy has historically been more integrative than systemic family therapy, incorporating a wide range of both systemic and nonsystemic theories, and this can be seen in the couples therapy approaches discussed in this book.

As you review the models that follow, consider your own beliefs about the nature of systems, the nature of reality, and the nature of change. Decisions about the model or models of therapy you will embrace as a family therapist are ethical and philosophical decisions, as well as practical ones (Keeney, 1982). The best outcome data we have on the efficacy of therapy suggests that the model of therapy chosen is not a key factor in successful outcome—but, paradoxically enough, the therapist's own belief in his or her model *is* a key factor (Lambert & Barley, 2001). The type of therapy you choose to practice will be influenced by what makes sense to you, and thus by your own theoretical understandings; your therapy and your clients will then influence your understandings in turn.

References

Anderson, H. (2011). *Postmodern social constructionist therapies.* Retrieved from http://www.harleneanderson.org/writings/postmoderntherapieschapter.htm

Bowlby, J. (1982). Attachment and loss: Retrospect and prospect. *American Journal of Orthopsychiatry, 52*(4), 664–678.

Burr, V. (2003). *Social constructionism* (2nd ed.). New York, NY: Routledge.

Doherty, W. J., & Baptiste, D. A., Jr. (1993). Theories emerging from family therapy. In P. G. Boss, W. J. Doherty, R. LaRossa, W. R. Schumm, & S. K. Steinmetz (Eds.), *Sourcebook of family theories and methods: A contextual approach* (pp. 505–524). New York, NY: Plenum.

Green, S. (2011, November/December). Power or pattern? A brief, relational approach. *Family Therapy Magazine, 10*(6), 9–11.

Hoyt, M. (1994). On the importance of keeping it simple and taking the patient seriously: A conversation with Steve de Shazer and John Weakland. In M. Hoyt (Ed.), *Constructive Therapies* (Vol. 1, pp. 11–40). New York, NY: Guilford Press.

Keeney, B. (1982). *Aesthetics of change.* New York, NY: Guilford Press.

Lambert, M. J., & Barley, D. E. (2001). Research summary on the therapeutic relation-ship and psychotherapy outcome. *Psychotherapy: Theory, Research, Practice, Training, 38*(4), 357–361.

Mingers, J. (1991). The cognitive theories of Maturana and Varela. *Systemic Practice and Action Research, 4*(4), 319–338.

For additional reading on all these systemic theories, please visit www.shss.nova.edu/familytherapyreview.

2

WHAT DOES IT TAKE TO BE A "GOOD" FAMILY THERAPIST?

Questions of Competence

AnnaLynn Schooley and Tommie V. Boyd

Gladwell (2008) estimates 10,000 hours of practice are required to become an expert at anything. This may well be a daunting prospect for the beginning family therapist. While in much of this book we will consider models of family therapy, as they offer useful guides for the beginning therapist in particular, we would be remiss not to point out that a mastery of basic relational and communication skills is also important. These skills have been discussed as common factors cutting across all schools of psychotherapy (Blow & Sprenkle, 2001). Those common factor skills most specific to family therapy are the ability to conceptualize in relational terms, to interrupt negative relational patterns, to expand the treatment system, and to expand the therapeutic alliance (Sprenkle, Davis, & Lebow, 2009). Varying models of family therapy approach these goals differently, but all can be seen as addressing these common goals. All models also address areas of thinking, feeling, and doing, although different models may focus on one or more of these areas (Sprenkle, Davis, & Lebow, 2009). (This will be discussed in greater detail in our compare and contrast chapters.)

Those broad overarching goals of conceptualizing, intervening, and expanding require microskills, basic communication skills that are the therapist's basic tool kit. One of us (Schooley) has created an exhaustive list of such microskills, which is presented in Appendix A (see website, www.shss.nova.edu/familytherapy review). In a parallel process, influenced also by developments within the world of academia, the Commission on Accreditation for Marriage and Family Therapy Education (COAMFTE) embarked in January 2003 on an ambitious project. A task force of nationally recognized scholars was convened to review and develop marriage and family therapist (MFT) core competencies for master's-level clinicians (Nelson et al., 2007). The task force identified six skill sets critical to becoming an independent practicing MFT: Admission to Treatment; Clinical Assessment and Diagnosis; Treatment Planning and Case Management; Therapeutic Interventions; Legal Issues, Ethics, and Standards; and Research and Program Evaluation.

Within each of the domains, more detailed subdomains broke these competencies down into conceptual skills, perceptual skills, executive skills, evaluative skills, and professional skills. COAMFTE-accredited marriage and family therapy training and education programs are now mandated to use these core competencies as a way to assess their students or trainees.

This is part of a larger shift, common to much of academia, toward a competency-based rather than input-based system of education; in other words, faculty are no longer evaluated on what they teach, but on what the students can be demonstrated to have learned (Gerhart, 2011). Miller, Todahl, and Platt (2010) identified results of this change, which may include revisiting a program's pedagogy, making curriculum changes, substantiating costs of data collection and implementation, and focusing on outcome and effectiveness. The feedback loop is complex and ongoing. Nelson and Graves's (2011) research on MFT trainees' competencies speaks to specific learning outcomes; however, there are still a number of gaps that future research will need to fill (Stratton, Reibstein, Lask, Singh, & Asen, 2011). These core competencies are listed on the website (www.shss.nova.edu/familytherapyreview).

There is current interest in the field in developing core competencies across mental health professions (Sperry, 2010), core competencies specific to particular models (Quick, 2011), and core competencies specific to populations/cultures (Sperry, 2010). It seems likely the basic building blocks of competence will continue to be debated in the field.

References

Blow, A., & Sprenkle, D. (2001). Common centers across theories of marriage and family therapy: A modified Delphi study. *Journal of Marital and Family Therapy, 27*(2), 385–402.

Gehart, D. (2011). The core competencies and MFT education: Learning-centered, outcome-based pedagogy. *Journal of Marriage and Family Therapy, 37*(3), 344–354.

Gladwell, Malcolm. (2008). *Outliers: The story of success.* New York, NY: Little, Brown.

Miller, J. K., Todahl, J. L., & Platt, J. J. (2010). The core competencies movement in marriage and family therapy: Key considerations from other disciplines. *Journal of Marital and Family Therapy, 36*(1), 59–70.

Nelson, T. S., Chenail, R. J., Alexander, J. F., Crane, D. R., Johnson, S. M., & Schwallie, L. (2007). The development of core competencies for the practice of marriage and family therapy. *Journal of Marital and Family Therapy, 33*(4), 417–438.

Nelson, T. S., & Graves, T. (2011). Core competencies in advanced training: What supervisors say about graduate training. *Journal of Marital and Family Therapy, 37*(4), 429–451.

Quick, E. K. (2011). *Core competencies in the solution-focused and strategic therapies: Becoming a highly competent solution-focused and strategic therapist.* New York, NY: Routledge.

Sperry, L. (2010). *Core competencies in counseling and psychotherapy: Becoming a highly competent and effective therapist.* New York, NY: Routledge.

Sprenkle, D., Davis, S., & Lebow, J. (2009). *Common factors in couple and family therapy: An overlooked foundation for effective practice.* New York, NY: Guilford Press.

Stratton, P., Reibstein, J., Lask, J., Singh, R., & Asen, E. (2011). Competences and occupational standards for systemic family and couples therapy. *Journal of Family Therapy, 33*(2), 123–143.

3

THE CHANGING MFT PROFESSION

Regulation, Technology, and Examination

Charles West

Editors' Note: This chapter will discuss regulation and licensure of the profession of marriage and family therapy (MFT) in the United States because licensure developed first in the United States. Canada, most nations in Europe, Australia, New Zealand, Russia, South Africa, Mexico, Ecuador, and Brazil currently have very active family therapy associations and offer voluntary credentialing, and there is ongoing interest and training in China, Japan, and Singapore (Ng, 2003). The trend is toward increased credentialing, and the story of the MFT profession in the United States, culminating in a mandatory licensing exam and state credentialing, can perhaps provide food for thought for our international readers as well. Increased regulation, as always, has both pros and cons, but it does appear to be the direction of the field, especially in countries where third-party insurance payment continues to be important.

Within the United States, the profession of marriage and family therapy has experienced significant growth and change over the past 30 years, evolving into a nationally recognized mental health profession. Although there have been many reasons for this growth, clearly one of the reasons has been the leadership of the American Association for Marriage and Family Therapy (AAMFT). This leadership included the instituting of comprehensive educational and training standards for marriage and family therapists, an increase in accredited graduate and postdegree educational programs, and an increase in the number of AAMFT-approved supervisors (Lee, Nichols, Nichols, & Odom, 2004). Perhaps most importantly, the AAMFT was influential in the battle for state licensure of marriage and family therapists, licensure that now exists in all 50 states and the District of Columbia.

With licensure comes regulation and regulatory boards, both of which exist to protect the health and safety of citizens. As part of this protection of the public, regulation limits who can practice in a profession by requiring individuals to meet specific qualifications. Regulation also protects the public by defining what a qualified professional can do (scope of practice) based on the individual's education, experience, and competency.

The Impact of Regulation

The growth of regulation has affected the profession of marriage and family therapy in numerous ways. One effect of licensure has been the creation of a patchwork of state standards regarding education and training standards, postgraduate requirements, supervisor qualifications, scopes of practice, and continuing education expectations. Different standards were adopted in part due to differing levels of opposition and/or cooperation with other mental health professions at the time licensure statutes were established in the different states.

A second effect is the inevitable tension that arises between regulatory boards and state professional associations. This is partly due to the reality that regulatory boards and professional associations have differing responsibilities and are primarily responsible to different constituencies. For example, professional associations are expected to primarily advocate for marriage and family therapists, the advancement of the profession, and helping professionals meet high standards, while state boards are primarily charged with the responsibility to protect the welfare of consumers and are concerned with the minimal requirements for competent practice (Sturkie & Bergen, 2001). In other words, while both regulatory boards and professional associations serve the profession and protect the public, the primary charge of the regulatory board to protect the public sometimes creates tension with state associations.

A third effect of regulation is the changing of standards for what qualifies an individual to be a marriage and family therapist. A study completed by West, Hinton, Grames, and Adams (in press) in 2007 broadly summarized state regulations regarding education, postgraduate, and supervisor requirements. They found significant variety in standards across states, and in a number of states these standards were lower compared to prelicensure AAMFT clinical membership standards (American Association for Marital and Family Therapy, 2004). They found that the number of core courses required by states for licensure varied from 6 to 13; that one-third of states did not met or exceed the AAMFT prelicensure clinical membership practicum standard of 1 year/300 hours of supervised direct client contact with individuals, couples, and families (several states did not specify a required number of practicum contact hours); and that while 35 states met or exceeded the AAMFT prelicensure clinical membership postgraduate requirement of 1,000 hours of clinical work experience in marriage and family therapy, only 10 states required postgraduate relational hours. In addition, postgraduate supervision requirements varied from 52 to 200 hours, and only 9 states required supervisors to be AAMFT-approved supervisors or meet equivalent training standards.

The Impact of Technology

Another continuing wave of change affecting the profession is related to the Internet and evolving technology. The American Counseling Association (ACA) has taken a leading role in responding to the impact of technology on the mental health profession, addressing benefits, limitations, appropriate use, access, and informed consent in the 2005 *ACA Code of Ethics* (American Counseling Association, 2005). In addition, the Council for Accreditation of Counseling and Related Educational Programs (CACREP) has evaluated and accredited several online marriage and family counseling programs (Council for Accreditation of Counseling and Related Educational Programs, n.d.), affecting both the form and delivery of education. At present, the Commission on Accreditation for Marriage and Family Therapy Education is evaluating and considering the question of online education.

Meanwhile, state regulatory boards have been establishing policies governing online education, service delivery, and online supervision. As of mid-2011, eight states have adopted distance counseling policies regarding MFTs: Arkansas, California, Illinois, Kentucky, Massachusetts, Ohio, Oregon, and Virginia. These policies address such issues as where online counseling is considered to occur for regulatory purposes (in the home state of the therapist, in the home state of the client, or in both locations) and how to handle confidentiality.

Four states specifically allow postgraduates under supervision to conduct distance counseling: California, North Dakota, Oregon (online supervision is the same as face-to-face), and Texas. Two states specifically disqualify any supervision conducted by electronic means (Maryland and Minnesota), while 14 states specifically allow electronic postgraduate supervision: Alabama (25%), Arizona (25%), Arkansas (50% by a supervisor with that specialized license), California (some settings), Colorado (50%, some settings), Iowa (50% or less), Kansas (in emergencies), Kentucky (if undue burden), Maine (25%), Missouri (if verbally/visually interactive), North Dakota (25%, considered the same as face-to-face), Oklahoma (50% or less), Oregon (75%), and Texas (25%, considered the same as face-to-face). Some of the reasons for this growth may be growing need for MFTs in both rural and urban settings, a growing interest in marriage and family therapy internationally, and the training needs of groups such as members of the military and their families.

In summary, the profession is changing, and regulatory boards, most notably as joined together in the nationwide Association of Marital and Family Therapy Regulatory Boards (AMFTRB), appear to be playing a major role in these changes. The next section outlines some of the history and impact of the AMFTRB.

The Association of Marital and Family Therapy Regulatory Boards

In 1987, existing marriage and family therapy regulatory board members decided that it would be beneficial to begin a formal association, and efforts were made that resulted in the Association of Marital and Family Therapy Regulatory Boards. Specifically, AMFTRB was established to enable regulatory boards to address common concerns, to encourage consistent training and credentialing standards, to act as a clearinghouse for information relevant to regulation, and to develop and administer the MFT national examination (Sturkie & Bergen, 2001). Following its inception, the AMFTRB "entered into a contract to develop a standardized examination acceptable to member states" (Lee & Sturkie, 1997). Today, almost all states require applicants to take the national examination, and graduate pass rates on the examination are considered an important outcome measure for COAMFTE-accredited programs (or those seeking accreditation) under the Version 11 COAMFTE Standards (American Association for Marital and Family Therapy, 2006).

The National Exam

The national examination for marriage and family therapists was first administered in 1988 (Association of Marital and Family Therapy Regulatory Boards, 2006), and in subsequent years there has been significant growth in the number of individuals sitting for this exam (Sturkie & Bergen, 2001). Due to increasing demands, the AMTFRB began offering a practice exam in 2005 and added a second practice exam in 2007. As of mid-2011, all states and the District of Columbia require a postgraduate examination and only California does not specifically utilize the AMFTRB exam to test potential licensees.

The examination is a standardized instrument, currently utilizing 200 multiple choice questions. Each multiple choice question has undergone a rigorous process "designed to maximize the content validity of the examination" (Association of Marital and Family Therapy Regulatory Boards, n.d.). Each question is typically written by an MFT professional, who is invited to participate by members of the AMFTRB and is typically drawn from family therapy academic programs and practicing professionals in both the United States and Canada. The resulting question is then submitted to a group of three MFT content experts to be examined for validity and accuracy. If the question remains viable, it is then passed to another three-person committee with expertise in the profession to ensure validity and accuracy (Association of Marital and Family Therapy Regulatory Boards, n.d.). Any question that survives this process must then be accepted by the Examination Advisory Committee "for accuracy, validity and overall quality, and revised as necessary" (Association of Marital and Family Therapy Regulatory Boards, n.d.). Only after this process can the question become an official part of the item bank maintained by the AMFTRB and considered for future use on a test form. Any item considered for use is "reviewed by psychometricians and editors on the PES [Professional Examination Service] staff" (Association of Marital and Family Therapy Regulatory Boards, n.d.) to ensure validity and is then reviewed yet again for possible approval by the Examination Advisory Committee for use in a particular window of the test. When a testing window closes, the statistical performance of the question is reviewed by Professional Examination Service employees and the Examination Advisory Committee prior to the scoring of the examination. After this last review, the final pass point (critical score) is set for the test administered in a test window. It is expected that those graduating from accredited family therapy programs will pass at a higher rate, although this is not always the case. In addition to the process outlined here, feedback from test takers and other professionals plays a vital role in improving and maintaining the quality of the examination.

Finally, the examination's passing percentage (cut score) is not arbitrarily determined, but rather is set using the Angoff method, a widely used, empirically based, standard-setting approach for examinations. The Angoff method utilizes a purposefully diverse group of subject-matter experts (SMEs) in MFT to examine the content of test items and then estimate the percentage of minimally qualified test candidates who would answer each item correctly. The predicted difficulty of the test is derived from the average of the SMEs' estimates, resulting in a recommended Angoff cut score.

The examination is designed to distinguish minimally competent candidates from less than minimally competent candidates (Association of Marital and Family Therapy Regulatory Boards, n.d.). Therefore, questions are expected to test candidates with 2 years' postgraduate clinical experience regarding relevant, current, and important information affecting the practice of marriage and family therapy. Questions are written with the goal of being clear and concise—free of jargon, ambiguous words, and nonessential information. Many questions seek to address a higher level of reasoning by asking test takers to assess problem scenarios requiring the application of facts, principles, theory, or techniques (Quin, Hinton, West, Adams, & Sims, 2006).

For more information about the regulation of the professions by states, or about the national examination, visit the AMFTRB website: www.amftrb.org.

Summary

The advent of regulation, technology, and national examinations continues to affect the profession of marriage and family therapy, including how we educate future MFTs, how we deliver services to clients, what is required to be a minimally competent therapist and supervisor, what is considered part of an MFT's scope of practice, and so on. While change brings anxiety and opposition, it also brings opportunity and growth.

References

American Association for Marital and Family Therapy. (2004). *AAMFT clinical membership evaluative track application*. Alexandria, VA: Author.

American Association for Marital and Family Therapy. (2006). *COAMFTE master accreditation manual: Policies and procedures*. Washington, DC: Author.

American Counseling Association. (2005). *ACA code of ethics*. Alexandria, VA: Author.

American Marriage and Family Therapy Regulatory Board. (n.d.). *AMFTRB national exam*. Retrieved from http://www.amftrb.org/exam.cfm

Association of Marital and Family Therapy Regulatory Boards. (2006, September). *20th annual meeting book*. Colorado Springs, CO: Author.

Council for Accreditation of Counseling and Related Educational Programs. (n.d.). *Directory*. Retrieved from http://www.cacrep.org/directory/directory.cfm

Lee, R. E., Nichols, D. P., Nichols, W. C., & Odom, T. (2004). Trends in family therapy supervision: The past 25 years and into the future. *Journal of Marital and Family Therapy, 30*(1), 61–70.

Lee, R. E., & Sturkie, K. (1997). The national marital and family therapy examination program. *Journal of Marital and Family Therapy, 23*(3), 255–269.

Ng, K. (2003). *Global perspectives in family therapy: Development, practice, trends*. New York, NY: Routledge.

Quin, M., Hinton, J., West, C., Adams, M., & Sims, P. (2006, October). *Marriage and family therapy: Regulating the profession*. Poster presented at the annual meeting of the American Association for Marriage and Family Therapy, Austin, TX.

Sturkie, K., & Bergen, L. P. (2001). *Professional regulation in marital and family therapy*. Boston, MA: Allyn & Bacon.

West, C., Hinton, W., Grames, H., & Adams, M. (in press). Marriage and family therapy: Examining the impact of licensure on an evolving profession. *Journal of Marital and Family Therapy*.

4

CULTURE AND DIVERSITY

A Lifelong Journey

Christine Ajayi, Martha Gonzalez Marquez, and Andrés Nazario

Editors' Note: The three authors contributed equally to the development of this chapter. Their names are listed alphabetically.

The content of this chapter is a product of several conversations that took place between the authors and is intended to present key components of the process of understanding diversity in clinical practice. We suggest that these issues be discussed in conversation as well.

Our Assumptions and Biases

A discussion of issues of diversity requires transparency on the part of the authors, clarifying their socially situated positions, their biases, and their assumptions. These assumptions are central to the types of conversations we suggest we should have with clients and colleagues, with supervisors, and among faculty and staff of any training program. We have several assumptions about family therapy, derived from oppression-sensitive family therapy (Nazario, 2007), that we would like to identify:

1. Therapy is always contextual. The therapeutic process involves an encounter between the client system's context and the context of the therapist.
2. Therapy is political: political in the sense of the multiple domains that influence the worldview of the clients and the worldview of the therapist.
3. Psychotherapy is not a neutral process, and we cannot avoid influencing our clients regardless of our therapeutic orientation.
4. Our socially situated position organizes our meaning making and organizes the therapeutic process.
5. Reality is culturally defined.

From this perspective, conversations with clients can only occur if therapists have been actively engaged in self-exploration of their socially situated positions and in conversation throughout the training program. This requires that faculty and supervisors also engage in these dialogues.

Who We Are: Recognizing Power and Privilege

An essential element of cultural competence is the continued awareness of our own social location. There are parts of each of us that are privileged, and there are other parts that are not. The interconnection of our varied selves shapes our values, experiences, and contexts (Aponte et al., 2009). With each part of self, the issues and intersections of power, privilege, and oppression must be considered.

We have each agreed that it is vital for us to locate ourselves in this chapter. In therapy, it is easy to expect our interactions with clients to consist of their transparency, as we serve as a sounding board of sorts. Yet the therapist is a whole person, and all parts of our selves—the privileged and oppressed parts—enter into the therapeutic experience, whether we are aware of it or not. Thus, we hope that our sharing of our selves will allow you to explore the dimensions of you, as a person, and how your many dimensions affect you as a therapist.

Christine: As I begin the process of deciding how to locate myself, it is interesting what comes up, and in what order. I will list them as they come to me: I am an African American, college-educated, heterosexual, Christian woman who is able-bodied; from Dallas, Texas; and from a middle-class, single-parent family. I am a first-year professor in a family therapy program and identify as a therapist committed to issues of social justice and equality. As I reflect on the social positions that influence my lived experience, I am reminded of the interconnectedness of my "identities." It is not that I am simply made up of multiple parts, but rather that my lived experience is shaped concurrently by these constructions. How can I speak solely from my African American self and be able to decipher which experiences were only a product of being Black, separate from being a woman, middle class, and the myriad of additional identities? The voices that have shaped me as a MFT are those of Paulo Freire, Ken Hardy, Monica McGoldrick, A. J. and Nancy Boyd-Franklin, Harry Aponte, Michael White, and a host of others.

Martha: As is the case with all human beings, each aspect that defines us is interrelated and affects each other. Some aspects that I believe help define me are that I am a female, first-generation Latina whose family immigrated to the United States from Colombia, South America, in the 1960s, by choice, for better work opportunities. I call myself American/Colombian, having been born in the Midwest to Colombian parents. I am also a heterosexual able-bodied woman, a mother, and a member of a large extended family mostly living within a few miles of each other. Many Colombian traditions have been embraced and continue to hold value in my life. I am middle class, graduate school educated, and I hold an administrative position in the university within which I work. I identify myself as being committed to issues of social justice and empowering the marginalized voices that exist in my life. I consider myself a "critical Catholic" as well and hold as one of my priorities my familial relationships. In some of these aspects I recognize that I have privilege, in others less so.

Andrés: My orientation to life and therefore to teaching, supervising, or practicing family therapy is shaped by a multitude of people, ideas, and situations that generate my multiple identities. Important influences in my life are my family of origin's commitment to issues of justice and equality as well as my social position as a political refugee, an immigrant, a gay person, a Latino, a male, an educated person, a member of the middle class, a nationalized citizen, a senior citizen, and many others. One other significant influence on who I am is my relationship of 34 years with a life partner who is U.S. born and of Anglo ancestry. These identities position me within a continuum of privilege and oppression. Other important influences in my development as a person and as an MFT have been the feminist critique of family therapy and the work of pioneers in issues of diversity such as Ken Hardy, Rhea Almeida, Marsha Pravder Mirkin, Gregory Herek, Robert-Jay Green, Joan Laird, Lillian Comas-Diaz, Celia Falicov, and many others.

Values and Politics of the Environment/Culture

Issues of diversity, and of social justice and inclusion, are complex and multidimensional, requiring attention at all levels throughout the process of becoming an MFT. In the corporate world, "diversity has become the underpinnings of mission statements, internal policies, business strategies and community outreach" (Larsen, 2011, p. 18). It appears that major U.S. corporations are actively pursuing diversity, yet it seems that in some MFT programs, social justice and inclusion are falling behind the corporate world.

Inclusion and social justice are developmental processes requiring a departure from and questioning of the sociopolitical prescription of the dominant culture (Anderson & Middleton, 2004). The dominant culture through its many venues invites us to conform and to ignore differences that could make us uncomfortable. Yet it is the recognition of those differences that forces us to situate ourselves in our social location and to recognize the social location of others.

Social Justice Versus Diversity: Is There a Difference?

Social justice, culture, and *diversity* are terms that are almost cliché, or buzzwords within the field of MFT. What does it mean to be a therapist who is committed to issues of social justice? How is this different from being culturally competent, or is there even a difference? Social justice is the value and advocacy of human rights for everyone and intentional participation in creating a society that is based on equality and inclusion for all persons. A critique of practicing therapy from a social justice paradigmatic view is that it goes beyond our scope as therapists. Yet all therapy is political. Whether a therapist is aware of his or her position or not, the therapeutic experience will be informed by the values of the therapist. That is why it is critical for therapists to continuously explore who they are, what informs their positions, and how who they are affects their work. The culturally competent practice of marriage and family therapy is the capacity to deliver relevant services to persons with diverse experiences, from diverse backgrounds.

Key Factors in Cultural Competency

1. Transparency is central. *Transparency* has become a common term in the sciences and humanities as part of an attempt to influence the social context in which we function to be more open, to increase communication, and to support accountability. In family therapy we view transparency as a process that increases open communication between therapists and supervisors about who they are and the values that guide their thinking beyond whatever therapeutic theory they may espouse. These conversations must occur in both directions: top down and bottom up.

   In order for transparency between therapist and supervisor, and client and therapist, to occur, they have to function within a culture of transparency supported and practiced within the institution where they operate. To be transparent in therapy does not mean disclosing our most intimate details, but rather to be engaged in conversations that identify our socially located position and to become accountable to those with less power than us. Therapists, supervisors, and faculty and institutions must constantly challenge themselves in terms of cultural issues, social inclusion, and creating a culture of transparency.

   In order to be a therapist who is aware and able to best address issues of diversity and justice, openness and authenticity must be practiced (Rastogi & Wieling, 2004). It must be an intentional way of being with others. When a therapist is able to be able to be transparent, it opens space for clients and colleagues to do the same. This gives way to conversation, although sometimes difficult, that can ignite awareness and connection.

2. Intersectionality is essential because cultural variables are interrelated. They have an impact on each other to the extent that their qualitative nature is changed due to their inter- and intrarelationships.

   Many can relate to the concept of gender differences between cultures. For example, when I (Martha) speak about motherhood from a perspective of my culture of origin, it is laden with respect, power, and much privilege. Most women in my family run their homes, as a CEO of a company might. Thus, a mother's role in my culture may have significantly different implications than in another culture. However, coupled with religious factors, the role of a mother in a Latina family may be altered to hold perhaps a different level of privilege.

3. Teach others how to think about social justice, compared to learning a formula. Since what is just differs for each individual depending on his or her individual aspects and cultural positions, to attempt to teach therapists about

what is or is not social justice is to minimize the complex nature of the concept. There is no actual formula to be memorized. Each person, couple, and family experience their social location differently and uniquely. One of the goals is for therapists to disregard previous assumptions and become curious about the client's experience. What follows should be a conversation about the client's own experience. The therapist, sitting in a position of privilege, is then charged with considering how justice is manifested.

Self-Exploration

The crux of the journey to an increased commitment to social justice and practicing competently is that of self-exploration on the part of the therapist as well as trainers and supervisors. Conversing about these issues exemplifies how these conversations are not always comfortable. Indeed, they often cause great discomfort. Embracing the discomfort is a priority to move forward. The corollary is to avoid the discomfort and run the risk of harming those with less power. As we engage in these explorations, we begin to realize that our lived experiences are not static, that they change in reference to our current social location, and that we can resonate with the experiences of students and clients. Challenging ourselves about our own power and privilege, recognizing our own intolerance, and facing tension head-on is often what we ask our clients to do. Thus, we need to have our own relationships with it as well.

The ultimate goal in this self-exploration is not certainty at all. It is actually the opposite. It is recognizing that there is much that can never be fully known as human lived experiences are dynamic and socially constructed. Our awareness of this nebulous state makes us more aware of our own values, biases, and social position. "Awareness forces you to do something" (Nazario, 2007). As this self-exploration occurs, we can formulate what our values are and realize how those values affect our thinking.

Once therapists are able to engage in this self-exploration, they can move smoothly into taking into account their responsibility in the therapeutic relationship. As therapists, regardless of model or orientation, we are in a position of power. To acknowledge this and recognize this means to also take responsibility for the conversation.

Myths About Cultural Competence

The concept of myths has been a powerful and influential theme in family therapy. Several books have dealt with the importance of addressing family myths. Within family therapy, especially in relation to culture and ethnicity, we have developed our own myths that deserve to be challenged.

"Cultural Competence Is Not Truly Attainable Knowledge"

There is an idea that diversity training or cultural competence education is, frankly, a waste of time. Some argue that there is no way to accurately measure if one is culturally competent and that we all should get the basic idea—"culture is important." We argue that cultural competence is knowledge that is not only attainable, but also a requirement for relevant and effective clinical practice. We all can (and should) endeavor to become more open and comfortable with differences, to learning about our own location and that of others and how it has an impact on our lived (or storied) experiences.

"Every Family Is a Culture in Itself"

Absolutely! Each familial system will have a uniqueness that can be deemed a culture. This does not diminish that a larger social context exists and is a valid entity to explore. Just as individual family members are situated into their family culture, every family is a part of a larger dominant framework. If little to no attention is paid to the family's interconnection, however, we argue that critical elements of this family are lost in the therapeutic experience.

"Culture Should Only Be Discussed If the Client Brings It Up: If They Do Not Bring It Up, It Is Not an Issue for Them"

Many clients are indeed raising issues of culture unbeknownst to the therapist. Therapists should listen for the opportunity to converse about issues of culture and should not assume culture is not an issue if the client does not bring it up. Therapists hold the power and comply with silence if they do not embrace these opportunities. Clients often follow the lead of the therapist due to the power differential.

"Therapists Should Be Colorblind and See All Families the Same"

To be colorblind is to simply be blind. In recent years, the idea that one cannot only see past color, but attach no meaning to it at all, has gained much steam. After the election of President Barack Obama, there was much discourse on America's shift to a "postracial" society. Although there is merit in the ideal of this philosophy, it does not account for the structural oppression and imbalance of power solely connected to race. When a therapist conceptualizes how he or she will work with a given client family, and does not even give a fleeting thought to issues of race, power, and privilege, much is lost from the process.

Indeed, clients can be harmed if the privileged therapist inadvertently imposes his or her position on a client. For many clients, this is a reexperiencing of oppression from previously abusive powers. Realities about how our culture has marginalized or oppressed some and privileged others should not be assumed nor dismissed.

"Therapists Should Remain Neutral on Social Issues That Are Brought Up in Therapy"

This runs the risk of complying with powers that oppress. A critique of therapy that explicitly addresses societal issues (racism, sexism, heterosexism, and all of the other -*isms*) is that we are beyond our scope of practice. A question often raised is, "If the clients are okay with an imbalance of power in their relationships, and see no connection to 'larger social issues,' who are we to challenge them?" We emphatically ask, "Who are we not to?" To effectively do this, we must first understand for ourselves how the larger social context is connected to clients' (and therapists') lived experiences. With that awareness, we not only are to allow but also create space for these oftentimes difficult conversations in therapy.

"Acknowledging Difference Is Negative and Oftentimes Perpetuates Stereotypes"

Perpetuating stereotypes occurs when assumptions are embraced unilaterally. Acknowledging differences can serve to open communication and increase transparency. Oftentimes it is not that therapists do not want to create any dissonance for clients, as most theoretical models make this call to clients. Yet it is therapists' discomfort with the conversation of cultural difference that does not afford this discourse in therapy.

"Not Everyone Has a Culture"

In most conversations on culture, the idea is expressed that someone (usually from the dominant group) is immune to having a culture. Everyone exists in a social location that situates him or her in regard to power and privilege. Some have more privilege based on social constructs, others have less. Oftentimes those from subjugated groups are more aware of their culture, as it may vary greatly from that of the dominant framework. This does not discount the fact that all members of society have a culture that is worthy of exploration. In fact, much is lost for members of the dominant and marginalized groups when culture is only attributed to the subjugated. This may often lead to little discourse or connection between members who are situated on alternate sides of the lines of privilege.

Conversations Revisited: The Importance of the Continued Conversation

We are not the same since we began conversing to write this chapter. Simply being a part of a discourse among ourselves expanded our understanding of who we are, our values, and our perceptions of our coauthors' experiences. Hearing their stories of their experiences has now become a part of our own experience. That is how change and growth occur—through relationships.

Relationships are built and maintained through conversation. The conversation that we are inviting you to have is an intentional one. Just as we ask our clients to sit with discomfort at times, we are not immune to this process. How we talk about these issues is important (Lawless, 2008). We must make ourselves accountable for not only having these conversations but also the manner in which we engage in them. These conversations need to be respectful, should demonstrate a responsibility on the part of the participants, *and* each participant must take responsibility that he/she is at fault when there is a misconception or misinterpretation. When issues of culture are discussed, it is oftentimes either a polite dance or an intense, emotional exchange. Either way, awareness emerges from interaction with the other.

Our experience working on this chapter brought forth many tangential discourses, especially about teaching these issues in coursework and in supervision. We were able to share our struggles, frustrations, and desires for more platforms to continue these discussions. We were each a bit sad when our conversations came to an end. We discussed how the sadness emerges from the lack of space for this vital discourse. Each therapist is charged with beginning and maintaining space for these conversations. If space does not exist, create it—it is not only for your own growth, but also the space where change and growth lives for us all.

References

Anderson, S., & Middleton, V. (2004). *Explorations in privilege, oppression, and diversity.* Belmont, CA: Brooks/Cole.

Aponte, H. J., Powell, F. D., Brooks, S., Watson, M. F., Litzke, C., Lawless, J., & Johnson, E. (2009). Training the person of the therapist in an academic setting. *Journal of Marital and Family Therapy, 35,* 381–394. doi: 10.1111/j.1752–0606.2009.00123.x

Larsen, R. (2011, September). Best companies 2011: Best diversity practices. *Hispanic Business,* 18–22.

Lawless, J. J. (2008). Transforming a racist legacy. In M. McGoldrick & K. Hardy (Eds.), *Revisioning family therapy: Race, culture, and gender in clinical practice* (2nd ed., pp. 191–196). New York, NY: Guilford Press.

Nazario, A. (2007). Counseling Latina(o) families. In W. M. Parker & M. A. Fukuyama (Eds.), *Consciousness-raising: A primer for multicultural counseling* (3rd. ed., pp. 205–222). Springfield, IL: Charles C. Thomas.

Rastogi, M., & Wieling, L. (2004). *Voices of color: First person accounts of ethnic minority therapists.* Thousand Oaks, CA: Sage.

5

EVIDENCE AND EFFICACY ISSUES

Ronald J. Chenail

In contemporary psychotherapy practice and research, the words *evidence* and *effectiveness* have both methodological and political issues (Sackett, Rosenberg, Gray, Haynes, & Richardson, 1996). From a methodological perspective, evidence can be the foundational information on which therapists base their beliefs in the usefulness, efficacy, and effectiveness of an intervention with individuals, couples, families, or groups. In this vein, evidence can also be seen by some therapists to offer support or to establish confidence in the potential effectiveness of a clinical approach with a particular clinical problem. Methodologically, this evidence of effectiveness can be derived from a variety of sense-making activities on the part of an observer or participant or yielded from a number of investigative designs ranging from the reflections of therapists on their clinical cases to highly controlled experiments wherein researchers conduct statistical analyses of effect size differences between the measured outcomes of participants who are randomly assigned to different treatments delivered by therapists operating from procedural manuals (Chenail, DeVincentis, Kiviat, & Somers, 2012).

From a political perspective, evidence can be a privileging and marginalizing process by which producers and consumers of clinical evidence establish hierarchies valuing one type of evidence over another when determining the effectiveness of a clinical intervention. In these scenarios, a term like *gold standard* can be used to create favoritism for the worth of effectiveness evidence generated from "highly controlled" experimental research designs such as randomized controlled trials (RCTs); at the same time, these imposed standards can be utilized to generate less partiality for the value of effectiveness evidence constructed from more naturalistic, discovery-oriented studies of therapists' and clients' experiences of their clinical encounters (Chenail et al., 2012).

A sizable body of evidence has been generated about couple and family therapy effectiveness over the last 50 years (Sprenkle, 2002). For many practitioners and researchers, the social constructional aspects of these relational therapies seemed to encourage the use of case study, qualitative, and reflective methodologies to conduct investigations into the exploration of outcomes, processes, and experiences (e.g., Chenail et al., 2011). For other curious observers, couple and family therapies presented an opportunity to apply research designs more readily associated with positivistic or postpositivistic worldviews (e.g., Chenail et al., 2011). These researchers typically conduct their research to explore questions of fidelity, efficacy, effectiveness, mechanisms of change, moderators, and mediators. Although at one time these two groups of investigators, both interested in learning about couple and family therapy effectiveness, seemed to have created two separate worlds of evidence for couple and family therapy resulting in a lack of ready conversation with each other, the contemporary landscape shows more dialogue and appreciation for a diversity of effectiveness evidence created using a variety of methodologies (e.g., quantitative and qualitative; Chenail et al., 2012).

This emerging middle ground for considering evidence encourages researchers and therapists to examine all levels of an "evidence pyramid" (see Figure 1) to seek out studies conducted by investigators employing a variety of methods to ascertain support for the use of certain interventions with particular clinical challenges from diverse perspectives (see chapter glossary for descriptions of the different study designs found in Figure 1). So, to minimize the political aspects of evidence and to maximize your attention to those accounts in which investigators, in the broadest sense of the word, attempt to make something evident, plain, or clear regarding outcome, process, or experience of a psychotherapy or relational theory encounter, I suggest you attempt to be methodologically pluralistic in your review and creation of clinical evidence in order to celebrate a diversity of designs and a vitality of difference in the contemporary landscape of therapy effectiveness research (American Psychological Association Presidential Task Force

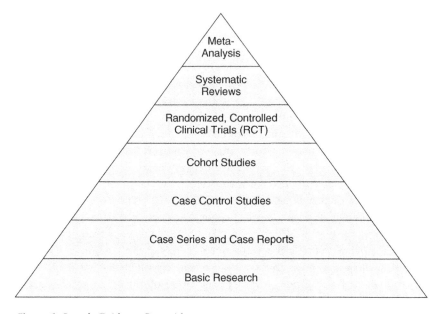

Figure 1 Sample Evidence Pyramid

on Evidence-Based Practice, 2006). By making this choice, you will be able to consider more research to inform your own clinical work and generate your own clinical evidence in pursuit of evaluating the effectiveness of the couple and family therapy you conduct.

Evidence-Based Practice

In response to calls for improved health care outcomes (e.g., Institute of Medicine, 2001), leaders in health and mental health care have called for clinicians to embrace practice values and recommendations similar to those expressed in the *Quality Chasm's 10 Rules to Guide the Redesign of Health Care* (Institute of Medicine, 2001, p. 8) and to take greater heed of the considerable body of research on what works in mental health care:

1. Care based on continuous healing relationships
2. Customization based on patient needs and values
3. The patient as the source of control
4. Shared knowledge and the free flow of information
5. Evidence-based decision making
6. Safety as a system property
7. The need for transparency
8. Anticipation of needs
9. Continuous decrease in waste
10. Cooperation among clinicians

In this effort to improve the delivery of clinical services, evidence-based practice (EBP) has emerged as a popular model for delivering and evaluating the effectiveness of psychotherapies, including couple and family therapy. Evidence-based practice in the mental health arena emerged from evidence-based medicine, which is

> the conscientious, explicit, and judicious use of current best evidence in making decisions about the care of individual patients. The practice of evidence based medicine means integrating individual clinical expertise with the best available external clinical evidence from systematic research. (Sackett et al., 1996, p. 71)

As is the case with evidence-based medicine, in EBP there is an expectation that you as a clinician are applying clinical models of practice and treatment protocols that have been demonstrated via research to be effective with the problem and population to which your client belongs. Based upon this assumption, you are expected to keep current with the clinical literature, to review research findings critically, to apply them in a way that allows you to customize your treatment to meet the unique circumstances of your clients, and to evaluate the results of your clinical work in order to make adjustments to treatment if necessary. EBP should not be confused with another popular research-based approach known as empirically supported treatment (EST), in which clinical models receiving a requisite amount of empirical evidence are deemed as being effective approaches to certain clinical maladies (American Psychological Association, 2002). Although ESTs may be considered as providing the best effectiveness evidence by therapists seeking guidelines for client care, EBP goes beyond simply following an EST by asking the therapist to consider this external EST evidence along with the therapists' own clinical judgment and the client's own perspective and circumstances to determine what course of treatment is most useful for a particular client being treated by a particular therapist for a particular problem. In other words, the evidence from the published research alone does not make a final clinical decision for you as the therapist, but rather the knowledge you learn from systematically reviewing the research literature can inform the care of your clients because in EBP you should integrate (a) the global research evidence; (b) the culture, values, and preferences of your client; and (c) your clinical expertise to deliver competent couple and family therapy. Evidence-based practice also goes one step further by asking you as the therapist to assess the local evidence of effectiveness from your direct practice, including bringing the client into the clinical decision-making process. Taken together, all of these steps in EBP are theoretically designed to enhance the opportunity for your client to achieve optimal clinical outcomes and quality of life (Duke University Medical Center Library and Health Sciences Library, UNC-Chapel Hill, 2010).

To practice EBP, therapists typically follow six steps (see Figure 2).

Assess the patient. In this step, it is critical you learn what your client is trying to achieve in couple or family therapy. In conjoint work, this process is especially

ASSESS the patient	1. Start with the patient – a clinical problem or question arises from the care of the patient
ASK the question	2. Construct a well-built clinical question derived from the case
ACQUIRE the evidence	3. Select the appropriate resource(s) and conduct a search
APPRAISE the evidence	4. Appraise that evidence for its validity (closeness to the truth) and applicability (usefulness in clinical practice)
APPLY: talk with the patient	5. Return to the patient – integrate that evidence with clinical expertise and patient preferences, and apply it to practice
ALL-AROUND evaluation	6. Evaluate your performance with this patient

Figure 2 The Steps in the EBP Process

Source: Adapted from Duke University Medical Center Library and Health Sciences Library, UNC-Chapel Hill, 2010, page 1 of 2.

challenging because different members of the family or couple may have varying perspectives on what constitutes the problem and the desired outcomes (Chenail et al., 2011). Under these circumstances, you may need to consider more than one problem or question in taking an EBP approach in conjoint treatment.

Ask the question(s). Based upon your assessment of the client, you pose a question that is based upon the circumstances of the case and that will allow you to search the research literature to find (a) evidence that supports your candidate approach for working with the couple or family, (b) evidence that does not support your candidate approach, or (c) evidence in support of some other clinical approach. One system you can use to construct a well-formed question is the PICO approach:

1. Patient/Problem: Include a component in your question in which you accurately articulate your client's particular circumstances and characteristics along with the problem or problems under treatment consideration.
2. Intervention: Include a component in your question that accurately presents the clinical model and/or interventions you propose using to help your clients.
3. Comparison (if any): Include a component in your question that helps you identify other candidate clinical models or interventions that might also be useful in the treatment of your client.
4. Outcome: Include a component in your question that describes the outcome desired by your clients. The outcome can be anything you and your clients are trying to achieve such as reducing incidents of a behavior, increasing what is working, or achieving new insights or perspectives. (Duke University Medical Center Library and Health Sciences Library, UNC-Chapel Hill, 2010)

Once you have identified the components, you can craft your basic search query. For example, if you are considering using solution-focused brief therapy with a married Hispanic couple, dealing with the wife's drinking and the husband's affair, who want to build a greater sense of trust in their relationship, you can create a question from these components or simply use them as search terms.

Acquire the evidence. Working from your PICO question or search terms, you can search online databases such as PubMed (www.ncbi.nlm.nih.gov/pubmed), a massive repository of published research, or use a more generic search tool such as Google Scholar (scholar.google.com) to begin your pursuit for publications related to your search terms. In couple and family therapy, there are also more focused resources for which authors have conducted systematic reviews to collect research on clinical topics such as solution-focused brief therapy (Franklin, Trepper, McCollum, & Gingerich, 2011), couples distress (Lebow, Chambers, Christensen, & Johnson, 2011), and couple and family alcoholism (O'Farrell & Clements, 2011).

Appraise the evidence. As you collect research pertaining to your clinical query, you will read the articles to determine (a) the results of the study (e.g., Did the participants in the study show positive outcomes?), (b) your confidence in the results (e.g., Did the authors of the study present a method and findings you find trustworthy?), and (c) how the results will help you in caring for your clients (e.g., How will this global evidence be relevant for the local concerns of your clients?). Knowing the likelihood that an external study will be completely isomorphic to the internal characteristics of your case is remote, you will need to consider the value of the body of evidence carefully as you integrate that knowledge with your own personal expertise and the perspectives of your couples and families.

Apply: talk with the patient. As you gather evidence from previously generated research you have reviewed and appraised, you can discuss the various courses of action with your clients to learn their wishes regarding their care. Part of this discussion with your clients can include information about the role other factors can play in the effectiveness of psychotherapy (e.g., building and maintaining positive client-therapist relationships; Sprenkle, Davis, & Lebow, 2009) and the possibility that a number of "effective" psychotherapies may be effective in their situation (e.g., many systematic reviews reveal different forms of psychotherapy can yield similar positive results; Wampold, 2001). As all these factors are discussed, a treatment plan can be formed, enacted, and evaluated for success.

All-around evaluation. As therapy ensues, EBP can be more accurately termed practice-based evidence (PBE; Gabbay & Le May, 2011). As you begin to evaluate evidence if the treatment plan is working, I suggest you not only reflect on your own sense of what is working and not working in the therapy with your couples and families, but also routinely consider the family members' viewpoints when reflecting on progress in therapy and make appropriate adjustments based on that feedback. In becoming more comfortable utilizing this all-around type of PBE evaluation, you may also benefit from viewing family members as your teachers and supervisors and doing therapy allied to this collective familial wisdom (Chenail et al., 2011).

As you become more familiar with couple and family therapy effectiveness evidence, I think you will find the research to be methodologically diverse and growing. You should be able to review controlled, confirmatory studies; naturalistic, discovery-oriented studies; outcome, process, and experiential studies; as well as systematic reviews including meta-analyses. I encourage you to favor inclusiveness in your searches for the "best evidence" by juxtaposing evidence from controlled and naturalistic designs with research based upon social constructionist or positivistic epistemologies. I suggest this pluralistic approach because I hold that all evidence has value when we are attempting to examine what researchers hold evident about couple and family therapy effectiveness. Last, I suggest you take seriously the role of producing your own practice-based evidence of effectiveness from a multiview perspective. This stance means you not only reflect on your own judgments of your cases' effectiveness evidence, but also you embrace the points of view of your clients by continually checking with them regarding what is and is not working in therapy from their perspectives.

From a methodological perspective, EBP is a simple process of integrating global research evidence of effectiveness with local evidence of our clinical effectiveness, but in the wise words of Karl Tomm (Chenail et al., 2011, pp. 20–21), "This, of course, requires genuine humility on the part of therapists" because "while we may think we know, on the basis of our wealth of experience as therapists, that we know what is better for our clients than they know themselves—this is seldom the case. And we certainly can never know their experiences better than they do." So please embrace your humility as a couple and family therapist when it comes to searching for evidence of effectiveness in your work.

References

American Psychological Association. (2002). Criteria for evaluating treatment guidelines. *American Psychologist, 57*(12), 1052–1059.

American Psychological Association Presidential Task Force on Evidence-Based Practice. (2006). Evidence-based practice in psychology. *American Psychologist, 61*(4), 271–285.

Chenail, R. J., DeVincentis, M., Kiviat, H. E., & Somers, C. (2012). A systematic narrative review of discursive therapies research: Considering the value of circumstantial evidence. In A. Locke & T. Strong (Eds.), *Discursive perspectives in therapeutic practice* (pp. 224–244). Oxford: Oxford University Press.

Chenail, R. J., St. George, S., Wulff, D., Duffy, M., Wilson Scott, K., & Tomm, K. (2011). Clients' relational conceptions of conjoint couple and family therapy quality: A grounded formal theory. *Journal of Marital and Family Therapy.* Advance online publication. doi:10.1111/j.1752–0606.2011.00246.x

Duke University Medical Center Library and Health Sciences Library, UNC-Chapel Hill. (2010). *Introduction to evidence-based practice* (5th ed.). Durham and Chapel Hill, NC: Authors. Retrieved from http://www.hsl.unc.edu/services/tutorials/ebm/index.htm

Franklin, C., Trepper, T. S., McCollum, E. E., & Gingerich, W. J. (Eds.). (2011). *Solution-focused brief therapy: A handbook of evidence-based practice.* New York, NY: Oxford University Press.

Gabbay, J., & Le May, A. (2011). *Practice-based evidence for healthcare: Clinical mindlines.* New York, NY: Routledge.

Institute of Medicine. (2001). *Crossing the quality chasm: A new health system for the 21st century.* Washington, DC: National Academies Press.

Lebow, J. L., Chambers, A. L., Christensen, A., & Johnson, S. M. (2011). Research on the treatment of couple distress. *Journal of Marital and Family Therapy.* Advance online publication. doi:10.1111/j.1752–0606.2011.00249.x

O'Farrell, T. J., & Clements, K. (2011). Review of outcome research on marital and family therapy in treatment for alcoholism. *Journal of Marital and Family Therapy.* Advance online publication. doi:10.1111/j.1752–0606.2011.00242.x

Sackett, D. L., Rosenberg, W. M. C., Gray, J. A. M., Haynes, R. B., & Richardson, W. S. (1996). Evidence based medicine: What it is and what it isn't. *British Medical Journal, 312,* 71–72.

Sprenkle, D. H. (Ed.). (2002). *Effectiveness research in marriage and family therapy.* Alexandria, VA: American Association for Marriage and Family Therapy.

Sprenkle, D. H., Davis, S. D., & Lebow, J. L. (2009). *Common factors in couple and family therapy: The overlooked foundation for effective practice.* New York, NY: Guilford Press.

Wampold, B. E. (2001). *The great psychotherapy debate: Models, methods, and findings.* Mahwah, NJ: Erlbaum.

Additional Resources

Patterson, J. E., Miller, R. B., Carnes, S., & Wilson, S. (2004). Evidence-based practice for marriage and family therapists. *Journal of Marital and Family Therapy, 30*(2), 183–195.

Rubin, A. (2008). *Practitioner's guide to using research for evidence-based practice.* Hoboken, NJ: Wiley.

University of Washington. *Evidence-based practice.* Retrieved from http://healthlinks.washington.edu/ebp

Williams, L. M., Patterson, J. E., & Miller, R. B. (2006). Panning for gold: A clinician's guide to using research. *Journal of Marital and Family Therapy, 32*(1), 17–32.

Glossary of Study Designs

Case series and **case reports** are studies in which the researcher reports on findings from one or many cases. The results of the therapy in these cases are not compared to the results of therapy conducted on a control group (i.e., clients who receive no treatment or receive a treatment other than the therapy being reported).

Case control studies are studies in which the researcher retrospectively investigates the circumstances of cases in which the clients had a specific condition and compares the results of their treatment with people who do not have the condition to identify factors or exposures that might be associated with the clinical problem.

Cohort studies are studies in which the researcher examines a large clinical population who are already receiving a particular treatment, tracks their progress over time, and then compares their results with a similar group that has not been treated by the clinical intervention.

Randomized, controlled clinical trials (RCTs) are experiments in which the researcher randomly assigns clients to intervention groups and control groups (i.e., no intervention) and then tracks the clients' outcomes to see if there are statistical differences in the effects of the treatments.

Systematic reviews are reviews of the research literature in which the reviewer focuses on a clinical topic to address a specific question. The reviewer collects and assesses the quality of the research and summarizes the results according to the preset criteria of the review question and method.

Meta-analysis is a review in which the analyst thoroughly examines a number of controlled studies (e.g., RCTs) on a topic and combines the results using statistical analysis methodology to report the results as if it were one large study.

6

FAITH AND SPIRITUALITY ISSUES

Melissa Elliott and Jacqueline Clarke

The family therapy field emerged with a radically inclusive focus on relationships and connecting systems, yet it followed the tradition of other mental health disciplines in excluding religion and spirituality from the therapy conversation. However, over the last decade the boundary that prevailed between religion, spirituality, and family therapy has been eroding (Griffith & Elliott Griffith, 2002; Helmeke & Bischof, 2007; Patterson, Hayworth, Turner, & Raskin, 2000; Richards & Bergin, 2010; Walsh, 2009). Family therapists and faith-based contenders are gradually rescinding the skepticism that placed behavioral science and spirituality at opposite ends of the spectrum in understanding people's lives. With this emerging perspective, more and more family therapists came to grips with the relevance of therapeutic interventions involving spirituality and religion. Spirituality and religion began to be seen as relationship issues rather than fragments that needed to be compartmentalized within the therapeutic process.

Aponte (2002, p. 14) indicated that religion and spirituality are at the heart of therapy, since "therapists have to access people's values behind clinical issues, and to determine within themselves and with their clients the values and morality upon which to base their therapy." For many people these values are grounded and worked out in their spiritual life or religious experience. For them these values offer an important perspective to include in the therapeutic dialogue—as important as issues of sexuality, power, intergenerational family patterns, and gender roles. This chapter will suggest some ways to include clients' spirituality and religion in therapy; some guiding principles; and some generative questions And we tell a story.

Perhaps what is most important to know is that one does not know about another's spiritual life, beliefs, or community, even if all these sound familiar or even if therapist and client state the same beliefs and share the same faith community (Elliott, 2009, p. 326). The conviction that one does not know sustains an attitude of humility when speaking with people about this most private and complex aspect of their lives. An attitude of humility provides the ground in which the cultivation of wonder can occur. The practice of wonder—being available to that which is not yet known or expected—is crucial to effective therapeutic conversations about spirituality.

There are some assumptions that foster an attitude of humility and the practice of wonder:

1. When meeting together with couples or families, a therapist may assume that differences in beliefs may not be speakable by clients or that speaking about these differences to an outsider might be an act of disloyalty to the family in the room, to their community, or even to their ancestors.
2. When listening to people describe their experience of God, a therapist may assume that this, like other relationships, is multistoried in ways that might even be contradictory (Elliott, 2009).
3. When hearing a person tentatively speak about religion, a therapist may assume that this person may fear being seen as ignorant, needful of a crutch, or psychologically unsophisticated because this perception has, in fact, been predominant in the history of mental health.
4. When asking about how spiritual practices support people's values or how religious tenets guide people's actions, a therapist may assume that, while people may speak some answers, they may not speak of the sense of shame stimulated by these questions, shame about their inconsistency with these practices or their failure to be true to these tenets. Therapists should remember that religious practices can be harmful as well as healing.
5. When witnessing or attending to the description of a ritual, a therapist may assume that a ritual is a container for mystery and that, while the acts of the ritual are set and predictable, what occurs inside this container may be unpredictable and inchoate (Imber-Black & Roberts, 1992).

There are a few good questions, gentle invitations for people to speak about their spirituality (Griffith & Elliott Griffith, 2002, p. 46). If spirituality is an important part of someone's life, questions like these can provide an opening for this conversation. However, these questions aim to not intrude on people's privacy and do not require a religiously oriented response.

*   What sustains your family in this difficult time?
*   Where do you find peace/solace/hope?
*   How did you decide not to take your life when you so yearned for the relief of dying?
*   When circumstances are so confusing, what is your way for finding wisdom and clarity?
*   For what are you most deeply grateful?
*   Who understands your innermost thoughts?
*   Or, less pointed than a question, a sympathetic statement like, "I don't know how you keep going from day to day" gives opportunity for a response.

These questions have been employed in many various clinical encounters, sometimes leading to conversations about spirituality, sometimes to conversations about people's pets, and sometimes to the response, "I don't know." This variety of responses suggests that they are truly open questions.

Though questions and prompts from a therapist may initiate a conversation about a client's spiritual life, the usefulness and relevance of such conversations hinge less on the therapist's questioning skills than on his or her listening skills. These skills include listening for cues, for example, a mention of a spiritual practice, a faith community, beliefs, or relationship with the divine, and then following the client's language and expanding the conversation with careful curiosity, asking often for direction about how to proceed. Opening our therapeutic ears to hear these cues, removing the blinding binds of stereotypes from our eyes, hinges on the continual and joyful work of opening our hearts. If I (Elliott) find that I am going for days with patients and clients saying what I thought they would say or if what I see serves to confirm my expectations, I take it as a sign that I am working in an unskilled, and unawake, way. The only reliable clue that I am genuinely engaged in this work is the experience of surprise. The following story of surprise occurred one evening on the psychiatric unit of the hospital where I practice both nursing and family therapy. Though it occurred while I was Sophie's nurse, it is just as relevant to my work as a family therapist because of the effects: to open my ears and eyes and heart, thus to prepare me to be more skilled and available, both as a nurse and as a therapist.

Sophie came to our unit from her assisted living home. Staff persons there had been concerned about her complaints of unremitting and severe headaches, and her recent behavioral changes warranted a safety concern for her and for the other residents. A 66-year-old woman severely developmentally delayed since birth, Sophie had always been dependent on her beloved and reliable mother. Her mother had recently died, and Sophie's life had been altered in every way.

A nurse from the assisted living home spoke with me, "Sophie didn't talk about it for two weeks after her mother died, and we thought she might be OK, but then she got agitated, striking out at us, hurting herself and screaming, constantly. She has never acted this way before and, given that there's no physiological explanation for this behavioral change, we think it must be because she's missing her mother. After all, they were together every day for 66 years. Her mother took care of her at home, then, when her mother came here, Sophie came too and has been her mother's roommate for the last 18 years."

When Sophie came to our unit, she complained, several times a day, about her head, in her high-pitched, childlike voice, "Nurse, my head hurts!" she would alert us at full volume whether calling from six rooms down the hall or six inches away from our ears, "I think it's gonna explode! Can't you help my head?" Our analgesics were ineffective, leading to a thorough workup and neurology consult resulting in the recommendation that this was a "typical tension headache" and should be treated as such. How could she not be tense, even terrified, as she faced the task of reordering her life after counting on the comfort and direction of her mother for 66 years? Perhaps her tension was exacerbated due to her difficulty in understanding this change or in verbally processing her grief, or in our lack of skills to understand what she was telling us.

Some hospital staff had been concerned about bringing up the subject of her mother, unsure of what Sophie understood of death and cautious about how to contain the overwhelming emotion that might arise. I also had been uncertain as to how to proceed until I heard Sophie say, quite matter-of-factly, to another patient, "Did you know my mama passed away?"

Attending to her language, a few hours later, I said, "Sophie, I heard that your mama passed away. I'm so sorry."

"Yes ma'am, my mama passed away about two weeks ago." Then she asked, "Did you know my mama?"

"No, I didn't, but I'd like to know about her. Will you tell me about her?" I asked.

"She was real pretty. She wore glasses." Sophie was calm. She seemed to have no more to say.

"I'll bet she loved you very much," I offered.

Then Sophie's tenses began to blur, past to present. It was the first time I had seen her smile, and she was beaming. "She loved me real good. She loves every little thing about me. She loves me more than anything!"

"Do you ever feel her close to you now?" I asked. "Can you feel her love? Do you feel her in your heart?"

"When I say my prayers I feel close to her." Then Sophie changed the subject, back to the headache she'd been complaining about for three days. "Nurse, my head hurts so bad. I think it's gonna explode. Can't you help my head?" I responded with a predictably ineffective analgesic.

Hours later, when helping her get to bed, I asked if her mother said her prayers with her at night. "Yes ma'am, she always did."

"Would you like for me to say your prayers with you?" I asked, quite tentatively.

"Yes ma'am. Of course I would," Sophie said.

"What would you like for me to do?" I asked.

"Just stand right there," she stationed me at her bedside, "and hold my hand."

I stood by her bedside in the darkened room, quietly, waiting for her to recite a verse, perhaps the familiar, "Now I lay me down to sleep, I pray thee Lord my soul to keep . . ."

But Sophie was quiet too. I wondered whether she was waiting for me to speak, whether her mother was the one who spoke first, but I remained silent, because I could not know what to say and because she had given me clear directions to just stand there and hold her hand.

Then she started to speak in a calm voice, one that was lower pitched than her usual child-like voice, "Heavenly father," she slowly began, "Help Sophie's head feel better. You know she is hurting. Help her feel better. Be with Sophie now and through the night. We ask you this in Jesus's name. Amen." Sophie released my hand, thanked me, and said, "Good night. You can go now."

Though I cannot know what this meant for Sophie, her demeanor was peaceful; she seemed comforted, was satisfied to stay in bed, and was no longer complaining of a headache. I cannot know if this differs from the way she prays every night, though I believe that a dimension is added by being witnessed (Weingarten, 2004).

As I left her room and walked down the hall, I was filled with gratitude to be doing this work and in awe that I had heard Sophie praying in her mother's voice. I was eager to share this story with a fellow nurse. First, though, I checked myself to see if I might be thinking too magically. I asked three staff members who were at the nursing station if they had ever heard Sophie voice her requests as "Help Sophie" rather than "Help me." My colleagues' responses, that Sophie never spoke that way, gladdened me. This fit with my sense that in this prayer, though Sophie was speaking, she had heard her mother praying for her. I was surprised and humbled. My purpose had been to offer some semblance of a comforting familiar bedtime ritual, but much more had occurred. I knew rituals to be the containers for mystery, but my stereotyping and limited imagination had led me to expect a rhyming children's prayer. Sophie's imagination was not so constrained.

This was a nursing experience, but it mirrors many of my therapy experiences in that it serves to reveal and unravel my assumptions and cultivate my capacity for wonder. It reminds me of the ways that the spirituality can be included in the care, whether through nursing or therapy, of the people with whom I work: offering to open doors, listening to their language, asking for and following their directions, holding expectations loosely, being happy to be wrong, and celebrating surprise. All these skills are rooted in humility, which is surely key to hosting conversations in therapy about spirituality and, possibly, about anything.

References

Aponte, H. (2002). Spirituality: The heart of therapy. *Journal of Family Psychotherapy*, *13*(1–2), 13–27.

Elliott, M. (2009). Opening therapy to conversations with a personal God. In F. Walsh (Ed.), *Spiritual resources in family therapy* (2nd ed., pp. 323–339). New York, NY: Guilford Press.

Griffith, J., & Elliott Griffith, M. (2002). *Encountering the sacred in psychotherapy: How to talk with people about their spiritual lives*. New York, NY: Guilford Press.

Helmeke, K. B., & Bischof, G. H. (2007). Couple therapy and spirituality. *Journal of Couple and Relationship*, *6*(1–2), 167–179.

Imber-Black, E., & Roberts, J. (1992). *Rituals for our times: Celebrating, healing, and changing our lives and our relationships*. New York, NY: Harper Perennial.

Patterson, J., Hayworth, M., Turner, C., & Raskin, M. (2000). Spiritual issues in family therapy: A graduate-level course. *Journal of Marital and Family Therapy, 26*(2), 199–210.

Richards, P. S., & Bergin, A. E. (2010). Toward religious and spiritual competency for mental health professionals. In P. S. Richards & A. E. Bergin (Eds.), *Handbook of psychotherapy and religious diversity* (pp. 3–26). Washington, DC: American Psychological Association.

Walsh, F. (2009). Integrating spirituality in family therapy: Wellsprings for health, healing, and resilience. In F. Walsh (Ed.), *Spiritual resources in family therapy* (2nd ed., pp. 31–61). New York, NY: Guilford Press.

Weingarten, K. (2004). *Common shock: Witnessing violence everyday: How we are harmed; How we can heal?* New York, NY: New American Library.

Section II

FAMILY THERAPY MODELS

PART A
PSYCHOANALYTIC/EXPERIENTIAL MODELS

7

A BRIEF HISTORY OF PSYCHOANALYTIC/EXPERIENTIAL MODELS

Anne Rambo, Charles West, AnnaLynn Schooley, and Tommie V. Boyd

This section discusses case studies from the psychoanalytic (Chapter 8), symbolic/experiential (Chapter 9), and human validation process (also often called experiential) (Chapter 10) traditions. We have chosen to group these models of family therapy together because, in our view, they share a focus on patterns of emotion. Congruence of affect and expressed emotion, emotional authenticity, and the emotional bond between therapist and client are important in all three of these models.

Psychoanalytic therapy, originated by Freud, is not in itself a systemic model. Yet there are systemic models of family therapy that focus on process and awareness in a way that resonates with this tradition. Nathan Ackerman, one of the founders of family therapy, was himself a practicing psychoanalyst and never gave up on the idea that family therapy could be combined with psychoanalysis, if the family itself were seen as a living system (Ackerman, 1958). Some psychoanalytic family therapy is still practiced at the Ackerman Institute for the Family in New York City, although this is no longer a primary focus (www.ackerman.org). Object relations family therapy is closely related, with a stronger focus on attachment theory, and the International Psychotherapy Institute (www.theipi.org) is a center of training and therapy in the object relations tradition, which includes family therapy among other modalities. Therapists outside the United States often do not see a sharp distinction between psychoanalytic approaches and systemic approaches; the history of family therapy in Europe and Australia was not marked by the outright rejection of psychoanalysis that was a feature of the early history of family therapy in the United States (Ng, 2003). We have chosen to present a blending of psychoanalytic and systemic ideas by Carmel Flaskas from Australia (Chapter 8).

We have chosen as well to group in this section as experiential two other models that are also focused on patterns of authenticity and congruence in emotional expression. These are the symbolic-experiential approach, associated with Carl Whitaker (Chapter 9), and Virginia Satir's human validation process model (Chapter 10). Both were developed initially in the 1960s. Whitaker's approach is difficult to replicate, except through intense cotherapy training. Augustus Napier, a trusted colleague of Whitaker's, now trains in this approach in Atlanta, Georgia, through the Family Workshop center (www. psychotherapy.net/interview/augustus-napier.html).

Satir's approach, meanwhile, has given birth to an entire international organization, the Avanta Network, dedicated to providing experiential workshops and trainings in her model (www.avanta.net). Satir's approach is clearly more educational and directive than Whitaker's, and both Whitaker's and Satir's are more deliberately experiential, focused in the present moment, than psychoanalytically informed family therapy. Yet all three of these models have a concern with process, with stimulating the authentic expression of emotion, and with growth rather than behavior change alone, which to us makes them worthy of joint consideration.

Considerations of managed care have made a practice in any of these models somewhat difficult in the United States, as long-term, insight-oriented models are less likely to be reimbursed by insurance. In Europe and Australia, however, these models continue to be quite influential. Their focus on self of the therapist in the moment makes them unique in their approach to training and supervision as well.

References

Ackerman, N. (1958). *The psychodynamics of family life*. New York, NY: Basic Books.
Ng, K.S. (2003). *Global perspectives in family therapy: Development, practice, trends*. New York, NY: Routledge.

Additional Resources

Bumberry, W., & Whitaker, C. (1988). *Dancing with the family: A symbolic-experiential approach*. New York, NY: Routledge.
Flaskas, C. (2002). *Family therapy beyond postmodernism: Practice, challenges, theory*. New York NY: Routledge.
Gerson, M. (2009). *The imbedded self: An integrative psychodynamic and systemic perspective on couples and family therapy*. New York, NY: Routledge.
Satir, V., Banmen, J., Gerber, J., & Gomori, M. (1991). *The Satir Model: Family therapy and beyond*. Palo Alto, CA: Science and Behavior Books.

8

A SYSTEMIC PRACTICE INFLUENCED BY SELECTED PSYCHOANALYTIC IDEAS

Carmel Flaskas

This chapter does not present a "pure" approach and serves instead as an example of a systemic practice influenced by selected psychoanalytic ideas. What do I mean by a systemic practice, and exactly which psychoanalytic ideas do I draw from? The systemic tradition of family therapy has an enduring and central interest in context and relationship, which shapes how the presenting problem is understood and how the therapy itself is undertaken. The orientation to context and relationship marks the continuity from the first generation through to the contemporary approaches. Alongside systemic ideas, which by their very nature all privilege the relational and interpersonal, I draw on some ideas from psychoanalysis that function as a "double description" in my practice. A summary list (Flaskas, 2002) would include the following: the unconscious and unconscious communication; transference, countertransference, projection, and projective identification; containment and the therapeutic "holding frame"; and knowledge about attachment and attachment patterns, allied as much with systemic as psychoanalytic therapy. Psychoanalytic ideas are most regularly in my mind with respect to the therapeutic relationship and my use of self.

The intake notes for this family consist of a bare one paragraph. I don't know the referral route, and for the purposes of this chapter we'll assume the family has contacted a government-funded child and adolescent counseling service. I will invite Mary, Fred, and Johnny to attend the first session. My inclination in child and adolescent work is to invite just the immediate family to the first session unless there are some good reasons to do otherwise (for example, cultural family forms or safety priorities around abuse). Though I note the information about the closeness of Mary's mother, Bess, to Mary and the family, I would not invite Bess to this first meeting. As yet, I have no information about how Bess's support for Mary is experienced by Fred and Johnny, or indeed who might be the least happy if I were to invite her to the first session.

Working from my systemic understandings, I walk into the first meeting with some relational and contextual hypotheses in my head. The process of hypothesizing in earlier Milan therapy (in the 1980s) was framed within positivist language: hypotheses were to be "tested" within session. But, even then, hypothesizing was seen as a tentative process, and the testing was not about whether a hypothesis was true or false, but instead about whether it was useful in opening out possibilities of change and whether it fit the family's situation. Systemic hypotheses frame the integrity of the presenting problem: how does the problem potentially make sense relationally and contextually? This practice theory still guides me in 2012, though now I am just as happy for initial hypotheses to stay in the form of interrelated questions rather than more organized scenarios, and to be lightly held in mind rather than tested.

From the intake notes, the presenting problem is around Johnny hating school, skipping class, possibly engaging in high-risk behaviors, and the anxiety and dilemmas for his parents. Mary has headaches she sees as related to this stress. Hypothesizing around developmental issues is a good starting point. And so I would wonder about family challenges when an only child (a son) turns 15 in a three-person, two-parent (heterosexual couple) family. Is Johnny engaged in the struggle of adolescent autonomy, trying to strike a balance of separating while staying connected to his parents? On the one hand, he could be making a bid for separation in skipping school and hanging out with who he wants while simultaneously inviting his parents to stay heavily involved in his life by alarming them with the dangers. From the parents' side of the challenge, I wonder about loss and anxiety associated with change. What might it mean to Mary for her son to be most definitely not a child anymore? Has Bess moved in closer to support Mary as she has become more worried and stressed? Is Johnny giving Bess a good reason to move in closer to support Mary? If Bess and Mary have become closer, what effect has this had on Mary and Fred's relationship (as a couple and as parents)? Or what might Fred's reactions as a father be to his son's growing up? What was his own time as an adolescent son like, and how might unworded thoughts/feelings be playing into the stance he is taking with Johnny? Could Johnny's behavior be allowing Fred to butch up with anger and hide his vulnerabilities? And while I am on this roll, I wonder about the forms of attachment and belonging, and the patterns of balancing intimacy and holding on to self, in Fred's and Mary's families' histories, and in earlier times in their family when Johnny was younger.

Another set of possibilities is sparked by a question in response to the intake notes: why exactly does Johnny hate school? Is he finding the academic work harder now? Does he feel bad about himself and ashamed? Does he fear disappointing his parents, and would he rather exit stage right from school altogether, with face-saving involvement with the group he has fallen in with—sparking the attendant relational fallout sequences in his family? Or has he been bullied or assaulted at school, too humiliated to talk to his parents about it, fearful of his mother's/father's distress or anger, and would rather handle it by exiting stage right from school?

So I meet the family. Culturally and in a gendered way I am low key and friendly and have cultivated as a therapist a calm presence (which is not to say

I am always calm!), and I use quite a lot of smiling and humor where it seems to fit. There are many different authentic ways to relate therapeutically, and I use what I can of my self in inviting a therapeutic relationship with the family, which I hope will serve as a holding frame for the challenges of the work ahead. I begin with the usual nonproblem talk introductions and from the start take responsibility for introducing a pattern within the therapy of inviting equal air-space and relating consistently in how I respond to the contributions of all three family members. Mary may want me to understand how worrying it is and may hope I can bring Fred around from his punitive reactions; Fred may be pretty lukewarm about the idea of therapy, polite but quite guarded/prickly about how I will respond; Johnny may want to show/tell me it's all a huge fucking waste of time and nothing to do with him anyway. As I invite each person in turn to tell me what they would like to come from today and what is on their mind most in coming to this counseling meeting, I convey that I am interested, that I want to hear and understand, and I ask questions assuming there will be complete good sense in what each person might choose to say. When I reflect back (which I do fairly sparingly), I phrase it as a form of checking and note the sense of the position from that person's point of view. In these reflections, I name strengths in a factual rather than complimentary way. At the end of this first part of the meeting, I note differences between the three of them clearly and calmly (conveying without words that there is nothing unusual about the level of differences). If Johnny isn't talking to me, I come up with two different things he might plausibly have said to me if he felt it was the right time and give his hypothetical contributions the same air space, relating to them in strictly the same way as I relate to his parents' ideas.

I tend to go slow with introductions and what people want from coming. Very often, I ask the family to tell me about a difficult recent time. Old-fashioned though it may be, a slow working-through of who does what to whom when where and why, inquiring about the meaning and emotion and not just behavior, has a lot of clinical mileage. I will ask the family about the immediate sequence between the three of them, and then the next level out, to each of them: who outside the three of you comes to know about this? If the only answer is Bess, and she is described as being there via and for Mary, I ask who outside the three of them understands most about what it is like for Fred and Johnny? I will ask other-oriented questions in this part of the interview, providing that everyone's anger and anxiety is contained enough to allow it: So, Mary, when Fred hits the roof when Johnny comes home drunk at 4 a.m., what do you think is really getting to him most as a father? (This would perhaps be followed by: Knowing your husband as well as you do, why do you think this is the thing about what Johnny is doing that gets to him the most?) I will use triadic questions around changes in closeness/distance at significant points in the timeline of the development of the problem—Fred, how have you noticed things change between Johnny and Mary, and between Johnny and you, since the start of Year 9? And,

Johnny, since the start of Year 9 and all the arguing, what have you noticed about how things have changed between your parents? (If Johnny still is not into talking, I might begin: I don't know, Johnny, if you'd want to give your ideas about this or not, but I've been sitting here wondering what you've noticed.) You can hear that these questions explore relationships held against context, and other-oriented and triadic questions invite different people to voice their understanding of other people and patterns. I would also be checking process to see if the questions and the discussions that emerge are (or are not) having the effect of containing anger and anxiety, opening up a more reflective rather than reactive space, and nurturing a more empathic and compassionate space rather than a blaming-counterblaming space.

I would follow the different stories that emerge from the naming of what needs to be changed, the discussion of sequences, the family's ideas about each person's meaning and spot, the relational changes since the beginning of the problem, and what sense they each make of the context of the problem. I would hold these stories against my earlier hypotheses, moving flexibly to other possible understandings that seem a better fit with what the family is telling me now, still drawing these understandings relationally and contextually and respecting the sense of each person's position while not denying the actual or potential damage/danger. I will take a 5–10 minute break after about 50 minutes, think about what the family has said, then give some feedback. I will start by noting strengths of different members of the family and of the family as a whole, then retell what I have heard about the advent of the problem and different people's perceptions and positions, highlighting the contexts and sense of each person's position, noting the changes to relationships, and drawing out commonalities of concerns/desires/hopes. I will also draw out my own (relational/contextual) wonderings that have come out of what's been said. If there has been a lot of talk, for example, about Johnny's high-risk activities, or whether he should or shouldn't change schools, I will directly talk about these concerns. I present the feedback as "ideas from today," framed as an offering rather than any expert edict. I may suggest a task that flows from this feedback. I will negotiate if the family want further appointments and go from there.

So far, I have flagged the systemic orientation as I have been describing this piece of practice. The psychoanalytic influences are less visible. However, some aspects of this practice share systemic and psychoanalytic orientations. You can hear that I give explicit attention to the process of containment, and this informs my style of therapeutic relating—containment is not about controlling emotions, but instead about allowing each person's experience to be voiced enough in words, which frees people to think about and relate to what is happening, rather than being held in its grip. The positioning of therapy as a space of reflection, with behavioral change following from changes in meaning and emotional experience, is central in the canvas of the psychoanalytic therapies. Reflecting processes are also at the center of post-Milan systemic and the dialogical tradition and, in a broader way, align with the centrality of meaning shared by narrative therapy. Treading a path of searching for commonalities while holding (not collapsing) differences is in alignment with the contemporary intersubjective tradition of psychoanalysis. Yet holding commonalities/differences is scarcely the sole province of an analytic orientation—indeed, it is one generic description of the challenge of human relating.

Reflective Practice Comes With the Territory of All Good Therapy

Using the idea of transference, I think about how I find myself pulled to relate to the family and to particular people in the family. I will look for the points during the interview when my own default behaviors show I am rattled, or when I find myself doing/thinking/feeling something that surprises me. I will assume my own responses make some sense—not that they are right, but that it's possible my responses relate to something about the family's struggle. So, after the first session, I think about the way I alternated between feeling protective of Mary then irritated with her, and being angry at points with Fred's punitive behavior and then cutting off the authenticity of my response to him, and a couple of times having turned to ask Johnny something when things got too hot between the parents. I also register a kind of helpless sadness in myself after this session, even a fatalistic tug relating to Johnny's trajectory (a countertransference belonging to my own stuff, or perhaps a countertransference that relates more to something in the family's experience). I then wonder about the dominant alternating emotions of anger and fear/anxiety in the session, with no expression of sadness/loss about anything current or historical. I think about the gendered division of who gets to feel/show anxiety and who gets to feel/show anger and about possible unconscious processes of projection in this division within the family. And I wonder if projective identification is at play in my being left feeling a helpless sadness, a feeling maybe not registered consciously in the family, but perhaps still somewhere a force in how they are relating to this crisis. These ideas, conditional and tentative, become another kind of hypothesizing, potentially bridging my own experience back to the family's experience.

This concludes my comments on a piece of systemic practice influenced by selected psychoanalytic ideas. However, I find I cannot resist adding a postscript: there are many kinds of families, many kinds of challenges faced by families, many kinds of settings of practice, many kinds of family therapists, and many kinds of good family therapy. One particular approach will not meet the breadth and depth of the diversity of cases. To acknowledge this does not detract from the value of the coherence and creativity embedded in particular practice approaches, but may instead offer choices for how we relate to the different offerings in family therapy practice theory. It may also offer us the freedom to use practice theory in pure or in blended ways in the interests of our clients.

Reference

Flaskas, C. (2002). *Family therapy beyond postmodernism: Practice challenges theory.* New York, NY: Brunner-Routledge.

Additional Resources

Bertrando, P. (2007). *The dialogical therapist: Dialogue in systemic practice.* London, England: Karnac Books.

Dallos, R. (2006). *Attachment narrative therapy: Integrating systemic, narrative, and attachment approaches.* Maidenhead, Berkshire: Open University Press.

Flaskas, C., & Pocock, D. (Eds.) (2009). *Systems and psychoanalysis: Contemporary integrations in family therapy.* London, England: Karnac Books.

Rivett, M., & Street, E. (2009). *Family therapy: 100 key points and techniques.* London: Routledge.

Vetere, A., & Dallos, R. (2003). *Working systemically with families.* London, England: Karnac Books.

9

USING FAMILY THERAPY À LA CARL WHITAKER

Dan Wulff

While my chapter will be responding to a common case, Carl Whitaker's approach to family therapy was one of responding in the immediacy of the face-to-face interactions. He often commented on hypothesized or truncated case examples, but those comments were understood with the proviso that family therapy emerges in the direct interaction that cannot be confidently predicted a priori.

I will be approaching this common case from my point of view, which has been significantly influenced by Carl, but I do not pretend that I could attest to what Carl would have done with this case. He was a strong advocate for family therapists to reach their own potential and style—he modeled courage on his path toward becoming a family therapist at a time when models and approaches were in short supply and despite criticisms he faced regarding his approach.

Carl routinely involved the entire family system, which to him included the extended family. In this common case, the parents, Johnny, and Bess (Mary's mom) would be included. Most likely, others in the family would be encouraged (expected) to attend as well (e.g., the other grandparents, siblings of Johnny, siblings of the parents). As an extension of this notion of inclusivity, I would also inquire about other nonfamily members who are involved or concerned with this family and their troubles and extend an invitation to them. This opening up of the conversation to other significant persons is also reflected in the work currently being done by Jaakko Seikkula in Finland (Seikkula & Arnkil, 2006). Families in trouble often tend to isolate themselves in their difficulties, and Carl's approach emphasized opening and stretching the family system in the therapeutic process. With this approach, the family's troubles would in effect become the lever with which to counteract the move toward isolationism.

Carl often stated that he did not "believe in individuals"; he believed that "individuals are merely fragments of a family" (Whitaker & Keith, n.d., p. 1). In order to address the dynamics involved in a behavior of a family member that was labeled and experienced as problematic, the family system is the place to look and to intervene. Without focusing on the context of that individual and his/her behavior, the behavior in question becomes ambiguous and perhaps mystifying. Carl also believed that no one "ever gets out of their family," and so Mary and Fred are still best understood within their families of origin. From this perspective, including their families of origin as much as possible is sensible and necessary if one is intent on addressing the processes involved in Johnny's behaviors.

The presenting problem is just an invitation to wade into the family. Carl often referred to the presenting problem as a "fake," merely serving the purpose of letting the family "audition" the therapist for his/her ability to address the more challenging work of working with the sensitive and central issues of the family. The presenting problem would thus not be the centerpiece of family therapy. Conversation could begin with the presenting problem, but it would serve mostly as a chance to observe the family and therapist interact. The family's interactions with the family therapist would create the substance of the therapy.

Carl focused on two processes that he termed the battle for structure and the battle for initiative. The therapist would want to win the first battle and lose the second. The battle for structure includes the ground rules for the therapy (e.g., who attends, the therapist's right to make decisions in therapy). The battle for initiative includes who will drive the therapy forward, who will invest in making changes. This is a battle the therapist must lose in order for the family to take initiative for change. From this perspective, the family therapist would avoid caring about change more than the family and would therefore not be working harder than the family.

Another hallmark of Carl's approach was to incorporate playful interactions into the therapy. It was his contention that a family that was restricted to only an overtly serious approach was narrowing its ability to mobilize resources to address the concerns they faced. Being playful was critical in making space for something new. The importance of this playful and humorous approach was underscored when Carl identified this quality as being central in assessing the health of a family system. The playfulness of his questions also carried very challenging components—they were curious questions that poked at some tough and sometimes sensitive issues.

A typical opening question with this family could include: "What's going on here and how do you think I can help?" There would be decided effort to not presume what path should be taken. I would want to understand as best I could the family's hopes and expectations rather than work from any theoretical understanding of how families work. One of Carl's most challenging and fascinating articles was entitled "The Hindrance of Theory in Clinical Work" (reprinted in Neill & Kniskern, 1982), and it underscores the importance of the therapist's parallel process with families over the tendency to categorize family types or intervention strategies.

Other questions or comments that I could envision coming up include the following:

- To Johnny: "Perhaps it is better to give up on school and go ahead and get a leg up on an occupation."

- To Johnny: "Do you think your parents will continue to fight with each other when you finally leave home?"
- To Fred: "Have you tried to get Bess [Mary's mom] on your team?"
- To Mary: "What do you think it is about men that make them so hard to live with?"

This approach to family therapy requires courage on the part of the therapist to risk being him/herself in relation to the family and necessitates steady supervision so as to not mix up one's issues with the client families and their issues. With this experiential and improvisational approach, it is not possible to plan therapy in a step-by-step manner and, because of this, traditional research practices struggle with how to capture and understand if and how this way of doing family therapy works. As a result, little formal research has been conducted on this approach. Rather than see this as an indication of therapeutic ineffectiveness, it seems to me to be more of an indictment of the research methods we have grown to trust. While Carl might question the importance of research in establishing therapeutic credibility, I would take the position that therapies like Carl's challenge research methodologies to evolve to be able to handle the not-made-to-order data of more behaviorally oriented approaches.

Carl's approach is personal and responsive. It is unique and hard to specify in an orderly set of steps. It demands a lot from the therapist and pushes the growing edges of both the family and the therapist. It resonates with the complexity and fluidity of families and encourages the family to engage with the therapist.

References

Neill, J. R., & Kniskern, D. P. (Eds.) (1982). *From psyche to system: The evolving therapy of Carl Whitaker.* New York: Guilford Press.

Seikkula, J., & Arnkil, T. E. (2006). *Dialogical meetings in social networks.* London: Karnac Books.

Whitaker, C. A., & Keith, D. V. (n.d.). *Family therapy as symbolic experience.* Unpublished manuscript.

Additional Resources

Napier, A. Y., & Whitaker, C. A. (1978). *The family crucible.* New York, NY: Harper & Row.

Whitaker, C. (1989). *Midnight musings of a family therapist.* Ed. M. O. Ryan. New York, NY: W. W. Norton.

Whitaker, C. A., & Bumberry, W. M. (1988). *Dancing with the family: A symbolic-experiential approach.* New York, NY: Brunner/Mazel.

Whitaker, C. A., & Malone, T. P. (1981). *The roots of psychotherapy.* New York, NY: Brunner/Mazel.

10

VIRGINIA SATIR'S GROWTH MODEL

Therapy as Intra- and Interpersonal Communication

Mary Hale-Haniff

In the mid-1970s, Richard Bandler and John Grinder, developers of Neuro-Linguistic Programming (NLP), studied the communication skills of three particular master psychotherapists for the purpose of deconstructing and replicating these skills in a manner that could become teachable and learnable. Virginia Satir was one of these three therapists. I had initially become familiar with many of her microskills and change patterns through the process of becoming certified by Bandler as an NLP trainer. However, when I watched Virginia in action, I felt that there was a large discrepancy between my experiences of her work and NLP's descriptions. Later, I met a Lakota Sioux medicine man and friend of Virginia's, Basil Braveheart, who sensed a connection between Satir and myself and put me in contact with her. During our first conversation, I told Virginia that I thought NLP's descriptions were missing something having to do with the holistic ways she used intentional and attention energy. She agreed and confided in me that she felt guilty that her gifts were being used by some to manipulate and control, rather than to heal, people. We had tentatively planned to meet in Palo Alto, once her traveling schedule subsided, for the purpose of making the patterns I was intuiting more explicit. Sadly, Virginia died after a brief illness later that year, and our meeting never materialized. What follows depicts how I currently interact with the communication model of Virginia Satir as applied to the hypothetical case provided. For more about how Virginia's work can be viewed in a holistic context, see Hale-Haniff (2004).

Prior to the first meeting, I would minimize what information I gathered via the telephone or from records because I would want to have full sensory access to the family's communications. This would enable me to perceive interrelationships between verbal and nonverbal communications, important because people communicate multiple simultaneous messages that often don't match or are incongruent. It is via the congruent and incongruent patterns in communication that I can identify both client resources and stuck patterns.

In considering even the skeletal information already provided, I would take careful note of what assumptions I might be formulating so I could later check out the accuracy of my hypotheses with the family. I would also ask myself whether any of the content of the presenting narrative might be triggering me to orient either to my own past experience or to previous experiences with other clients. Otherwise, I might inadvertently—and unconsciously—find myself gathering information to fill in my own outline, rather than leaving space to be filled in with information from the client family. Obviously, this would be at odds with my intention of making contact with the family and would, a priori, inhibit the flow of communication between me and the client system. In my view, the aim of therapy is to restore a flow of intra- and interpersonal communication within, between, and among the clients, and my role, as the person of the therapist, is to catalyze that flow. For these reasons, I need to be mindful of what information is coming from where so that I can be fully available to myself and the client family in the moment-by-moment doing of therapy.

Ultimately, I would see the entire family, but who I would see first, and in what sequence, could vary with the clients' preferences and emerging characteristics as well the therapeutic context. One approach would be to begin by working first with Mary and Fred. To begin with them would emphasize their role as mates over their role as parents and leaders of the family. I would include their son only after having had a session or two to provide the couple with some tools to loosen up the fixed, repetitive patterns of perceiving and communicating they were currently manifesting.

For example, I could help them identify and congruently express the positive intention(s) each has for the other and for their child (e.g., to nurture and support each other, to teach their child the skills he needs to become an independent adult, etc.). Then, I would ask each person to separate their positive intention from their current behavior so they would be in a position to evaluate whether their current actions (e.g., arguing with each other, punishing Johnny, etc.) were congruent with their stated intentions. That is, are the actions each is taking useful or not useful in leading them toward the intended direction? If the actions are deemed to be incongruent with their positive intentions, the couple can be encouraged to generate several alternative behaviors that would lead them toward their desired outcomes.

This process helps the couple cocreate a shared intention, which serves as a basis from which to generate coordinated actions (as opposed to arguing). At the same time, it provides each spouse with a vehicle for examining their own actions in a nonjudgmental manner—important because being judged and/or judging oneself as bad or wrong stops the flow of communication between and within people. When clients instead perceive their undesired actions as simply not useful, they regain their ability to self-focus without experiencing the painful emotions of guilt/self-judgment. This skill, in turn, is a prerequisite to being able to take responsibility for one's own actions.

A complementary approach would be to invite each individual to perceive a person they currently feel at odds with as a worthwhile person engaging in less than useful behavior. That is, each person is worthwhile and valuable although their actions may not always be in concert with that value and their positive intentions—the highest of which is generally the desire to love and be loved.

It is likely that, having experienced the efficacy of these alternate communication strategies—within themselves and between each other—the couple would be in a more fluid state of perception. Having restored hope that their family does have the potential to heal, they may have genuine desire and curiosity to explore with Johnny his positive intentions vis-à-vis his current behavior. With practice, over time they may perceive the value of implementing these patterns (and other patterns) as ways to gain more intimacy at the same time as they coparent their son. Having resolved their conflict as a couple and as parents, it is likely that the issues with Mary's mother and the headaches would dissolve.

The questions I would ask focus on emotion as well as communication and would include the following:

- Dad, what else are you feeling inside while you are saying that Johnny should be punished?
- Mary, when you frown and shake your head while you tell us that you think Johnny needs a more nurturing school, what are you experiencing?
- How are the various ways you've been trying to help Johnny affecting your closeness as a couple?

This model focuses both on addressing presenting concerns and facilitating longitudinal growth. Goals would be actualized by restoring a flow of congruent communication within, between, and among family members. An additional focus might be to identify individual family members' deepest yearnings and to identify ways that family members can facilitate each other's dreams.

In summary, dysfunctional communication patterns result from judgmental and disempowering communication with the self coupled with each individual applying rules he or she learned earlier in life to the present situation—and not noticing they are not working. The coping stance of each member (blaming, placating, being super reasonable or irrelevant) is supported by other family members who are also not communicating congruently. Each of these coping stances functions by omitting attention to self, other, or context. I would help the clients add in what they are missing so they can restore the well-being and health that defines congruent communication with self and other. This is a holistic, growth-oriented model that considers emotion as well as behavior and attempts to bring the two into congruence.

Reference

Hale-Haniff, M. (2004). *Transforming NLP's meta model to enhance listening skills in postmodern family therapists.* Unpublished doctoral dissertation, Nova Southeastern University, Fort Lauderdale, FL.

Additional Resources

Andreas, S. (1991). *Virginia Satir: The patterns of her magic.* Palo Alto, CA: Science and Behavior Books.

Satir, V. (1967). *Conjoint family therapy* (Rev. ed.). Palo Alto, CA: Science and Behavior Books.

Satir, V. (1988). *The new peoplemaking.* Palo Alto, CA: Science and Behavior Books.

Satir, V., & Baldwin, M. (1983). *Satir step by step: A guide to creating change in families.* Palo Alto, CA: Science and Behavior Books.

Satir, V., Banmen, J., Gerber, J., & Gomori, M. (1991). *The Satir model.* Palo Alto, CA: Science and Behavior Books.

Virginia Satir Global Network (formerly AVANTA). http://www.avanta.net

11

PRACTITIONER'S PERSPECTIVE

Practicing Psychoanalytic and Experiential
Therapies Today

Edith Huntley and Mary Hale-Haniff

A recent study (Huntley, 2010) explored the extent to and manner in which psychoanalytic and experiential family therapy content was taught in COAMFTE-accredited master's and doctoral programs. Program requirements and course descriptions from COAMFTE-accredited master's and doctoral MFT programs were examined through content analysis. In addition, thematic analysis was utilized to analyze the interviews of designated spokespersons of these same programs. Themes that emerged indicated that these models continue to be an important influence in clinical training, and may have been part of the training of clinical supervisors, but are not at this time a primary focus of course content in any of the accredited programs. COAMFTE-accredited programs in general appear to be moving to a greater focus on evidence-based practice. In practice, this has meant a focus on structured, directive brief therapy models, for the most part. In the United States, the MFT field has become a formalized and licensed entity, complying with requirements of managed care and insurance companies. In Europe, in particular, experiential and psychoanalytic approaches have been less constrained by these exigencies.

Psychoanalytic and object relations family therapy approaches are represented in the United States at postgraduate training institutes like the International Psychotherapy Institute (www.theiep.org). These approaches by their nature are longer term, growth oriented, emotion centered, and difficult to quantify. There has been an increasing movement toward seeking empirical validation for psychoanalytic family therapy and work with children in particular, however, and early results are promising (Midgley & Kennedy, 2011).

Experiential approaches to family therapy with their origins in existential and humanistic psychology and philosophy focus on catalyzing generative, on-the-spot change in individuals and families in the immediate present time of therapy. That a person is an inseparable part of a family and larger community was a preliminary assumption of both Satir's and Whitaker's models. Similarly, they felt that therapists were more effective when they communicated authentically and demonstrated the sensory acuity and flexibility to customize interventions in unique and creative ways that fit the particular persons/families they were working with. Their experiential models thus avoid cookie-cutter techniques and view interventions as processes that evolve from therapeutic orientation. They center on amplifying one's multisensory experience and shifting ineffectual interpretations of those experiences, particularly emotional experiences. Emotions are interpreted as both intrapersonal and interpersonal in nature. Experiential therapy thus avoids established technique and views techniques as something that evolve from relationship. This process orientation has worked against empirical validation in the past. However, empirically validated emotion-focused therapy (Greenberg, Elliott, & Lietaer, 1994; Greenberg, Watson, & Lietaer, 1998), which is "solidly grounded in explicit theory and technical skills" (Brubacker, 2006, p. 142), has become an effective vehicle that includes experiential ideas and practice.

The field of family therapy in general is moving toward more empirically validated treatments and models and an increased focus on outcome-based education, especially in the United States (Levant, 2004). Yet in the process, valuable clinical skills and experience could be lost. The field is invited to consider a perspective that values the art as well as the science of therapy.

References

Brubaker, L. (2006). Integrating emotion-focused therapy with the Satir model. *Journal of Marital and Family Therapy, 32*(2), 141–153.

Greenberg, L. S., Elliott, R., & Lietaer, G. (1994). Research on experiential psychotherapies. In A. E. Bergin & S. L. Garfield (Eds.), *Handbook of psychotherapy and behavior change* (4th ed., pp. 509–539). New York, NY: Wiley.

Greenberg, L. S., Watson, J. C., & Lietaer, G. (1998). The experiential paradigm unfolding: Relationship and experiencing in therapy. In L. S. Greenberg, J. C. Watson, & G. Lietaer (Eds.), *Handbook of experiential psychotherapy* (pp. 3–27). New York, NY: Guilford Press.

Huntley, E. (2010). *Virginia Satir: Locating a founder.* Unpublished dissertation, Nova Southeastern University, Fort Lauderdale, FL.

Levant, R. T. (2004). The empirically-validated treatments movement: A perspective. *The Michigan Society for Psychoanalytic Psychology, 14*(2), 1–6.

Midgley, N., & Kennedy, E. (2011). *Psychodynamic psychotherapy for children and adolescents: A critical review of the evidence base.* Retrieved from http://www.tandf.co.uk/journals/RJCP

12

COMPARE AND CONTRAST

Psychoanalytic and Experiential Models

Anne Rambo, Charles West, AnnaLynn Schooley, and Tommie V. Boyd

We will begin with what these models of therapy share. Note the particular importance each of these models places on the person and the emotions of the therapist. Strong feelings on the part of the therapist, whether negative or positive, are seen as valuable information for the therapy, rather than something to be overcome, worked through, or reasoned away. This is a unique feature of these models.

Note also the reluctance to intervene with "here's what you need to do" type directives. The models in this group are growth oriented, rather than focusing solely or primarily on behavior change. Thus, even in what could be seen as an urgent situation (such as the potential school failure in our hypothetical case), the therapist keeps a focus on growth over time. This is in contrast to more action-oriented models, such as structural/strategic (IIC) and brief therapy models (IID).

Common factors researchers have identified that all successful models of therapy involve intervening in the areas of feeling, thinking, and doing (Blow & Sprenkle, 2001), but it is clear different models differentially privilege these areas of intervention. The models in this section, psychoanalytic/experiential, focus on the area of feeling. Successful family therapy requires that the therapist conceptualize in relational terms, interrupt negative relational patterns, and expand both the treatment system and the therapeutic alliance (Sprenkle, Davis, & Lebow, 2009). Psychoanalytic/experiential models conceptualize the system of the family as a whole, interrupt negative relational patterns by providing insight, and expand by involving and relating to all family members.

In terms of underlying theories, the models in this group show the influence of both attachment theory and general systems theory. Note the emphasis on emotional attachment (attachment theory) and on working with the couple or family system as a system (general systems theory). While there is no explicit influence from social constructionist theory, these models do share with two groups of models heavily influenced by social constructionist theory, narrative (IIE) and collaborative (IIF), a common interest in changing understandings and meanings, rather than behavior. Thus at times there can be at least a partial compatibility. The author of our psychoanalytic chapter, Carmel Flaskas, incorporates social constructionist theory into her work (see Chapter 1 for more discussion of theories).

There is a different type of compatibility, though, between psychoanalytic/experiential and structural/strategic (IIC) models. This different type of compatibility is based on a common appreciation of attachment theory as well as general systems theory. Healthy families from a structural standpoint do share appropriate hierarchy, but also sincere attachment and congruent, age-appropriate expressions of affection and concern. The structural/strategic models share with the psychoanalytic/experiential models these common understandings based on attachment theory and general systems theory.

In general, this group of models (psychoanalytic/experiential) shares a focus on feeling (as opposed to thinking or doing) and a clear influence from both attachment theory and general systems theory. Having discussed what the models in this section share, we now turn to some important differences.

Satir's model (Chapter 10) does show some influence from Batesonian concepts of cybernetics and communication theory as well. While Satir was at one point early on the training director of the Mental Research Institute (MRI), her model nonetheless clearly diverges from the MRI model (IIDc) in its focus on emotion. This aspect of Satir's work, as well as her focus on large-scale, public, growth-oriented workshops, may have been a factor in her departure from MRI and her dismissal from the board of Family Process (Huntley, 2010). Human process validation has gone in a growth-oriented direction influenced by Satir's work with Esalen and not altogether compatible with traditional family therapy settings.

Whitaker's symbolic experiential model (Chapter 15) is closer to psychoanalytic but involves a unique focus on the here-and-now experience. Napier has stated Whitaker privileged the here-and-now experience over the family's history (Aponte, 2009). Psychoanalytic family therapy would presumably balance the two, history and present emotional experience. So there are certainly differences between the models in this section, but we see common themes in the focus on growth over time, as opposed to rapid problem resolution, and on depth of emotional expression.

References

Aponte. (2009). *Augustus Napier on experiential family therapy*. Retrieved from http://psycho therapy.net/interview/augustus-napier

Blow, A., & Sprenkle, D. (2001). Common factors across theories of marriage and family therapy: A modified Delphi study. *Journal of Marital and Family Therapy, 27,* 385–402.

Huntley, E. (2010). *Virginia Satir: Locating a founder*. Unpublished dissertation, Nova Southeastern University, Fort Lauderdale, FL.

Sprenkle, D., Davis, S., & Lebow, J. (2009). *Common factors in couple and family therapy: The overlooked foundation for clinical practice*. New York, NY: Guilford Press.

PART B
INTERGENERATIONAL MODELS

13

A BRIEF HISTORY OF INTERGENERATIONAL MODELS

Anne Rambo, Charles West, AnnaLynn Schooley, and Tommie V. Boyd

The second group of models we will consider are the intergenerational models, which have in common a focus on rebalancing across generations. They could be, and at times are, grouped with the preceding psychoanalytically informed models as they also are concerned with patterns across generations and increased insight. However, these intergenerational models, Bowenian and contextual, are set apart by their unique mutual interest in the individual's progress toward increased differentiation. Differentiation is a concept from natural systems theory, the overarching model of systems developed by Murray Bowen. But it is reflected in contextual family therapy as well. As Iván Böszörményi-Nagy noted, "It is the claim of the contextual approach that there is a dynamic linkage between steps towards differentiation and an engagement in the process of balancing one's debts and entitlement" (Böszörményi-Nagy & Ulrich, 1981, p. 171). Balancing one's debts and entitlement are key elements of Böszörményi-Nagy's concept of relational ethics, in which the individual must find a balance between obligations to family and obligations to self. The therapist in both of these intergenerational models coaches the client toward increased differentiation and/or a more relationally balanced life ethic.

Iván Böszörményi-Nagy was originally from Hungary and came to the United States to escape Stalinist repression. He retained close ties to European family therapy (www.eftacim.org/doc_pdf/ivannagy.pdf), and his wife and fellow contextual therapist, Catherine Ducommun-Nagy, met him at a family therapy training program in Switzerland. Her interest in biological psychiatry has also informed the model (Ducommun-Nagy, 2003). Böszörményi-Nagy founded the Eastern Pennsylvania Psychiatric Institute, which later became the Family Institute of Philadelphia. He also taught for many years at Hahnemann University, now Drexel. His work continues at both locations.

Murray Bowen first trained at the Menninger Institute, where he developed an interest in family systems. He directed the National Institute of Mental Health

(NIMH) until he ran into political troubles for hospitalizing entire families (consistent with his model that pathology did not reside in one individual alone). He also applied his model to relations between and among staff at NIMH, beginning what would be a fruitful application of intergenerational therapy to organizational consulting. He founded the Georgetown Center for the Study of the Family, now known as the Bowen Center for the Study of the Family, in Washington, DC. Michael Kerr continues his work at the Bowen Center.

Like the psychoanalytic/experiential models (IIA), intergenerational models have not always fared well at the hands of managed care. Nor have they lent themselves easily to the requirements of evidence-based practice. However, a questionnaire has been developed that provides empirical support for certain aspects of intergenerational theory (Bray, Williamson, & Malone, 1984). Intergenerational therapy has also enjoyed great popularity when applied to organizational consulting (Sagar & Wiseman, 1982). And it remains the therapy of choice for many family therapists interested in their own growth and development (Lee & Everett, 2004).

References

Böszörményi-Nagy, I., & Ulrich, D. (1981). Contextual family therapy. In A. S. Gurman & D. P. Kniskern (Eds.), *Handbook of family therapy* (pp. 159–186). New York, NY: Brunner/Mazel.

Bray, J., Williamson, D., & Malone, P. (1984). Personal authority in the family system: Development of a questionnaire to measure personal authority in intergenerational family processes. *Journal of Marital and Family Therapy, 10*(4), 167–178.

Ducommun-Nagy, C. (2003). Can giving heal? Contextual therapy and biological psychiatry. In P. Prosky & D. Keith (Eds.), *Family therapy as an alternative to medication* (pp. 111–138). New York, NY: Routledge.

Lee, R., & Everett, C. (2004). *The integrative family therapy supervisor: A primer.* New York, NY: Routledge.

Sagar, R. R., & Wiseman, K. K. (Eds.). (1982). *Understanding organizations: Applications of Bowen family systems theory.* Washington, DC.: Bowen Center for the Study of the Family.

Additional Resources

Böszörményi-Nagy, I., & Spark. G. (1984). *Invisible loyalties.* New York, NY: Routledge.

Framo, J. (1992). *Family of origin therapy: An intergenerational approach.* New York, NY: Routledge.

Kerr, M., & Bowen, M. (1988). *Family evaluation.* New York, NY: W. W. Norton.

Williamson, D. (2002). *The intimacy paradox: Personal authority in the family system.* New York, NY: Guilford Press.

14

BOWEN FAMILY SYSTEMS THERAPY

Christopher Burnett

It is imperative for a clinician working from this model to understand the (a) emotional context and (b) relational anxiety that frames all individual behaviors in a family system. Working from this point of view, the first thing that a clinician seeks to do is construct a genogram of the family system. This process is started as early in the first session as is practical. It is obvious that Mary, Fred, Johnny, and Bess are all currently operating under a high level of family tension and stress. Doing a genogram is a very effective clinical tool for reducing the immediate overall level of anxiety in a family system. By not immediately asking "What brings you here today?" the therapist prevents Fred, Mary, and Johnny from going into their well-rehearsed reactions to one another. This reduces the amount of automatic emotional reactivity in the emotional triangle that the three of them form. If the three of them cannot enact their automatic emotional postures with one another, it may then allow for a different kind of conversation than they have had with anyone else.

The first session would definitely include Fred and Mary, and possibly Johnny. It would be most important to see Fred and Mary in therapy because it is assumed that as the adults in the family, they have the greatest capacity to think clearly and act accordingly. However, they may be very invested in the idea that Johnny is "the problem" and, as such, he is the one that needs to be seen, not them. If this were the case, then the therapist would talk about how this kind of work is based on thinking about things from a holistic, systems-based point of view and that it makes little sense to talk about any single individual being the problem. The therapist would also make it clear that from such a point of view, it would be very unlikely that any changes Johnny made would be sustained for any amount of time without their full and informed participation.

At this first session, the therapist would then begin the process of constructing a genogram. A genogram at first focuses on the factual information about the family system. Fred, Mary, and, if he was present, Johnny would be asked about things like the dates of birth, marriage, separation, divorce, death, and so on not only in their own generation but as far as possible in the generations of their parents, grandparents, and great-grandparents. *Is Johnny the only child in the family? If not, how many others are there? Where in the family birth order does he fall? Is he the oldest? Are either of you two oldest children within your families?* This broadens the idea of the family as a system and has a way of moving people off of a here-and-now focus. It also serves the function of not making Johnny the immediate focus of the therapy process.

The therapist must be careful at this stage not to be so focused on gathering factual genogram information that he or she fails to acknowledge the family's current emotional distress. However, gathering such factual genogram information can effectively serve the clinical goal of reducing the overall level of relationship anxiety in the system. It is a way that everyone can participate in the session without anyone feeling like they are being put on the spot or singled out as a problem.

Once the therapist has established sufficient rapport with each of the family members, he or she may begin asking more relationship-based questions about the history and quality of relationships between various members of the family. Again, this is done in as much of a neutral and fact-gathering tone of voice as possible. It might be important to ask each of them about the nature and history of their relationship with Johnny. *Which of the two of you would you say Johnny is closer to? Has this always been the case? If it has changed over time, when did that happen? Was there anything else going on in the family then that you think was related to that change? Are there any other adults in the family that Johnny is close with, like grandparents, aunts, or uncles? Is he close with any of his cousins?*

Eventually, once the overall level of anxiety in the emotional triangle is reduced to a more manageable level, it would be important to ask Fred and Mary about the history of their relationship and marriage. *How would each of you describe your marriage today? Has it always been that way, or have things changed over time? If they have changed, how have they changed? Fred, when would you say you noticed things were different? Mary, when you would say you noticed that things were different in your marriage? Around the time that you noticed things were different with the two of you, did you notice any changes going on with Johnny or any of your other children?*

It sounds like Mary's mother, Bess, also plays a large part in the family's day-to-day affairs. It would be important to gather more information about just what kind of relationship Bess has with each of the members of the emotional triangle in order to get a more accurate assessment of the family as a system. *Mary, do you talk with your mother daily about this situation? If it is not daily, then how often is it, would you say? If so, what kinds of things does she say about what's going on? Fred, are you able to talk with Bess about Johnny yourself? Fred, when does Mary usually talk with Bess about Johnny? Once she does, what kinds of conversations are you and Mary able to have afterward? Does Johnny know that you talk to his grandmother about him and his situation? What kind of relationship does he have with her? Is he more or less likely to do things if she tells him to do them?*

The overall goal of this kind of structured, neutral, relationship-based inquiry is to allow two things to happen simultaneously. First, it allows for some kind of emotional cooling down among all the participants. It should be clear that the therapist has no interest in making any one of them the focus of the therapeutic process. Instead, each of the participants should believe that the therapist understands their particular point of view of the family and is sympathetic to what they are managing. Once it is established that there are not going to be the usual emotional reactions to doing or saying things in therapy that there are at home, it is hoped that this can lead each of the participants to become more thoughtful and less reactive with one another. Second, this kind of structured, relationship-based line of questions helps the therapist create his or her first-draft impression of how this particular family system operates and the larger relationship processes that undergird it. With more and more information, this preliminary understanding transforms, but it is important for the therapist in this model to have, and continually refine, a hypothesis about what is going on here as a system of interlocking relationships. Further questions can then be asked in order to confirm or refute these hypotheses, leading to greater clarification for everyone about what exactly can be understood about this family as a system.

After doing the initial genogram exercise, it may then be possible for the therapist to ask, "What do you folks hope to accomplish by coming here to family therapy?" By establishing the therapist's own differentiated presence with the family, the therapist is able to affect the overall level of reactivity in the family. By not allowing herself to become "triangled" by them, she is showing that she is able to absorb some of the family's relationship anxiety. This establishes her as a source of stability and allows clients to articulate their goals as individuals as well as members of an emotionally connected system. If Fred and Mary agree they want Johnny to attend school again, it's easier to seek this goal as a family unit when the prospect of doing so does not trigger the same old reactions to each other they always have.

Regardless of the stated behavioral change goals of the family, the overarching goals of a Bowen family systems approach is almost invariably to (a) reduce the level of relationship anxiety in the family system and (b) introduce increased abilities to think about how the family operates as an emotional system. Highlighting, understanding, and reducing the automatic emotional reactions people have to one another help move people to a different level of understanding themselves, the people around them, and the interconnections that help shape the behaviors of individuals as well as families.

In this process of moving to a different level of understanding, it is necessary for the therapist to both connect empathically and avoid the fixer role. I would first try to connect as empathically as I could with the struggles that Fred and Mary are having in dealing with a son who has become as disruptive and concerning as Johnny has. I would do everything in my power to try to understand their situation as a family rather than an individual issue and to communicate this to them without any kind of blame shifting or evasive language. While doing my best to be empathic, I would also not let myself get put in the position of understanding their difficult situation from only one single point of view. I would explore with

Fred and Mary if Johnny's recent behaviors could best be understood as a recent aberration or a much longer standing pattern of disrespect and defiance on his part. Regardless of the answers they provided, I would then seek to understand this behavior in the context of their own nuclear as well as extended family processes. I would constantly be exploring with them how best to make sense of the situation they are currently in and what kind of adaptive choices are available while they are in it.

I would resist as much as I could any appeals they presented me to fix their problem. I would try to deflect any pleas, no matter how desperate, to step in and offer them a solution. Instead, my work would be directed at helping them understand, challenge, and then better navigate the complexities of their complex family emotional system. While staying in emotional contact with each of them, I would also seek to remain in a position where I could also challenge the accuracy or utility of their more entrenched relationship positions vis-à-vis one another.

In many cases like this one, the development of behavioral symptoms in a child or adolescent is attributed to the presence of high levels of unresolved anxiety in the nuclear family emotional system. I could not just assume that this was the case with Fred and Mary, but I would be interested in testing out with the family some hypotheses about how Johnny's recent changes could be seen as being related to his being a member of an emotional triangle with Fred and Mary. When Fred and Mary have such very different views of how best to discipline their teenage son, it is not farfetched to think that they have been unable to agree on other important things in the marriage as well. If this was the case over an extended period of time, I would be interested to know about how else this relationship anxiety has been expressed in the course of the marriage.

It is also plausible to speculate on the role that Bess has played in forming another emotional triangle with Fred and Mary during the course of the marriage. If Bess has been a consistent ally with Mary, I would be curious as to how this has affected Fred. Has he sought out others that he can "triangle" in times of emotional disturbance? Has he tried to put Johnny in the position of being his ally? Does he invest himself in people or activities outside of the family system as a way to manage the relationship anxiety inside of it? Does doing this fuel Mary's sense of isolation from him and strengthen her relationship with Bess or Johnny?

Clinical issues and symptoms arise when the intensity and duration of relationship-based anxiety exceeds the capacity of the relationship system to successfully manage and adapt to it. Accurately tracking the various routes, and understanding the various expressions relationship anxiety takes in nuclear and extended family systems, is one of the primary ways a Bowen family systems therapist is of help to client families. There is no single or complete way to accomplish this. The journey of family therapy is best thought of as an ongoing process of reflective, thoughtful exploration and education in the ways that family relationships constantly move closer together or farther apart. There are real relationship consequences of such movements, but they are often not apparent unless one is able to take a more distanced point of view on the entire family relationship process. Any member of a family system who is able to gain and maintain this sense of perspective is able to make more thoughtful, considered choices as to the ways they participate in their own family functioning.

Resources

Bowen Center for the Study of the Family, Georgetown Family Center. http://www. thebowencenter.org

Gilbert, R. (1992). *Extraordinary relationships: A new way of thinking about human interactions.* New York, NY: Wiley.

Guerin, P. J., Fogarty, T. F., Fay, L. F., & Kautto, J. G. (1996). *Working with relationship triangles: The one-two-three of psychotherapy.* New York, NY: Guilford Press.

Kerr, M. E., & Bowen, M. (1988). *Family evaluation.* New York, NY: Norton.

McGoldrick, M., Gerson, R., & Petry, S. (2008). *Genograms: Assessment and intervention* (3rd ed.). New York, NY: Norton.

15

CONTEXTUAL FAMILY THERAPY

Terry D. Hargrave and Miyoung Yoon Hammer

Contextual family therapy (Böszörményi-Nagy & Krasner, 1986) is an integrative approach in dealing with the family that fits within the framework of a family of origin or psychodynamic therapy. The focus of the approach is the interplay between the four dimensions of relationships (Hargrave & Pfitzer, 2003). The first of these dimensions is facts—objectifiable realities about the individuals in the family—which include such elements as health factors, socioeconomic realities, and history of events. The second dimension is individual psychology, which relates to the individual personality perspectives of each member of the family and the psychodynamic forces that have shaped behavior and motivation. Family and systemic interactions are the third dimension of contextual family therapy and have to do with the communication and processes in the family that govern aspects of family power, hierarchy, structure, and beliefs.

These three dimensions are helpful in assessment and conceptualization of cases and by themselves give the therapist much information. The fourth dimension, however, is the element of this approach that sets it apart and is the essential contribution of contextual family therapy. The dimension of relational ethics deals with the intergenerational balance of justice and trustworthiness in families and describes the relational resources of love and trustworthiness. In this dimension, as family members are able to trust and rely upon one another, they are free to give to family members in loving and trustworthy ways themselves. When there is a lack of love and trustworthiness, there is a sense of violation among members (often traced back to the family of origin), and they tend to act out in dysfunctional ways that are self-justifying. These actions are described as destructive entitlement and are the source of much of the pain and distress in family relationships (Hargrave & Pfitzer, 2003).

When coming to the common case example of Mary, Fred, and Johnny, the contextual family therapist will have the focus of all four dimensions but will have particular sensitivity to the issues of love and trustworthiness that exist in the fourth dimension. We would have interest, for instance, in Mary's frequent headaches and whether or not Johnny has some organic learning difficulty. These elements would both relate to the dimension of facts. In addition, we would be interested in the intrapsychic processes of how both Mary and Fred were raised and what their histories were concerning discipline in their families of origin. This is representative of the dimension of individual psychology. As well, we would assess the structure of the family by observing process and power. For instance, we would notice who in the family is closest to whom and who tends to get his or her way in the interaction processes. These elements would all be reflective of the dimension of family and systemic interactions. But since the contextual therapy process sees the fourth dimension as being the most powerful and influencing all the dimensions of relationships (Böszörményi-Nagy & Ulrich, 1981), relational ethics is where we will concentrate our main analysis and suggestions here for discussion.

In this approach, we would want to see the entire family in each session. It is absolutely essential in the contextual approach to realize that individual pain, dysfunctional patterns, and violations of love and trustworthiness tend to follow from one generation to the next. Our assumption would be that Johnny's behavior of failing school is connected to individual pain he feels about his sense of self and/or lack of safety he feels in the context of relationship. From the contextual perspective, pain concerning identity is developed because of lack of love in relationships, and pain over lack of safety is developed because of a lack of justice or trustworthiness in relationships. As seen in Figure 3, when an individual feels such pain, he or she will tend to act out or cope with the pain through behaviors

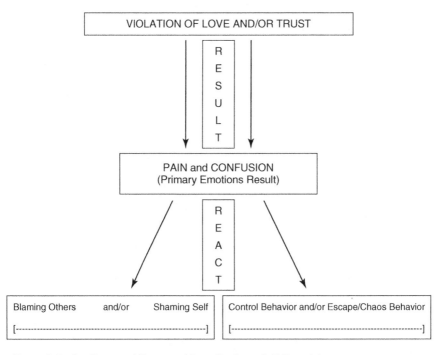

Figure 3 Lack of Love and Trustworthiness Produces Self-Reactivity

that are blaming (someone is to blame because I do not feel good about myself), shaming (I am deserving of the lack of worth and love I feel), control (I can only make myself safe by controlling the situation and limiting my vulnerability to others), and escape/chaos (I cannot make myself safe and therefore I must leave to get away from the pain). These coping behaviors are called self-reactivity and are largely responsible for destructive entitlement (Hargrave & Pfitzer, 2011).

From the case description, we as the therapists would at least consider the possibility that Johnny feels some type of pain from the lack of love and trust-worthiness and is reacting by possibly shaming himself (a sense of inadequacy) and escape/chaos (not attending to school and hanging out with friends). We would further hypothesize that Mary and Fred carry these same or similar senses of violations and that Mary likely reacts in a controlling manner (we need to help Johnny by getting him more nurturing) and Fred reacts in a blaming fashion (we just need to get aggressive and punish Johnny to force him to be responsible). Further, the assumption would be that the grandmother, Bess, carries violation and also reacts by controlling behavior. We would see the family together to get to the bottom of the story concerning these violations of love and trustworthiness. As the therapist hears the stories of violations, it creates in the individual a more relaxed stance as his or her story is validated or credited. In addition, the dialogue between therapist and family member is the initial step in building trustworthi-ness between the two and is a precursor to the family members restoring lov-ing and trustworthy behavior with one another (Böszörményi-Nagy & Krasner, 1986). As the therapist and family members hear pain and credit each other, there is less reactivity and destructive entitlement and more opportunity for love and trustworthy actions (Hargrave & Pfitzer, 2003)

Because the therapeutic dialogue is so essential to the idea of crediting and having an attitude of multidirected partiality toward all family members (Böszörményi-Nagy & Krasner, 1986), it is essential that the therapist get a sense of each person's story and history of love and trustworthiness. We would ask all family members questions like the following: When you experienced this unpleasant situation, how did you feel about yourself? What are the situations that make you feel un-safe? How do you tend to cope or what do you do when you have these feelings? More specifically, we would ask Fred about how he feels about himself when his son is seemingly out of control. To Mary, we would ask specifically the pain she feels when she and Fred disagree about Johnny and how it feels when Bess and she agree. To Johnny, we would want to know the parallel of feelings between being at school and being at home.

From a contextual perspective, the overall goal would be to establish the fam-ily having more loving and trustworthy relationships. As this occurs, dysfunction would tend to diminish with regard to reactivity (Hargrave & Pfitzer, 2003). Specifically, however, we would want Fred and Mary to be closer in their re-lationship as well as Johnny feeling secure enough to attend school. An exten-sion of the contextual approach is found in the restoration therapy approach

(Hargrave & Pfitzer, 2011). In this extension of contextual therapy, the therapist would work with identifying destructive patterns and developing peaceful patterns using mindfulness.

In the contextual approach, the therapist must balance concerns in all four dimensions of relationships but specifically be concerned about reestablishing love and trustworthiness in interactions. The therapist, therefore, works using techniques such as multidirected partiality, understanding, helping the clients reparent themselves, relating to other generations, and forgiving, which are more associated with intrapsychic work. In addition, the therapist works in a very cognitive/behavioral manner identifying patterns, suggesting new cycles, and pointing clients toward mindfulness. Combining contextual family therapy with the newer restoration model actually gives the therapist a "one-two punch" in being able to work both psych-dynamically and cognitively (Hargrave & Pfitzer, 2011). In either instance, however, the therapist is very active in listening, suggesting, and practicing alternative ideas and responses that will build a context of loving and trustworthy behavior among members.

References

Böszörményi-Nagy, I., & Krasner, B. (1986). *Between give and take: A clinical guide to contextual therapy.* New York, NY: Brunner/Mazel.

Böszörményi-Nagy, I., & Ulrich, D. N. (1981). Contextual family therapy. In A. S. Gurman & D. P. Kniskern (Eds.), *Handbook of family therapy* (pp. 159–186). New York, NY: Brunner/Mazel.

Hargrave, T. D., & Pfitzer, F. (2003). *The new contextual therapy: Guiding the power of give and take.* New York, NY: Routledge.

Hargrave, T. D., & Pfitzer, F. (2011). *Restoration therapy: Understanding and guiding healing in marriage and family therapy.* New York, NY: Routledge.

Additional Resources

Hargrave, T. D. (1994). *Families and forgiveness: Healing wounds in the intergenerational family.* New York, NY: Brunner/Mazel.

Hargrave, T. D. (2001). *Forgiving the devil: Coming to terms with damaged relationships.* Phoenix, AZ: Zeig, Tucker, and Theisen.

16

PRACTITIONER'S PERSPECTIVE

Intergenerational Models and Organizational Consulting

Brian Rosenberg

Bowenian approaches in particular and intergenerational approaches in general have received some empirical validation from studies linking emotional distress to level of differentiation (Miller, Anderson, & Keals, 2004). Nonetheless, the focus by managed care organizations in particular on structured brief therapy approaches has at times affected the ability of intergenerational family therapists to practice in agencies (Webeter & Cebula, 2009). Interestingly, however, the real growth area for intergenerational family therapists may lie in taking their skills to a different but related field: that of organizational consulting. Since the 1970s, intergenerational family therapy models based on natural systems theory have been directly applied to organizations and businesses (Sagar & Wiseman, 1982).

This is the type of work that I do. I have both a master's and a doctoral degree from a COAMFTE-accredited marriage and family therapy program, but all of my work is organizational consulting. I work in the health care industry. Over the past 12 years, I have had the position of organizational development leader in several large and well-respected organizations. I have worked in a multihospital health care system and a large national physician management group. My daily role consists of either facilitating workshops or training events that are focused on interpersonal relationship skills. I find myself teaching doctors and business leaders the art of effectively sending their messages so they can be received in the way they were intended. If a boss sends an important message that is tied up in emotions, the person expected to receive the message may totally misunderstand the intensions and make the issue into something it is not. For example, if manager A needs to encourage the front office staff to deliver better customer service to the patients in the waiting room, yet goes about this by standing in front of the group in an angry and fear-inducing way, the staff might respond—but will the behaviors be implemented and sustained or will the behaviors only occur while the difficult boss is watching? In my experience, people tend to be so emotionally charged by similar experiences that they might do the opposite behavior when the boss is not watching just to retaliate.

These relationship skills often do not come easily to physicians. The process of becoming acculturated as an MD is an exacting, arduous, fact-filled, and often-times emotionally devoid experience. Doctors are taught to act quickly, to believe in themselves enough to make very complex decisions totally independently, to not ask for help, and to act on their own. What do you think these traits do for relationship building, empowering the nursing staff, and building teams? As you might have guessed, sometimes it is difficult. When it comes to the realm of human relationships, there are no black-and-white constructs like there are in medicine. We can invent a new reality, believe in it, and act as if it were the truth. Here is an example. Doctor A is working as the medical director for a very large and busy practice. He is becoming more and more upset with his new colleague, a physi-cian who just joined the team the previous year. Doctor B has her own style of working with her patients, she is clearly just trying to get the job done, and she has been described as abrupt, quick to act, not a good listener, abrasive, and not a good team player. Doctor B is well liked by her patients, but the office staff and the other physicians have clear concerns about how she makes everyone feel in the office. She demands perfection and is easily frustrated if her charts are not in the correct place, the lab work is not clearly indicated, and the patients are not in her exam room on time; and she blasts the staff on a daily basis. I was invited in to offer some assistance. Doctor B was eager to share details about how everything that she is doing is for the best interest of her patients and everyone else just needs to "suck it up" and do a good job. She felt that there really were no issues except for overly sensitive staff, and she also believed that her colleague physicians could learn a few things from her approach. Doctor A and Doctor B are locked in an impasse, and both have some valid points. Does this scenario sound familiar to you? Does this sound like business consulting or family therapy? Well, it sounds and feels like a therapy session to me as well. My role became one of a coach and interpersonal communication leader. I gathered all the perspectives that I could find, separated out the facts from the perceptions, found ways to help key individuals have direct conversations about their goals, helped everyone clarify their intentions for what they were doing, and, most importantly, helped everyone refocus on taking great care of the patients and each other. In the process, I used the concepts of transmis-sion of anxiety and intergenerational patterns I learned as a family therapist.

Moving from the role of an MFT-trained therapist to that of a business con-sultant has required adjusting the language used while working with clients. But overall the skills that have helped me be a successful consultant are the same skills that have made me a successful therapist. I am appreciative of the MFT training and my experiences and am extremely grateful that I am working directly in the health care environment in a manner that I do not have to deal with managed care contracts, health insurance, and payment issues. As an organizational development professional, I use intergenerational family therapy on a daily basis, and it has served me very well.

References

Miller, R., Anderson, S., & Keals, D. (2004). Is Bowen theory valid? A review of basic research. *Journal of Marital and Family Therapy, 30*(4), 453–466.

Sagar, R., & Wiseman, K. (1982). *Understanding organizations: Applications of Bowen family systems theory.* Washington, DC: Bowen Center for the Study of the Family.

Weber, T., & Cebula, C. (2009). Intensive family of origin consultation: An intergenerational approach. In J. Bray & M. Stanton (Eds.), *Handbook of family psychology* (pp. 272–285). Madden, MA: Wiley-Blackwell.

17

COMPARE AND CONTRAST

Intergenerational Models

Anne Rambo, Charles West, AnnaLynn Schooley, and Tommie V. Boyd

As already noted, these intergenerational models share a concern with patterns across generations with the psychoanalytic/experiential models already discussed (IIA). History is important here, as it is also in the psychoanalytically informed models (less so with the experiential). Yet Bowenian and contextual approaches are distinctive in their concern with differentiation and with rebalancing the relationship between the individual and the system.

The concept of differentiation in particular is a very inclusive one that can explain the behavior of microscopic cells and nation states, as well as families. Like cybernetics, it offers a perspective on all of life, not just the family (see Chapter 1). Contextual theory also borrows from attachment theory and general systems theory, as noted in Chapter 9, but Bowenian therapy rests almost exclusively on natural systems theory. Both these models are set apart, in our opinion, by their ties to natural systems theory. Of the two, contextual therapy is the more integrative.

Intergenerational therapy tends to be longer term, or at the very least not brief by design. Nor is the intergenerational therapist actively directive in the way of the structural, strategic, or brief family therapist. These are growth-oriented models, not rapid-change models, and the therapist takes on a more consulting or coaching role. These models, like psychoanalytic/experiential models (IIA), are not focused on strategies of immediate behavior change.

Yet there are important distinctions. With respect to common factors, while all therapies affect feeling, thinking, and doing (Blow & Sprenkle, 2001), these intergenerational models appear to focus on changes in thinking. It is important that the client have insight into generational patterns. While the client's experience may be at times emotionally intense, that is not the focus of the therapeutic work; the focus is on acquiring insight into family patterns and subsequently actively rebalancing those patterns.

Common-factors research suggests all models of family therapy, if done well, involve systemic conceptualization, intervention to disrupt dysfunctional patterns, and expansion of the therapeutic system and alliance (Sprenkle, Davis, & Lebow, 2009). In these terms, the intergenerational models conceptualize the system of family dynamics over time and over generations, intervene by coaching the client to increase differentiation or consider relational ethics, and expand the system by shifting to a focus on patterns across generations.

The focus on relational ethics leads to an interesting alliance of sorts between intergenerational therapists (IIB) and narrative family therapists (IIE). It is a natural outgrowth of both sets of models for the therapist to be deeply concerned with restorative justice issues, as Hargrave and Yoon Hammer note in their chapter on contextual therapy for this book (Chapter 15). This is despite the fact that the theory bases are quite different, with narrative models (IIE) drawing on social constructionist theory and the ideas of Michel Foucault. Nonetheless, the ideas of natural systems theory lead practitioners of these intergenerational models to similar reflections on the need for social justice.

References

Blow, A., & Sprenkle, D. (2001). Common factors across theories of marriage and family therapy: A modified Delphi study. *Journal of Marital and Family Therapy, 27,* 385–402.

Sprenkle, D., Davis, S., & Lebow, J. (2009). *Common factors in couple and family therapy: The overlooked foundation for clinical practice.* New York, NY: Guilford Press.

PART C
STRUCTURAL AND STRATEGIC MODELS

18

A BRIEF HISTORY OF STRUCTURAL/ STRATEGIC MODELS

Anne Rambo, Charles West, AnnaLynn Schooley, and Tommie V. Boyd

In this section, we have grouped together structural family therapy, as developed by Salvador Minuchin and colleagues; strategic family therapy, as developed by Jay Haley and Cloe Madanes (but as distinct from MRI therapy, covered in Chapter 29); and several evidence-based, community-focused models that utilize structural and strategic ideas: multidimensional systemic family therapy (developed by Howard Liddle), multisystemic therapy (developed by Scott Henggellerr), functional family therapy (developed by James Alexander and Thomas Sexton), and the University of Miami brief strategic model (developed by Jose Sapoznik and University of Miami colleagues). These models have in common a focus on family organization. All also show the influence of the originating model in this section, structural family therapy.

Structural family therapy is generally considered to have originated at Wiltwick School for Boys, in the 1960s, when Salvador Minuchin and his colleagues (Braulio Montalvo and Charlie Fishman) first experimented with a more directive, brief form of therapy. Minuchin had been trained in classic psychoanalytic therapy (Nathan Ackerman, the originator of psychoanalytic family therapy, was his training analyst), but in his experience, this model did not work well with the multiproblem, low-income families whose sons were ending up at Wiltwick, a residential treatment center largely populated by young men in trouble with the law. Instead, Minuchin and his colleagues developed a way of working that focused on restructuring the family hierarchy and putting parents back in charge of their families—hence the term *structural*. Minuchin later left to become director of the Philadelphia Child Guidance Center.

In 1967, Jay Haley, one of the originators of the MRI model (Chapter 29), left the West Coast and his work with MRI and moved to the East Coast, where he took a job at the Philadelphia Child Guidance Center. He and Minuchin carpooled in together every day from New Jersey; this famous carpool affected two major models of family therapy (Haley, 1991). Their discussions influenced Minuchin to some extent, and one can note the attention to patterns of communication also present in structural family therapy. Haley was also influenced, and the model he developed, strategic family therapy, combines MRI-like indirect techniques (derived from Erickson) with structural theories about the nature of the family. Haley himself stated strategic family therapy utilizes techniques from the communications theory of MRI, along with structural understandings of the family (Haley, 1991). Strategic family therapy was also influenced and cocreated by Cloe Madanes, originally an Argentinian student of Minuchin's from Argentina, who is a cofounder of the model. (She and Haley were also married for a period of time, one of several influential husband/wife teams in family therapy—other such teams are Insoo Kim Berg and Steve de Shazer, who are jointly credited with originating solution-focused therapy [Chapter 30]; Iván Böszörményi-Nagy and Catherine Ducommun-Nagy, for contextual therapy [Chapter 15]; and Cheryl and Michael White for narrative therapy [Chapter 35].) Haley/Madanes strategic therapy is often grouped with MRI brief therapy due to the common influence of Erickson (Chapter 28). However, Haley/Madanes strategic therapy, like structural therapy, has as a goal the reorganization of the family, moving away from less desirable to more desirable patterns of organization (Piercy, Sprenkle, & Wetchler, 1996). MRI brief therapy (Chapter 29) is concerned only with patterns of interaction, not with altering the structure of the family (Piercy et al., 1996). Thus, we have chosen to group structural and Haley/Madanes strategic together. Structural and Haley/Madanes strategic are often combined in practice, as in functional family therapy (FFT; Chapter 23) and University of Miami (UM) brief strategic (Chapter 24).

The Philadelphia Child Guidance Center, now under the direction of Marion Lindblad-Goldberg, remains a center of structural family therapy training and practice. The Minuchin Center for the Family in New York City is another such center. Minuchin now lives in West Palm Beach, Florida, where he works with teams of Nova Southeastern University family therapy students (see Chapter 25). A center of strategic family therapy on the East Coast is the Family Therapy Center of Washington, DC; since 2001, there has also been a center for strategic family therapy training at MRI, dedicated to the work of Jay Haley (recognizing the common Ericksonian influence; however, the two models—MRI brief therapy and Haley/Madanes strategic—remain distinct and are housed separately at MRI). Cloe Madanes trains with organizational consultant Tony Robbins at Robbins-Madanes Training in Ashland, Oregon. In addition, structural and strategic models have been a strong influence on the development of a range of evidence-based, community-based models: multidimensional family therapy (MDST), multisystemic therapy (MST), FFT, and UM strategic. All these models are discussed in the chapters in this section.

References

Haley, J. (1991). *Problem-solving therapy.* San Francisco, CA: Jossey-Bass.

Piercy, F., Sprenkle, D., Wetchler, J., & Associates. (1996). *Family therapy sourcebook.* New York, NY: Guilford Press.

Additional Resources

Aponte, H. (1994). *Bread and spirit: Therapy with the new poor: Diversity of race, culture, and values.* New York, NY: W. W. Norton.

Haley, J., & Richeport-Haley, M. (2003). *The art of strategic therapy.* New York, NY: Routledge.

Madanes, C. (1990). *Sex, love, and violence: Strategies for transformation.* New York, NY: W. W. Norton.

Minuchin, S., & Fishman, H. C. (2004). *Family therapy techniques.* Cambridge, MA: Harvard University Press.

19

ECOSYSTEMIC FAMILY THERAPY

Marion Lindblad-Goldberg

The ecosystemic structural family therapy model (ESFT), developed by Dr. Marion Lindblad-Goldberg and colleagues at the Philadelphia Child and Family Therapy Training Center, is an empirically supported adaptation of the structural family therapy model originated by Salvador Minuchin and colleagues. The ESFT model targets treatment for children and adolescents with moderate to severe emotional and behavior disturbance and their families in outpatient and in-home/community settings. The ESFT model is integrated with respect to its theoretical foundations. ESFT is a biological/developmental/systemic strength-based, clinical model that examines the biological and developmental influences of family members as well as current and historical familial, cultural, and ecological influences. ESFT is based on the fundamental assumption that child, parental, and marital functioning are inextricably linked to their relational environment. Five interrelated constructs guide ESFT therapists in their understanding of clinical problems: family structure; family and individual emotional regulation; individual differences (e.g., historical, biological, cultural, developmental); affective proximity (e.g., emotional attachments between parents and child and between parents); and family development. ESFT is organized around four stages of treatment and four targets of change. The four treatment stages are as follows: stage 1 constructs the therapeutic system; stage 2 establishes a meaningful therapeutic focus; stage 3 creates key growth—promoting interpersonal experiences; and stage 4 solidifies change and discharge planning. The foci of change during ESFT treatment are (1) co-caregiver alliance, (2) caregiver–child attachment and caregiver-caregiver attachment, (3) executive functioning, and (4) individual and family emotion regulation.

The Common Case

An ESFT therapist would approach this case situation first with a view to constructing a therapeutic system that would include joining the family and its individual members and having the family identify their informal and formal supports. Joining is not a minor part of the therapy process for therapists working from this model, nor is it a process we rush. We take our time to truly get to know the family and help them feel comfortable with us. This alliance building, particularly between the therapist and the parent(s), is a crucial part of the process. For families with young or school-aged children, the therapist may meet first with the caregivers (in this case, Mary and Fred) and then include the identified child (in this case, Johnny) and siblings later in the first session or in a second session if more time is needed to connect with the parents. Our experience is that most parents want to check out the therapists before exposing their child to this new situation. In this first meeting, we would begin by getting to know Mary and Fred as individuals, apart from the problems they may be facing. "So, Fred, are you from Philly and are your parents or brother/sisters in Philly?" As we talk, we would observe the interactions between Mary and Fred as well as mentally constructing a genogram, allowing us to develop a picture of the entire extended family system as well the family's informal and formal helpers. Much of the information we gather is strengths based—What does each parent like to do for fun? What does each parent do to relax? What are each of their interests, hobbies? When hearing about the challenges each parent has encountered in their life, we elicit the coping skills each has used to meet these challenges. As we talk, we begin to get a picture of their family system and how it operates. Questions I generally like to ask teens include "What do you do to relax?" and "What would one of your good friends say I should know about you?" In talking with Johnny, I would ask what he wants to change and what he does to feel better when he is challenged within the family, in school, or with friends. In a session with Mary, Fred, Johnny, and any siblings, I would observe family process— for example, watching Mary's reactions as Fred talks to Johnny. Also, I would link parent(s) and child through comments that connect: "So, Johnny, did you know your dad was also a baseball fan?" As I interact with the family, I look for a repetitive core negative interactional pattern that keeps the family stuck. I would talk about the core negative interactional pattern with the family: "Just like the two of you, Mary and Fred, sometimes don't support each other, but instead give up on each other and withdraw, that's what happens when Johnny's behavior leads you to give up on him, and he, in turn, gives up on himself and his school responsibilities." I would work to enlist the parents' and Johnny's support in changing this pattern. However, I would also assess other possible foci of change. It could be that Johnny has an undiagnosed learning disability or the biological/trauma-induced reactivity of one or both of the parents needs to be addressed. I would also assess whether Mary and Fred need to rebuild their emotional attachment to each other as well as to Johnny before working on their executive functioning as coparents. Within collaborative partnerships between myself and Mary, Fred, and Johnny, we would work together to construct the best treatment plan for change.

Training and Research

Comprehensive training, including distance learning and training in outpatient or in-home/community family therapy, is available through the Philadelphia Child and Family Therapy Training Center (www.philafamily.com). Ecosystemic structural family therapy builds on one of the most solid records of evidence-based research in the family therapy field. Structural family therapy (SFT) and other SFT modifications are listed as highly effective means of treatment by both the Office of Juvenile Justice Model Programs Guide (www.ojjp.gov) and the Substance Abuse and Mental Health Services Administration (www.samhsa.gov). Ecosystemic structural family therapy is a highly effective treatment as well for severely emotionally disturbed children (Hansen, Litzelman, & Salter, 2002). In 1986, Dr. Marion Lindblad-Goldberg and the Children's Bureau within the Pennsylvania Office of Mental Health and Substance Abuse Services developed Family Based Mental Health Services (FBMHS) for families with severely emotionally disturbed children (SED); the program featured the ESFT model conducted in the home and community. Initially there were 10 pilot programs. After an ESFT clinical effectiveness study demonstrating significant clinical changes with 1,968 treated families, all 67 of Pennsylvania's counties are now served by FBMHS/ESFT programs. Recent trends in the field of family therapy have been toward evidence-based practice and increasing work in homes and communities; structural family therapy was ahead of its time in its early focus on both treatment outcomes and meeting families where they are, wherever and however we can be most useful. We at Philadelphia Child and Family Therapy Training Center continue this tradition using the ESFT model in close partnership with the parents we serve.

Reference

Hansen, M., Litzelman, A., & Salter, B. (2002). Serious emotional disturbance: Working with families. In D. Marsh & M. Fristad (Eds.), *Handbook of serious emotional disturbance in children and adolescents* (pp. 375–391). New York, NY: Wiley.

Additional Resources

Jones, C. W., & Lindblad-Goldberg, M. (2004). Ecosystemic structural family therapy. In F. Kaslow & R. Massey (Eds.), *Comprehensive handbook of psychotherapy: interpersonal/humanistic, 3,* (pp. 3–34). New York, NY: Wiley.

Lee, Yueh-The. (2011). Structural family therapy: With an interview with master therapist Marion Lindblad-Goldberg. In L. Metcalf (Ed.), *Marriage and family therapy: A practice oriented approach* (pp. 229–254). New York, NY: Springer.

Lindblad-Goldberg, M., Dore, M., & Stern, L. (1998). *Creating competence from chaos.* New York, NY: W. W. Norton.

Lindblad-Goldberg, M., Igle, E., & Simms, S. (2011). Ecosystemic structural family therapy with couples. In D. Carson & M. Casad-Kehoe (Eds.), *Case studies in couple's therapy: Theory based approaches* (pp. 121–131). New York, NY: Routledge.

Lindblad-Goldberg, M., Jones, C. W., & Dore, M. (2004). *Effective family based mental health services for children with severe emotional disturbances in Pennsylvania: The ecosystemic structural family therapy model.* Harrisburg, PA: CAASP Training and Technical Institute.

20

STRATEGIC FAMILY THERAPY

James Keim

Cloe Madanes used to advise trainees of the following hierarchy of intervention, "Keep them alive, keep them coming, solve the problem." This remains the emphasis of strategic therapy, although the model has advanced in its understanding of alliance building, client feedback, and intervention.

Although it has evolved in ways demonstrated in the following case, the guiding map of strategic remains focused on the constructs of hierarchy and sequence to guide change and avoid harm. There is still a special interest on the interplay of multiple levels of communication. There remains an optimistic view of human difficulties as "love gone wrong" as described by one of the founders of strategic, Don Jackson. And, as with many current models of therapy, strategic has integrated advances in the use of constructs such as attachment, neuro-endocrine functioning, and self-regulation. (Space does not permit dealing with all of these issues within this short case description.)

The alert reader will note elements of structural therapy (the aforementioned focus on hierarchy) and of MRI (the multiple levels of communication and interest in interrupting stuck sequences). Thus, classic strategic therapy is an integrative model, drawing on both structural and Ericksonian/MRI elements.

The theory of change is common to both. If a system can be supported so that it continues to experiment creatively with solving challenges, the chances of resolving a problem are maximized. Experimenting creatively involves some combination of giving up on what is not working, repeating what has worked in the past, and trying some new approaches (John Weakland, personal communication, 1993). Clients tend to come to therapy because they are worn out or are finding it difficult to be flexible and/or rigid, and the therapist's contribution to the change process may include the following:

1. Encourage the discouraged. This usually includes elements of novelty; playfulness; reawakening of feelings of love, connection, and support; and the coaching of self-care.
2. Encourage experimentation. The therapist encourages experiments in systemic flexibility and rigidity in ongoing problem solving.

3. Encourage competence. Clients tend to integrate second-order change to the degree to which they feel it flows from their own competence, effort, and love.

Applications to the Case

When Fred first called for therapy, he noted that he had a son who was "quite possibly the most oppositional adolescent in his whole school." He sounded quite frustrated and even ashamed about the problem, but he was still eager to find help. I asked who the most important people in the system were and ended up agreeing with him that he, his wife, and Johnny should all attend the first session.

Mary, age 40, and Fred, age 42, arrived with Johnny, age 15. They were ushered into my office after signing the first session paperwork. After introductions, the structure of the session was described, with the family understanding that for the first segment of the hour they would be seen together, then the parents would be seen alone, and then Johnny would be seen. If there was time, the whole family might be brought in together again at the end. I then asked the family the following:

1. to describe some examples of fun that they like to have as individuals and together;
2. to describe something difficult that they overcame individually and together.

My goals in asking these questions are numerous. One is to anchor the therapy in a sense of competence in problem solving and in an ability to enjoy life. These questions anchor the therapy in their more competent selves and interactions, and each time they come to therapy or evoke the thought of therapy, it is hoped that this more competent and optimistic self and system are evoked. Another goal is to begin to create some confidence in the clients that I (the therapist) can keep order and a safe emotional tenor in the session and to additionally give them a sense of the inclusiveness and listening that is involved. A third goal is to get a sense of the nature of hierarchy and sequence around this discussion. Does even a positive question such as this quickly evolve into fighting? Are the parents able to authentically compliment their children? Are the children able to receive the compliments as offered? This first part of the interview looks more at the functioning of the soft side of the family hierarchy. By "soft side," I mean the attachment rather than the executive functioning of the parental system.

Johnny's problem behavior is not addressed in the family portion of this first session because I already have a concern (given the symptoms) that Johnny might feel singled out and blamed. In order to preserve the alliance not only with Johnny but also with his tired parents who seemed overwhelmed, I am going to wait for a safer time to have family discussion around his problem behaviors. After getting the family to address the first two questions, and when the mood of the family is colored by the questions about fun and competence, I ask Johnny to go to the waiting room so that I can speak to his parents alone. I asked Mary and Fred to describe their view of Johnny's difficulties. I specifically ask these questions:

- What happens when there is a problem?
- What are your views of the history of this problem?
- What do you do to try to solve the problem?
- What are the rewards for your children? What are the consequences?
- How do you take care of yourselves as parents and have fun?
- Who encourages you? Who do you feel blames you for not doing the right thing with Johnny?
- When does the problem not happen?

Mary and Fred describe Johnny as having had an oppositional temperament "since he was just a few months old." Unlike his older siblings, he was colicky and difficult to soothe. Until middle school, he would only wear stretch pants without a belt as he did not like the feeling of belts. Because of my interest in self-regulation, I am particularly interested in this early history of difficulties.

Because of some academic difficulties, Johnny was diagnosed in seventh grade with an auditory processing problem that did not require transfer to special classes but that certainly had an impact on his performance and that required some alternative teaching approaches from his very experienced seventh and eighth grade teachers. His behavior at home at this point was occasionally oppositional but not to a degree that severely affected his family relationships or school performance.

In ninth grade, Johnny's behavior took a turn for the worse. There were no changes in the family or friendship systems that the parents were aware of. His behavior became increasingly oppositional, and he would challenge his parents' authority and seemed at times to "cut off his nose to spite his face" when faced with increasingly severe punishments as his parents tried to correct his behavior. Fred and Mary even tried "tough love" approaches but found that they did not work.

By 10th grade, Johnny was skipping classes and was spending time with friends who, though good at heart, were similarly discouraged about school and were occasionally skipping class to play computer games together and perhaps smoke pot. At home, Johnny was at times explosive when his parents tried to talk to him about his behavior problems or school performance. He quickly was able to turn conversations around and blame his parents for his problem.

I ask about Johnny's experiences with teachers in the 9th and 10th grade, and Fred and Mary reported that Johnny had had a particularly hard time with a teacher who took a "law and order" approach to classroom difficulties. Johnny reported to his parents on a number of occasions that he felt singled out and humiliated by this teacher.

As Johnny's oppositional behavior became worse, it seemed to focus more on his father. While Mary worked full-time, Fred worked half-time and had much more parenting responsibility. Fred had a much more oppositional relationship with Johnny, and Mary, though she experienced it some, was less likely to be involved in heated power struggles with Johnny. They had purchased numerous books on dealing with behavior problems, had tried the techniques (point system, etc.), and had met with much failure.

I congratulated the parents on the times when they succeeded in creating situations where Johnny had succeeded (with a tutor, and when Johnny was in a sports-related setting). I then noted that what was helpful in my own evaluation was that they had done what normally works with problem behavior, and, interestingly enough, Johnny had not responded as expected. I further noted that their other two children had responded quite nicely to their approach. Fred noted of those situations, "But he was this way with other people. Why should we take credit for how he is with his ball team and with the tutor?" I responded with the question, "Who arranged for Johnny to have these successful experiences?" "I guess we did," answered Mary, looking hopefully at Fred. I finished by saying, "With your permission, I suspect that we are going to have to throw out the 'book of normal' and try some rather unusual approaches to this situation." Fred and Mary stepped out feeling relieved that they had not been blamed and had not been made to feel like bad parents.

I next met with Johnny. When I interviewed Johnny, I wanted not only to join with him and get his view of the problem; I also wanted to understand issues of harm or even suicidal thoughts, although I addressed these issues at the end of our individual portion of the interview after joining with him in a way that allowed me to broach these from a position of some initial trust in our relationship.

Johnny was energetic in asserting that he was not responsible for the things he was accused of, that his parents were unfair, and that he hated school. We discussed his feelings about various teachers. We discussed why he felt his father was unfair to him. I asked him for ideas about what he wanted to get out of the therapy even though it wasn't his idea to come. I also asked him how his family could have more fun, though I was not sure if I could encourage anything specific. He perked up at this question. He noted that his parents were boring and needed to get out more. He mentioned a few specific concerts he thought they should attend. He also noted that he wouldn't mind a family trip to an amusement park. I thanked him for these ideas. It is important to organize an interview so that the therapist ends up honestly admiring the clients, and I ended this interview with transparent and authentic appreciation for Johnny's ideas about family fun.

I brought the parents back in and spoke to them alone. I told them that I concurred with their description of the problem, that this was a case of oppositional behavior that did not respond to normal parenting techniques. I noted that "as parents, we are equipped with a sense of what our parents did that worked, what our parents did that didn't work, and with norms of average parenting. If you have a child who needs an approach outside of these three categories of knowledge, it is a real challenge. You have a real challenge on your hands. The good news is that we know a process that works to alleviate some of your frustration as parents and that should help to get Johnny back on track." I asked the parents to come back without their children the next session. I then asked their permission to do something that would help keep Johnny engaged in therapy. I asked them if it would be okay if he got to suggest a fun family activity and a parent activity to be completed in the next month. Sympathizing with my plight in having to keep Johnny interested in therapy, and secure in the knowledge that I did not blame them for being bad parents, they agreed. Fred noted, "We probably need to have more fun. We have so many terrible arguments with Johnny that it sucks the life out of the family sometimes. Out of our marriage sometimes." I noted that most parents felt similarly stressed.

When the parents returned without their child, I asked them about their statement that "Johnny would cut off his nose to spite his face" when pushed regarding behavior and consequences. I noted that this was a very, very important clue as to how to proceed because most normal parenting methods assume just the opposite. I noted that as a way of describing the problem, "cuts off his nose to spite his face" was a bit of a mouthful, and asked what they would like to call it. "Let's call it oppositional behavior," Fred replied, looking at me a bit strangely.

I described an approach to oppositional behavior that I had had some success with and that I had had occasion to teach others. It has four steps. And it is based in the idea that normal parenting guides are for kids who won't cut off their noses to spite their faces.

The steps are the following:

1. developing an empowering definition of the problem and starting to deal with blame issues;
2. stepping back from what is not working and focusing on self-care (the goal of this stage is not to change the oppositional behavior but rather for the parents to give themselves permission and practice stepping back from approaches that they have proven not to work; it is facilitated by the creation of an individualized parenting guide that records the ongoing experiments of the caretakers);
3. reworking rules and consequences;
4. empowering the parents further by coaching them through soothing discussions of the "hottest" topics in the session.

Using this four-step intervention focuses on both the hard and soft sides of hierarchy: change is associated with the benevolent empowerment of parents that happens when they more efficiently use the soft side versus the more common overemphasis on battling over hard-side issues. Parents are given the opportunity to soothe their children in relation to discussions of the most inflammatory and difficult topics in the family system. And, in the end, parents are newly encouraged to parent.

21

MULTIDIMENSIONAL FAMILY THERAPY

A Science-Based, Developmental Approach for Adolescent Problems

Howard A. Liddle

Adolescents drop out of various forms of therapy at alarmingly high rates. In one national study of clinics treating adolescent substance abuse and behavioral problems, 77% of the sample of clinically referred teenagers left treatment before the end of the 90-day program. Reviews have estimated that a 40%–60% dropout rate for teenagers is normative. At the same time, consider how the experts come to the aid of clinicians working with teenagers; they use terms such as the tough adolescent, the defiant adolescent, the difficult adolescent, and the aggressive adolescent. Creating as much as reflecting reality, these descriptors show an author's hand. They are a *tell*.[1]

This chapter is part of the story of the evidence-based practice movement that is relevant for but exists very much outside of today's family therapy. Multidimensional family therapy (MDFT) is a specialized treatment for adolescent substance abuse and delinquency. I developed this treatment in the mid-1980s, having spent the initial dozen years of my career teaching family therapy, running training clinics that we operated like community agencies, writing about integrative therapy, and formulating supervision and training ideas. MDFT has been tested in 12 controlled clinical trials since 1985, in varied geographic and routine care clinical settings, and with diverse multiethnic and multinational clinically referred adolescents. In studies where MDFT is compared to active treatments like cognitive behavioral therapy (CBT) and manual guided group therapy, for instance, MDFT achieved clinically superior outcomes that remain stable at one-year follow-up and beyond. These outcomes are consistent across a range of problems, including substance use, antisocial behavior, school failure, and other co-occurring externalizing and internalizing problems. MDFT process research has demonstrated a capacity to change critical targets of problem development and maintenance and increase areas of functioning that promote positive current and future development, including the individual developmental tasks of youth, parents, and family relationships.

Getting to the case, we would first disentangle the details and try to make sense of the information that we have so far. This is always the first thing that one does, regardless of approach. In this case, we approach the case from the mind-set and outline of a particular evidence-based therapy. Among other things, this means that the therapy is well specified in a practically oriented manual. Therapists use a good manual and supplementary how-to protocols at the beginning of their training and throughout all of their cases. These materials are used differently as clinicians gain skill in the approach. The protocols can take the form of checklists about the key steps and parts of an approach or the key challenges that one usually faces in clinical work with a particular kind of problem. Thinking developmentally is essential in any family therapy. In MDFT, thinking developmentally also includes the developmental issues of the therapist, of training, and, most of all, of the inner workings of therapy and the therapy model itself. MDFT conceptualizations about change and how to prompt it are specified in terms of stages. In practice, this way of organizing one's work is not as lockstep as one might think at first. It's actually quite logical, even intuitive for most therapists who work our way. Thinking in terms of what one has to accomplish first, we start with adolescent and parent engagement, beginning with fundamental activities to not only engage in but to *accomplish*. Although there are common methods in each, every engagement operation with the parents and the youth are different. They require different mind-sets, knowledge, and skills, all of which are developed over time in the initial training but mostly in the seeing of real cases, over a period of months, watching other therapists, and receiving extensive weekly coaching on how to grow MDFT competence. Watching the core MDFT DVDs—videos illustrating the ABCs of the approach—the problems that always arise in implementation, and the varieties of clinician style that help deliver the approach in a flexible way, are essential. Unsurprisingly, since the therapy model is multidimensional, the training and supervision model, and the logic model of clinician change, are all multidimensional as well.

The MDFT manual and materials overview the entire approach. They describe in unabashed how-to terms how to move from phase to phase and how to work in each of the four critical domains—with the adolescent alone, the parent(s) alone, the family as a unit, and the family members in relation to outsiders and the social systems that are involved with one or more family members (probation officers, school teachers, counselors, or administrators). Therapists begin the case conceptualization process on the basis of the information that one first receives. It's not a problem to have incomplete background information. Moving quickly to meet and hear the story of the adolescent, the parents, and the overall case gives more than enough to build relationships, focus on what's important, and begin to grow motivation all the way around.

Interpreting the Facts in MDFT Terms

Several bits of information are available so far. But initially, these pieces are static. Like photographs, they can reveal useful things, but it's only in action, in relationships, and in the process of meeting a case and beginning therapy that the action comes to life, as it needs to, for one to begin to get the most useful kind of information. Here, I pose some questions and raise issues to illustrate the MDFT way of proceeding, processing, and, most critically, using the initial information that one receives to create the foundation for change.

Mary and Fred are the parents. Get to know the parents, their life stories, occupations, and so on. In overall terms, you're trying to retrack the family's developmental functioning. MDFT is a developmental approach. I think of what we do as a *natural* approach to treatment. Given the family's ongoing importance in all aspects of the youth's successful development and life outcomes, regardless of what has happened previously, we know that true change across a wide range of families and family situations is possible. The trick lies in what a therapist does, or what he or she is willing to do to help the parents and the youth do what it takes to get on a healthy life course.

What about the family's living circumstances? Where do they live? In the first conversation with the family on the phone, we raise the treatment's home visit component. MDFT sessions with the youth and /or parents are conducted both in the clinic and in the family's home or apartment. Access and convenience are vital. Clinicians work right from the start to use the presenting problem, and whatever urgency or crisis may be accompanying the presenting problem, as a lever for contact and getting the ball of treatment rolling. Sessions are held in an office in the school, a family or drug court, a detention center, a medical clinic, a cinema, a park bench, a diner, or a fast food restaurant. Home visits are interesting, challenging, informative, and intimidating for many clinicians. MDFT clinicians are aware that assessment is only a part of the purpose of a home visit (to meet the family in their natural environment). Relationship building is vitally important as well. We ask about previous therapy or program attempts and use details of those treatments—respectfully, of course—to draw distinctions between those treatments and the services we offer. Our studies show that MDFT can engage and retain between 90% and 95% of the kids and families in this relatively brief service approach, which typically extends in a once-or-more-a-week session mode over four or five months.

Johnny, age 15. What's his grade level? Is he on target, level-wise? What about previous problems, including academic problems in school? J says he hates school and skips to hang out with his friends. Asking J about his friends is vital, as is getting a dynamic picture of his comings and goings. We want to know his day-to-day schedule in and around the house and also in his outside-of-the-house activities. Have there been any arrests, even minor violations, trouble with neighborhood folks? What about aggressiveness and substance use? Does J smoke cigarettes? Do his parents smoke? In or around the house? How about alcohol experimentation and use by J or his parents? How does he come across to the therapist? What kind of kid is he? How would the therapist describe him to a colleague? Does the youth show a sense of humor? Is he funny, does he seem sad? Is his expressiveness limited, or perhaps it's too soon to tell, and he's just wary. How does he dress, handle himself physically? What does he like to do? How does he use his time, day to day? Details are important in terms of assessment and are also a way of getting to know the adolescent. MDFT therapists are very concerned about how all members of the family interpret what the therapy (the program) is, what it will try to do, and what will be required of them. And adolescents in particular know that talk is cheap; following this, if a therapist says that he or she wants the MDFT program to be a place where the youth, in addition to the parents, can get something out of the program for himself or herself, well, that therapist better deliver.

Mary and Fred argue about how to handle this situation. Arguing per se is not a sign of dysfunction. But if parent-teen conflict is chronic, escalated, and emotionally hurtful, and/or if disagreement between the parents exists and is affecting the parental subsystem, then a problem does exist and it's grist for the mill of MDFT or, surely, any family-based therapy. Compromises in individual parent functioning or the parental team are known to put a child's development at risk. J's missing school is not thought of as serving a function in the family. In fact, *function of the symptom* attributions, in addition to being wrong, unprovable, and narrow in conceptualization of why a behavior comes about or stays in place, do not immediately lead to constructive action on anyone's part. In MDFT the focus is on development and unlocking the keys to positive and prosocial development of the youth and the parents together. So the parental disagreements should be explored and discussed. See each parent alone, get their point of view, ask what they have tried, ask about how each sees the disagreement with the other parent, and emphasize that disagreement is normal but that chronic disagreement and arguing hurts them and their child. The father's preference for punishment can be part of a solution or part of the problem solving that occurs, but we think more in terms of consequences that are fair and that are more thought of in terms of limit setting than punishment per se. The emotions of the father—his anger, perhaps embarrassment, about his son's behavior—are explored, and the mother's emotional reactions to her son's behavior are important to work with as well. The mother's attribution of her headaches to stress is quite useful as a scaffolding on which to define the need for immediate action on everyone's part. At the same time, physical symptoms should be checked out fully through the usual medical means. The mother's mom seems to be a relevant part of the initial presentation, so she should be met and consulted as well. Perhaps she has the potential to help the mother and father get a break from some of their parenting demands now and then. As with all aspects of the case, it is important to seek out and mobilize the strengths of family members to take on the events that concern them.

The program brings parents together to work out more effective ways of raising their child. The sessions with the parents and youth progress to having parents discuss house rules, the importance of going to school, and why these outcomes are important to them. Putting parental requests or demands within a bigger picture and expressing their love and commitment to their child, while at the same time detailing their concerns about the current problem and where it may be headed, is standard work but vital. Critically, however, family sessions also permit the adolescent to talk, to state his case and tell his story about what's going on, why going to school is uninteresting, what's on his mind, what's his point of view about school, his friends, and his parents and family. J's capacity to express himself in these ways is facilitated through individual meetings with him.

Mary thinks perhaps Johnny would benefit from a more nurturing school environment. This could very well be. This is why MDFT therapists do not see changing family interaction as generally sufficient to bottom-line or lasting youth outcomes. A therapist needs to get on the phone with the school, help the parents deal with the school officials, and arrange meetings for all concerned at the school. The objective is not to take on the school's policies or procedures to engineer change in this or any aspect of the youth's social environment, as influential as those structures and institutions may be. Rather, therapists work with the family, parents and adolescents, to help them change their ways of thinking about, and relating to, institutions and influential aspects of the environment including juvenile justice.

Note

1. A tell in the card game poker is a change in a player's behavior or demeanor that is claimed by some to give clues to that player's assessment of his or her hand.

Resources

Introduction to MDFT [Video]. http://www.youtube.com/watch?v=FiOiOERc82o, http://www.youtube.com/watch?v=YzjGqlPlU-g&feature=related; http://www.you tube.com/user/CTRADA#p/u/11/yHKSI5bv9Q8

Liddle, H. A. (1991). Empirical values and the culture of family therapy. *Journal of Marital and Family Therapy, 17*(4), 327–348.

Liddle, H. A. (1994). The anatomy of emotions in family therapy with adolescents. *Journal of Adolescent Research, 9*(1) 120–157.

Liddle, H. A. (2010). Treating adolescent substance abuse using multidimensional family therapy. In J. Weisz & A. Kazdin (Eds.), *Evidence-based psychotherapies for children and adolescents* (2nd ed.). New York, NY: Guilford Press.

Liddle, H. A., Dakof, G. A., Turner, R. M., Henderson, C. E., & Greenbaum, P. E. (2008). Treating adolescent drug abuse: A randomized trial comparing multidimensional family therapy and cognitive behavior therapy. *Addiction, 103,* 1660–1670.

Liddle, H. A., Rowe, C. L., Dakof, G. A., Henderson, C.E., & Greenbaum, P. E. (2009). Multidimensional family therapy for early adolescent substance abusers: Twelve month outcomes of a randomized controlled trial. *Journal of Consulting and Clinical Psychology, 77*(1), 12–25.

Liddle, H. A., Rowe, C. L., Diamond, G. M., Sessa, F. M., Schmidt, S., & Ettinger, D. (2000). Towards a developmental family therapy: The clinical utility of research on adolescence. *Journal of Marital and Family Therapy, 26*(4), 485–499.

Liddle, H. A., Rowe, C. L., Gonzalez, A., Henderson, C. E., Dakof, G. A., & Greenbaum, P. E. (2006). Changing provider practices, program environment, and improving outcomes by transporting multidimensional family therapy to an adolescent drug treatment setting, *American Journal on Addictions, 15,* 102–112.

Liddle, H. A., Rowe, C. L., Ungaro, R. A., Dakof, G. A., & Henderson, C. (2004). Early intervention for adolescent substance abuse: Pretreatment to post treatment outcomes of a randomized controlled trial comparing multidimensional family therapy and peer group treatment. *Journal of Psychoactive Drugs, 36*(1), 2–37.

MDFT in Practice [Video]. http://www.youtube.com/watch?v=tu-r27w6mgg

Shelef, K., Diamond, G. M., Diamond, G. S., & Liddle, H. A. (2005). Adolescent and parent alliance and treatment outcome in multidimensional family therapy. *Journal of Consulting and Clinical Psychology, 73*(4), 689–698.

22

MULTISYSTEMIC FAMILY THERAPY

Trahern LaFavor and Jeff Randall

Multisystemic therapy (MST) is an evidence-based therapy model designed to treat youth with serious antisocial behavior and their families (Henggeler, Schoenwald, Borduin, Rowland, & Cunningham, 1998; 2009). While there are several components of MST, this chapter will only focus on techniques considered necessary for first sessions.

The following principles are fundamental to MST. Principle 1: The primary purpose of the assessment is to understand the fit between the identified problems and their broader systemic context. Principle 2: Therapeutic contacts emphasize the positive and use systemic strengths as levers for change. Principle 3: Interventions are designed to promote responsible behavior and decrease irresponsible behavior among family members. Principle 4: Interventions are present focused and action oriented, targeting specific and well-defined problems. Principle 5: Interventions target sequences of behavior within and between multiple systems that maintain the identified problems. Principle 6: Interventions are developmentally appropriate and fit the developmental needs of the youth. Principle 7: Interventions are designed to require daily or weekly effort by family members. Principle 8: Intervention effectiveness is evaluated continuously from multiple perspectives with providers assuming accountability for overcoming barriers to successful outcomes. Principle 9: Interventions are designed to promote treatment generalization and long-term maintenance of therapeutic change by empowering caregivers to address family members' needs across multiple systemic contexts (Henggeler et al., 1998, 2009).

The MST Analytic Process

The MST analytic process guides the MST therapist in treatment planning and interventions (Henggeler et al., 1998, 2009). Although there are several components of the analytic process, this chapter will focus on conceptualization of the "fit." "The term 'fit' or 'fit circle' is derived from principle 1 of MST" (Henggeler et al., 2009, p. 22). The fit is crucial because it aids the MST therapist in assessing and understanding presenting behaviors (Henggeler et al., 1998, 2009).

In the common case example given, Mary and Fred are frustrated due to Johnny's skipping classes. Given that they are key participants, vital to treatment, Mary, Fred, and Bess (the maternal grandmother) are central in obtaining and sustaining progress (principle 9). The presenting problem is skipping classes; therefore, an overarching goal will consist of increasing classroom attendance.

After ascertaining referral behaviors, desired outcomes, and overarching goals, the MST therapist assesses and conceptualizes multiple factors contributing to Johnny's behavior. To accomplish this goal, MST considers five systems in a youth's ecology: family, individual, community, school, and peer. Within context of these systems, the assumption is that one or more drivers (i.e., factors) within the systems have an influence on the youth's presenting behaviors. For instance, factors related to Johnny's skipping classes are likely negative peers (i.e., peer system) and Mary, Fred, and Bess not being on the same page (i.e., family system) concerning how to address Johnny skipping classes.

Initial Interviews

The initial stage of therapy consists of engaging and identifying family strengths, which will be used as leverage for change (Henggeler et al., 1998, 2009). For example, in the aforementioned case, Johnny's two biological parents as well as his grandmother are concerned about his behavior. Their concerns will be leverage to get the three adult caregivers to reach a consensus concerning treatment goals. Consistent with MST, family and key participants must be engaged for treatment to be successful. Examples of some key participants might include friends of the family, neighbors, coaches, and clergy (Henggeler et al., 1998, 2009). According to principle 9, interventions are designed to promote treatment generalization and long-term maintenance of therapeutic change by empowering a youth's adult caregivers to address family members' needs across multiple systemic contexts (Henggeler et al., 1998, 2009). To generate positive outcomes, progress must be sustained through a collaboration of multiple systems. Therefore, in Johnny's case, engaging his grandmother in treatment is also essential inasmuch as she could assist with supporting the two biological parents daily with interventions (principle 7).

Assessment

Johnny is skipping classes. This behavior is most likely causing him to fail his grade. According to principle 1, the goal of assessment seeks to make sense of client behavior within context, while determining each factor that contributes to his behavior. A peer factor (i.e., Johnny's association with negative peers) and a family factor (i.e., adult caregivers not being on the same page regarding what to do about Johnny skipping classes) would be examined for possible fit. Assessment is an ongoing process with the MST therapist obtaining information from multiple systems maintaining the problem, such as individual, family, peers, school, and neighborhood/community (Henggeler et al., 1998). Through assessing systemic ecological factors, case conceptualization becomes clear and leads to concrete goal and intervention development.

After collaborating with family and gaining a definitive understanding of factors contributing to behavior, fit factors are prioritized, and goals are developed to tackle the behaviors. In this case, the MST therapist and family members might prioritize Johnny's association with negative peers and his adult caregivers not being on the same page as fit factors that treatment goals should target. To obtain some additional information, the MST therapist and Johnny's adult caregivers might schedule a parent-teacher conference to obtain a clear picture of client behavior within the environment of the school setting. Given that the MST therapist's work hours are flexible, he or she has the luxury of being present with family during any school conference to aid the family in assessing any additional factors related to Johnny skipping classes.

Once the analytic process is complete, fit is developed, and goals are established, interventions would be implemented. Potential interventions to address Johnny's association with negative peers might include ascertaining who the negative peers are and connecting with parents of negative peers to enhance adult supervision of Johnny's peer associations. Agreement between the adults as to consequences for Johnny would also be important. Interventions are typically straightforward and directive and aimed at reinforcing family hierarchy and appropriate parenting.

After interventions are developed, the MST therapist would work together with the family to implement the strategies. Given that MST engagement is ongoing, treatment progress includes continuous effort (principle 4) and evaluating of progress toward goals in order to maintain progress during and after treatment is completed (principle 9). It should be noted that the aforementioned work does not occur in one session but over the course of several sessions.

MST is an evidence-based treatment model that has demonstrated success in treating families who present serious clinical problems; therapists collaborate with caregivers to overcome barriers, helping them achieve success (Cunningham & Henggeler, 1999). MST has demonstrated improved outcomes for juvenile offenders, substance use, prevention of out-of-home placement, and also improving family, school, and peer functioning. In addition, MST therapists who practice MST are available to families 24 hours a day, 7 days a week, and have a low caseload of four to six families. Therefore, they are able to address the many barriers leading to behavior problems (Henggeler, Melton, & Smith, 1992; Henggeler et al., 2009; Schaeffer & Borduin, 2005). MST continues to provide effective treatment to youth and families who experience behavior problems.

References

Cunningham, P. B., & Henggeler, S. W. (1999). Engaging multiproblem families in treatment: Lessons learned throughout the development of multisystemic therapy. *Family Process, 38,* 265–286.

Henggeler, S. W., Melton, G. B., & Smith, L. A. (1992). Family preservation using multi-systemic therapy: An effective alternative to incarcerating serious juvenile offenders. *Journal of Consulting and Clinical Psychology, 60,* 953–961.

Henggeler, S. W., Schoenwald, S. K., Borduin, C. M., Rowland, M. D., & Cunningham, P. B. (1998). *Multisystemic treatment of antisocial behavior in children and adolescents.* New York, NY: Guilford Press.

Henggeler, S. W., Schoenwald, S. K., Borduin, C. M., Rowland, M. D., & Cunningham, P. B. (2009). *Multisystemic therapy for antisocial behavior in children and adolescents.* New York, NY: Guilford Press.

Schaeffer, C. M., & Borduin, C. M. (2005). Long-term follow-up to a randomized clinical trial of multisystemic therapy with serious and violent juvenile offenders. *Journal of Consulting and Clinical Psychology, 73*(3), 445–453.

23

FUNCTIONAL FAMILY THERAPY

Kim Mason, Holly Waldroon, and Michael Robbins

Functional family therapy (FFT) is an evidence-based family therapy model focused on helping troubled youth and their families by improving relationships and developing prosocial behaviors of individual family members. FFT is an integrated approach that combines family systems with cognitive and behavioral theories and intervention strategies to reduce risk factors and enhance protective factors at the level of individual family members, the family system, and the social ecology of the family. FFT consists of phases of treatment: engagement, motivation, relational assessment, behavior change, and generalization. Each phase is associated with distinct goals, assessment focus, and intervention techniques that provide a guide for therapists as they navigate the complex interactions that occur in sessions and develop treatment plans to address the unique needs of each individual family member and the family as a whole.

The first phase of treatment, engagement, is quite brief, intended primarily to maximize family members' initial expectations of treatment and to establish the therapist as a credible helper. This phase involves establishing contact with all family members to ensure their participation during the initial session. Separate calls may be necessary to engage each family member by presenting treatment in a way that enhances their perception that they have something to gain by engaging in the treatment process. In these early calls, therapists carefully match their behavior to the family's style, language, and pace of communication and demonstrate a deep respect for the families' beliefs, feelings, values, and culture. Individual differences are accepted in a nonblaming and nonjudgmental way.

Determining which family members to include in treatment is an ongoing clinical assessment. Additional family members, significant others, or nonfamily members may be brought in during the different phases of intervention as needed to facilitate the change process. For example, the therapist would typically discuss the possibility of a grandmother living with the family being included in the services due to the role she plays in the family.

During the first session, the basic strategies of the engagement phase are quickly replaced with more sophisticated clinical interventions that are intended to create a context in which family members are motivated for change. The goals of the motivation phase, generally the first two to four sessions of treatment, include (a) continuing to build a balanced alliance with all family members, (b) reducing negativity and blame, and (c) building hope for the future. FFT therapists systematically disrupt patterns of negativity and blame to create a more positive relational focus, as opposed to individual target child focus, through the utilization of process-based change focus techniques, such as interrupting negative interactions or relationship-based process comments, as well as more sophisticated change meaning techniques, such as relational reframing. With respect to the former, for example, the therapist may highlight positive relational connections by using process statements like "Mary (Mom?) and Frank (Dad?), I notice you all nodding your heads every time I mention how protective you all seem of one another... so this is something that you are all pretty well aware of. Is that right?" Or, with respect to the latter, the therapist may follow up later with a reframe that assigns some nobility to Johnny's misbehavior by reframing it as, "It seems that Johnny is very tuned in to what is going on with you guys. I wonder if part of his acting up at school involves bringing some attention to himself so that you two, mom and dad, have to come together to work out your differences." It is through the utilization of these techniques that therapists create a context in which family members are willing to try out something new.

While the therapist is moving the family toward a new definition of the problem that enhances their motivation to change, they are also working to identify the *relational functions* or interpersonal relational payoffs of individuals' behaviors in the family. Relational assessment involves identifying patterns of interpersonal antecedents and consequences of behavioral patterns relevant to dysfunctional behavior. Relational functions represent inferred internal motivations of family members based on overtly expressed (behaviorally, verbally, emotionally) patterns within the family. The focus is not on the inferred internal process, but rather on the resulting patterns that emerge from family interactions.

The assessment process also examines the functional relationships and problem behavior patterns outside the family. The primary focus of relational assessment involves determining the degree of interpersonal connection that is expressed in the behavior patterns that directly or indirectly affects another person (or persons) in the family (and other systems). The degree of connection can involve high levels of contact, closeness, and interpersonal connection, and high levels of separation, distance, independence, or autonomy; or can involve a significant blending of behaviors that reflect aspects of both closeness and distance—a relational function referred to as "midpointing." These dimensional anchors are not considered to be fixed and invariant points along a single dimension. Instead, we consider closeness and distance independently. We look to the combination of contact or closeness with separation or distance in consistent behavioral patterns in the family to determine which relational function—closeness, distance, or midpointing—best characterizes the ongoing relationship of each family member's relationship with each other family member. Imagine a couple in an ongoing relationship: they are not *always* close or *always* distant or *always* a mixture of both. In general, however, couples can be distinguished in terms of whether their pattern is generally close and connected, generally distant and autonomous, or generally variable. Whatever the behavioral pattern over time, the relational functions of each family member with each other family member are not targeted for change, but rather are accepted, consistent with the FFT core principal of the *respectful acceptance of the diversity that all family members bring*. In the case of Johnny, therapists would assess all of the relational functions of each dyad (including the grandmother or other therapy participants). The therapists would consider whether Johnny's misbehavior or truancy at school leads to more contact with or distance from mom or dad and, at the same time, if this behavior also leads to more contact/closeness for mom with dad or with the grandmother.

FFT does not attempt to change peoples' relational functions. The goal is to enhance the *quality* of the relationships in the family, but not specifically to promote youth moving closer to or establishing independence from their parents. Youth and parents can have healthy close relationships without being enmeshed as well as autonomous relationships without being disengaged. Similarly, the goal is not to facilitate more intense contact for mothers with each of their children or to help them become less involved with them. Therapists assess the relational functions present in each dyad and then integrate these relational configurations into a sustainable plan for changing maladaptive behaviors in the family. This is accomplished by working *with* the relational configurations they already have developed, providing them *adaptive* and *acceptable* ways to express these configurations differently...and better! This is core to FFT and distinguishes FFT from many other intervention approaches.

The next phase of treatment, behavior change, is focused on replacing maladaptive behaviors with adaptive behaviors. These behaviors include referral problems such as truancy, delinquency, or drug use, as well as other problems in the family, such as inappropriate anger outbursts or parenting strategies. In developing behavior change strategies, the focus is on creating changes that provide family members with adaptive alternative behaviors that maintain their relational functions in the family. FFT utilizes two broad classes of techniques for behavior change. The first class is represented by *general skill-building* processes such as communication training, problem solving, and conflict management techniques. These techniques are possible for many families, and they represent skill development that is useful to family members when they interact, but also generalize nicely to other extrafamily systems (school, work, friendships). The second class of techniques represents *problem- or syndrome-specific techniques* that may apply to some people and families but not others, including: (a) skill-building techniques, such as anger management, relaxation training, and so on; (b) techniques for overcoming challenges unique to some families, such as a single parent with a physical disability that precludes the use of many parenting strategies; and (c) techniques specific to youth with developmental disorders.

Prior to initiating the behavior change phase, the therapist determines the relational functions of each family member dyad and reviews the risk and protective factors present in the family. Then, once behavior change has begun, the therapist works to assist the family in developing skills that would still meet each of their relational functions in a way that replaces maladaptive behaviors with adaptive or healthy ones, reduces the impact of risk factors on the family, and fosters the development of or strengthens existing protective factors. Initially the therapist might help parents focus on the positive adolescent behaviors and overtly reinforce these behaviors to encourage them. They might also work with the family to develop effective problem-solving strategies. The behavior change phase is complete when all the presenting or primary problems in the family have been addressed.

Finally, during the generalization phase, the focus shifts to generalizing change into multiple systems in the youth's and family's social ecology. Interventions address the complex networks of social, legal, cultural, economic, community, and other systems in which families are embedded. Unlike generic treatment planning, which sometimes provides multiple services to families and family members with little consideration of family dynamics, FFT focuses on each individual family's interpersonal and systemic needs when considering adjunctive support services. For example, participation in a community program may not be supported by the mother if it replaces the father's role with his son and in doing so enables the father to further disengage from the family. In the generalization phase, other family members who were not part of the core FFT sessions could also be included in the therapy sessions. The focus would be to help the family generalize the skills they have learned with each other, such as problem solving or focusing on the positive, and now apply these same skills in their relationship with other family members (e.g., grandmother) and the school. These other family members could also be a part of sustainability planning as to how they can help the family maintain the positive changes they have made.

Resources

Alexander, J., & Parsons, B. V. (1982). *Functional family therapy.* Monterey, CA: Brooks & Cole.

Alexander, J. F., Robbins, M. S., & Sexton, T. L. (2000). Family-based interventions with older, at risk youth: From promise to proof to practice. *Journal of Primary Prevention* 21(2), 185–205.

Alexander, J., Waldon, H. B., Newberry, A. M., & Liddle, N. (1990). The functional family therapy model. In A. S. Friedman & S. Granick (Eds.), *Family therapy for adolescent drug abuse* (pp. 183–199). Lexington, MA: Lexington Books/D.C. Heath and Company.

Sexton, T. L., & Alexander, J. F. (2002). Functional family therapy for adolescents and their families. In T. Patterson (Ed.), *Comprehensive handbook of psychotherapy.* New York, NY: Wiley & Sons.

24

BRIEF STRATEGIC FAMILY THERAPY

Monica Zarate, Ruban Roberts, Joan A. Muir, and Jose Szapocznik

Brief strategic family therapy (BSFT) was developed in a 35-year program of research at the University of Miami's Center for Family Studies (Szapocznik & Williams, 2000; Szapocznik, Hervis, & Schwartz, 2003). The BSFT model is a 12- to 16-week intervention for the prevention and treatment of adolescents with serious behavior problems and drug use. A series of randomized clinical trials have demonstrated that the BSFT model is efficacious in treating adolescent drug abuse, conduct problems, associations with antisocial peers, and impaired family functioning (Szapocznik et al., 1989; Santisteban et al., 2003; Robbins et al., 2009). Because the family is an important context for adolescent development, the BSFT model intervenes directly at the level of the family system, diagnosing and restructuring maladaptive interactions. These maladaptive interactions are considered to contribute to or maintain the presenting problem and are therefore the targets of change in therapy.

When preparing to work with a family, a therapist using the brief strategic family therapy model needs to determine the answer to two important questions: (1) What are the family's patterns of interaction that are sustaining the problem behavior? and (2) How can the family exchange maladaptive patterns of interaction to more adaptive ones while preserving their interdependency? BSFT therapists look to the family system to obtain the information to plan and achieve change and rely on three important principles to achieve this change. The first principle is that the BSFT model is a family systems approach, which views family members as interdependent and therefore able to influence one another. The second principle is that patterns of interaction in a family are repetitive and predictable and therefore influence the behavior of each family member. The third principle involves careful planning of interventions that target those patterns of interaction that are directly linked to the adolescent's problem behavior.

Given the common case study, we would utilize the following steps: (a) engaging the family in treatment, (b) joining with all involved family members and observing interactions for diagnostic purposes, (c) developing a treatment plan for the entire family system, (d) restructuring the family's maladaptive interactions, and (e) closing the deal.

Engaging the Family

In the case of Johnny's family, the BSFT therapist would invite all family members who have regular contact with Johnny and who give input in his rearing to participate in the sessions. It is important to invite all family members to sessions in order to fully assess how family members interact and observe these exchanges directly. Working with partial family systems will give an incomplete picture of that family system and will hamper treatment plans and therapeutic goals. BSFT therapists rely on direct observation in order to understand how the family system functions as a whole and to develop a working diagnostic map of the family that will lead to effective treatment. Successfully engaging all family members to participate in sessions is not always an easy task, so BSFT therapists rely on well-developed BSFT engagement strategies that ensure participation (Santisteban et al., 1996; Robbins et al., 2009). There are two important strategies for effective engagement of families: (1) the same family dynamics that are associated with the symptom (e.g., truancy, substance use, and other delinquent behaviors) also cause resistance to engagement; and (2) the clinician's behaviors affect engagement and retention. Therefore, to engage families into treatment, therapists diagnose the failure to engage and use practical strategies to get around resistant patterns and change them later during treatment (Szapocznik et al., 1988; Szapocznik & Kurtines, 1989). These practical strategies may include the following: (a) conveying to family members acknowledgement and understanding of their point of view, (b) exploring individual gains from participation in treatment, (c) exploring obstacles to regular participation in sessions, and (d) offering more positive perspectives of individual family members or the problem situation. BSFT therapists work diligently to persuade family members to participate actively in the process of change and to trust the therapist to guide them to create that change.

Joining the Family

The first session in the BSFT model has two important goals: (1) joining with the family and (2) diagnosing maladaptive patterns of interaction. The first goal is crucial to treatment because it allows the therapist to establish the therapeutic relationship. Joining enhances motivation in family members to follow the BSFT therapist's directives and prepares the family for change. In joining, the therapist may use different techniques to prepare Johnny for change, which may include temporarily aligning with him, acknowledging and validating Johnny's point of view. The BSFT therapist will also need to connect with his parents and grandmother by validating and conveying understanding of their differing points of view. In joining with the family, the therapist works toward establishing trust and gaining a position of leadership to create therapeutic change. The second goal in a first session involves developing a diagnostic map of the family that will help the therapist develop a treatment plan. The treatment plan will lay out the interventions that will help the BSFT therapist change the maladaptive patterns of interaction that are sustaining the symptom in place. Hierarchal misalignment, marital discord, enmeshed dyadic relationships, and triangulated relationships are a few examples of maladaptive family patterns that could give rise to the symptomatic behavior that Johnny demonstrates. The therapist would need to know how Mary and Fred are interacting as the executive subsystem of the family. Do they present a united front to Johnny? Does the executive subsystem need strengthening? How is Johnny interacting with his parents? Does he seem connected to them? How is Bess interacting within the family? Is she usurping the authority of his parents?

Diagnosis

In the BSFT model, diagnosis refers to identifying interactional patterns (structure) that sustain symptoms in place. Problematic patterns of interaction in the family are diagnosed by focusing on family process using five dimensions: (1) organization, (2) resonance, (3) developmental stage, (4) identified patienthood, and (5) conflict resolution. These dimensions are the areas where BSFT therapists will work to achieve change in the family system.

The dimension of organization focuses on assessing leadership functions, subsystem formations, and communication flow in the family. The BSFT therapist will want to know the following: Who takes charge when the family needs to accomplish a task? Is leadership in the appropriate hands? How are decisions made in the family? Who supports whom when there is conflict or difference of opinion? Do family members speak directly to one another? This dimension will provide the BSFT therapist with a good understanding of how power and status are distributed in the family, how the family keeps order, and how the family provides direction and instruction, as well as knowledge about family member affiliations and the flow of communication.

The dimension of resonance assesses the permeability of boundaries between individuals and subsystems. Interactions that are enmeshed (boundaries are too permeable) and interactions that are disengaged (boundaries are too rigid) can cause problems and give rise to symptoms. This dimension helps BSFT therapists assess how much affect or emotion can get through from one person to another. It is important to note that resonance needs to be assessed in the context of culture because culture may dictate the distance or closeness between family members. BSFT therapists need to consider cultural differences and address these with great sensitivity when an interaction, though typical to a culture, might be giving rise to symptoms.

The developmental stage dimension assesses the adaptability of the family to negotiate effectively the various transitions and role changes in the family life cycle. BSFT therapists assess four major tasks and roles when examining this dimension: (1) parenting roles and tasks: Is parenting occurring at a level consistent with the age of the children? (2) spousal roles and tasks: How well are spouses cooperating and sharing family responsibilities? (3) sibling/child roles and tasks: Are children behaving at their age level? Is a child parentified? Is a child immature for her/his age? (4) extended family members' roles and tasks: Is a grandparent undermining the leadership of the parent? Contradicting parents? Treating a parent like a child?

The dimension of identified patienthood assesses the extent to which the family views the family's problems as embodied in one single individual, usually the symptom bearer. The BSFT therapist will want to know these elements: Do family members focus negatively on any one member of the family? Often criticize that person? Is that person considered the cause of all the family's problems? This dimension can be an excellent measure of a family's flexibility. The more the family insists that the problem is found in one single person, the more challenging it will be to bring about change. However, if the family is able to acknowledge that more than one family member contributes to the problem, the family demonstrates more flexibility and hopefully will be more open to change.

The dimension of conflict resolution assesses the family's ability to express, confront, and negotiate solutions to conflicts. There are five different conflict resolution categories: (1) denial, (2) avoidance, (3) diffusion, (4) conflict emergence without resolution, and (5) conflict emergence with resolution. It is important to note that BSFT therapists assess conflict on a continuum from the least adaptive to the most adaptive behaviors. However, BSFT therapists also use considerable judgment in determining which style of conflict resolution is appropriate given the circumstances family members are confronting at any one time. For example, if Johnny is angry or tired, it may be reasonable to table the conflict until Johnny is ready to have a meaningful discussion. Mary and Fred will have to make sure to set aside a time when they can come back to the discussion; if they postpone it and do not come back to it, it is a sign of avoidance.

Restructuring the Maladaptive Family Patterns

Enactments afford the BSFT therapist the opportunity to observe family interactions directly so that the BSFT therapist can later intervene directly in the family's process to create change. As the BSFT therapist observes interactions, the BSFT therapist begins to notice that Mary and Fred become increasingly negative with one another and Mary becomes more protective of Johnny, which only serves to isolate Fred and mobilizes Bess to support her daughter. The BSFT therapist then notices that Johnny's symptomatic behaviors begin to increase. As these exchanges continue, more of the maladaptive patterns become evident, and the BSFT therapist mobilizes to decrease the negativity between Mary and Fred and work toward strengthening their parental relationship. This strategy will serve to address the overinvolvement between Mary and Johnny, solidify the executive subsystem, and establish clearer relational boundaries among family members. This is the beginning of the restructuring process in the BSFT model.

Closing the Deal

The process of restructuring requires that the BSFT therapist be active and directive in facilitating alternate interactional patterns. Emphasis is on family members doing rather than talking. This process, however, can be stressful for family members, which can manifest as resistance. Thus, the BSFT therapist needs to work throughout the process of change toward maintaining a joined position with family members to maintain motivation and secure a new more adaptive family structure.

Toward the close of treatment, the BSFT therapist will need to ensure that Johnny's family system has made adaptive changes such as a reduction in Johnny's symptoms as a result of Mary and Fred resolving conflict, Bess being more of a support to Mary and Fred, and Johnny having a more appropriate relationship with his parents and grandmother. These new interactions should be discussed in session prior to closing the case. The goal is for the therapist to guide the family in acknowledging the new interactional patterns of behavior and preparing them to address future setbacks to avoid falling back into the old patterns of interactions (homeostasis) when conflicts reemerge. Johnny now has a family system that is functioning in a more adaptive and supportive way. The family system is not without error; however, the family now has a set of skills to assist in the management of crisis situations, which has a positive impact on the reduction of symptomatic behaviors not only for Johnny, but for all members of the family.

References

Robbins, M. S., Szapocznik, J., Horigian, V. E., Feaster, D. J., Puccinelli, M., Jacobs, P., Burlew, K., Westlein, R., Bachrach, K., & Brigham, G. (2009). Brief strategic family therapy for adolescent drug abusers: A multi-site effectiveness study. *Contemporary Clinical Trials, 30*, 269–278.

Santisteban, D. A., Coatsworth, J. D., Perez Vidal, A., Kurtines, W. M., Schwartz, S. J., LaPerriere, A., & Szapocznik, J. (2003). The efficacy of brief strategic family therapy in modifying Hispanic adolescent behavior problems and substance use. *Journal of Family Psychology, 17*(1), 121–133.

Santisteban, D. A., Szapocznik, J., Perez-Vidal, A., Kurtines, W. M., Murray, E. J., & Lapierre, A. (1996). Efficacy of intervention for engaging youth and families into treatment and some variables that may contribute to differential effectiveness. *Journal of Family Psychology, 10*, 35–44.

Szapocznik, J., Hervis, O., & Schwartz. (2003). *Brief strategic therapy for adolescent drug abuse.* (NIH Publication No. 03-7451). Rockville, MD: National Institute on Drug Abuse.

Szapocznik, J., & Kurtines, W. (1989). *Breakthroughs in family therapy with drug abusing and problem youth.* New York, NY: Springer.

Szapocznik, J., Perez-Vidal, A., Brickman, A., Foote, F. H., Santisteban, D., Hervis, O. E., & Kurtines, W. M. (1988). Engaging adolescent drug abusers and their families into treatment: A strategic structural systems approach. *Journal of Counseling and Clinical Psychology, 56*, 552–557.

Szapocznik, J., Rio, A., Murray, E., Cohen, R., Scopetta, M., Rivas-Vazquez, A., Hervis, O., Posada, V., & Kurtines, W. (1989). Structural family versus psychodynamic child therapy for problematic Hispanic boys. *Journal of Consulting and Clinical Psychology,* 57(5), 571–578.

Szapocznik, J., & Williams, R. A. (2000). Brief strategic family therapy: Twenty-five years of interplay among theory, research, and practice. *Clinical Child & Family Psychology Review, 3*(11), 7–134.

Additional Resources

Briones, E., Robbins, M. S., & Szapocznik, J. (2008). Brief strategic family therapy: Engagement and treatment. *Alcoholism Treatment Quarterly, 26*(1/2), 81–103.

Coatsworth, J. D., Santisteban, D. A., McBride, C., & Szapocznik, J. (2001). Brief strategic family therapy versus community control: Engagement, retention, and an exploration of the moderating role of adolescent symptom severity. *Family Process, 40,* 313–332.

Horigian, V., Robbins, M. S., & Szapocznik, J. (2004). Brief strategic family therapy: Brief strategic and systemic therapy. *European Review [inaugural issue], 1,* 251–271.

Robbins, M.S., Feaster, D.J., Horigian, V.E., Puccinelli, M.J., Szapocznik, J., & Henderson, C. (2011). Therapist adherence in brief strategic family therapy for adolescent drug abusers. *American Psychological Association, 79,* 43–53.

Robbins, M. S., & Szapocznik, J. (2000). *Brief structural family therapy with behavior problem youth.* Office of Juvenile Justice and Delinquency Prevention Bulletin, Office of Justice Programs, U.S. Department of Justice: Washington, DC.

25

PRACTITIONER'S PERSPECTIVE

Fridays With Minuchin

Charmaine Borda

Clearly, as earlier chapters in this section have demonstrated, structural family therapy is alive and well. In its original form, as the ecosystemic variation currently practiced at Philadelphia Child Guidance, and in the evidence-based community-centered models developed from its influence, the model is widely practiced and abundantly evidence based. Structural therapy has the highest possible "highly recommended" rating from the U.S. government mental health services (www.samsha.gov).

It is important to note, however, that the model is not set in concrete but is constantly evolving. I have had the opportunity for the past 4 years to supervise the experiences of family therapy master's and doctoral students who attend weekly case consultations with Dr. Salvador Minuchin in his home. Specifically, students have committed to present and view the clinical work of their peers for 10-week sessions at a time for the purpose of growing, expanding, and widening their lenses as systemic family therapists. In return, they receive a once-in-a-lifetime opportunity to have their clinical work supervised and critiqued by Minuchin. He contends: "To provoke is as important as to love," or, in other words, in order to develop at your best, you must be prepared and willing to consider "respectful challenge."

Over the years, the students have learned many things, including how Minuchin came into his structural ideas:

> I am a brand, like Tylenol. Historically, there were 7–8 people that were the pioneers of family therapy; all of them were systemic. Each one of them were systemic, but they were competing for students, so each one of them took a name—Tylenol, Advil, Aleve. But each one of them was working on one corner [of the world]; we were all systemic therapists (who had different ways and ideas theoretically of how systemic ideas would work in families). I read a book about structures and anthropology—but my techniques

of family therapy were called structural but they were not structural. Structural was my way of looking at families with groups, subgroups, alliances, coalition, and so forth. Families are an organism, and they are subsystems, and complex. (Salvador Minuchin, personal communication, May 8, 2008)

While much about Minuchin's model of therapy has changed over time and is open to evolution, he continues to focus on a basic four principles: opening up the presenting complaint, highlighting problem-maintaining interactions, conducting a structurally focused exploration of past patterns of behavior, and exploring alternative new ways of relating. This is and remains the core of structural models of family therapy.

26

COMPARE AND CONTRAST

Structural/Strategic Models

Anne Rambo, Charles West, AnnaLynn Schooley, and Tommie V. Boyd

Note that all the authors in this section, whether directly and forcefully or more indirectly but still persuasively, attempted to get the parents in this hypothetical case situation to work together more as a team. "Well, of course," the reader may be thinking, "any family therapist would do that. Obviously these parents need to work together." Well, as a reading of the rest of this book will verify, not every family therapist would work toward that goal. An MRI therapist might well encourage the parents to stop trying to agree, so as to interrupt the stuck solution behavior and free them up (Chapter 29); a therapist practicing the Internal Family Systems model would begin by working individually with the teen (Chapter 46). It is a tribute to the pervasiveness of the structural/strategic models in the field, however, that many family therapists would indeed think first of this essentially structural goal: to reorganize the parents into a more appropriately hierarchical team.

Structural ideas and their strategic variations are quite pervasive in the field, in part due to the large numbers of family therapists trained in these models since the 1970s. Structural and strategic family therapists as a group also carry on the tradition of community involvement started by Minuchin and his colleagues at Wiltwick School. The Philadelphia Child Guidance Center is heavily involved in community mental health throughout the state of Philadelphia. Jim Keim, author of our classic strategic family therapy chapter, has taken the model to crisis situations including Sri Lanka after the tsunami and his work with the Children's Organization of Southeast Asia. Many if not most therapists working in child welfare, juvenile detention, and other crisis-oriented settings have been trained in structural/strategic family therapy; variations of structural and strategic models (including MDFT, MST, FFT, and UM strategic) are listed as model programs by the U.S. federal government for situations involving substance abuse and at-risk youth (Office of Juvenile Justice and Drug Prevention, 2012; SAMHSA National Registry of Evidence-Based Programs and Practices, 2012).

The community-based models derived from structural and strategic ideas (MDST, MST, FFT, and UM strategic) are practical, intensive, and aimed at high-risk populations. Structural and strategic models in general have an impressive array of research evidence and are considered among the most evidence-based models. This is especially true of the manualized models, MDST, MST, FFT, and UM strategic. Proponents of these models have typically not been drawn to social constructionist ideas and have thus not shied away from empirical research studies. Specific differences between these closely related models may be explored in their respective chapters; it may be of interest to note that MDST is a specialized treatment for adolescent substance abuse and delinquency; MST utilizes a specific analytic process; FFT emphasizes accepting the family's own preferred relational functions; and UM strategic puts particular emphasis on the therapist finding a fit with the family (as described in Chapters 21–24).

In terms of our systemic theories (IA), the primary theoretical influence on structural family therapy is general systems theory. Elements of hierarchy, boundary, systems, and subsystems are key components of this model and draw directly on general systems theory. Strategic models, both classic (Chapter 20) and community based—FFT (Chapter 23) and UM brief (Chapter 24)—draw also on Batesonian cybernetic ideas and Ericksonian techniques (Chapter 28). Structural/strategic models—all the models in this chapter—share an emphasis on working with the family as a whole, even if not all family members are seen together. Those groups of models more influenced by social constructionist theory—the brief therapy (IID), narrative (IIE), and collaborative (IIF) models—can work as easily with individuals as with families. Minuchin has argued that therapists from these models are not truly family therapists (Minuchin, 1998). Minuchin's strong emphasis on seeing the family as a whole, and the commitment to working with couples and families as units that structural/strategic therapists share, relates to the influence of general systems theory (see IA).

One may also note an influence of attachment theory in the structural/strategic models. However, in contrast to the psychoanalytic/experiential models, similarly influenced by attachment theory (IIA), structural/strategic models clearly emphasize doing rather than feeling. Structural/strategic models are action oriented and tend to be brief. In terms of the thinking/feeling/doing trilogy, mentioned in earlier compare and contrast chapters, these structural/strategic models clearly come down on the side of changing behavior (doing). In terms of the common factors of all successful family therapy (Sprenkle, Davis, & Lebow, 2009), structural/strategic family therapists conceptualize systemically by considering the family organization—boundaries, subsystems, and hierarchies—and often the role of the community as well; intervene quite directly to interrupt dysfunctional family patterns; and expand the therapeutic system by joining with all family members and significant adults in the community as well.

References

Minuchin, S. (1998). Where is the family in narrative family therapy? *Journal of Marital and Family Therapy, 29*(4), 397–403.

Office of Juvenile Justice and Drug Prevention. (2012). *OJJDP model programs guide*. Retrieved from http://ojjdp.gov

SAMHSA National Registry of Evidence-Based Programs and Practices. (2012). *National registry of evidence-based programs and practices*. Retrieved from http://www.nrepp.samhsa.gov

Sprenkle, D., Davis, S., & Lebow, J. (2009). *Common factors in couple and family therapy: An overlooked foundation for effective practice*. New York, NY: Guilford Press.

PART D
BRIEF THERAPY MODELS

27

A BRIEF HISTORY OF BRIEF THERAPY

Anne Rambo, Charles West, AnnaLynn Schooley,
and Tommie V. Boyd

The originating model in this group, the Mental Research Institute model of family therapy, derived its name when the MRI Brief Therapy Center was founded in 1965 by Richard Fisch, John Weakland, and Paul Watzlawick (Fisch, Ray, & Schlanger, 2009). The MRI model is based on the communication theory earlier created by what is known as the Palo Alto research team: Gregory Bateson, John Weakland, and Jay Haley. Haley would go on to found his own school of family therapy, together with Cloe Madanes (Chapter 20). The MRI model was also very much influenced by Milton Erickson, a prominent hypnotherapist (Chapter 28), and by Don Jackson, a creative psychiatrist and prolific writer who became interested in the MRI ideas (Fisch, Ray, & Schlanger, 2009). These MRI ideas, the foundation of the brief therapy models, represent a dramatic break from conventional mental health notions of pathology and health. The goal of therapy becomes to assist the client in becoming unstuck from overly rigid patterns of behavior and communication in a brief and noninvasive manner. The emphasis on noninvasiveness comes from Bateson; the emphasis on efficiency and efficacy comes from Erickson. The original Milan team studied the MRI model and the work of both Bateson and Erickson, and the influence is clear in their work (Piercy et al, 1996). The MRI model was also the original inspiration for what became solution-focused brief therapy; in fact, the husband/wife originators of that model, Steve de Shazer and Insoo Kim Berg, met each other while training with John Weakland at MRI (Yalom & Rubin, 2003). We have grouped these models together due to their common history and their common focus on solutions—stuck solution behavior on the part of individuals, which is to be interrupted (MRI, Chapter 29); spontaneous solutions (again, of particular individuals) that are working and should be encouraged (SFBT, Chapter 30); and stuck solution behavior on the part of the family as a whole, which is made overt and thus neutralized (classic Milan, discussed in Chapter 31). It should be noted that the original Milan team split in 1979, and two of the original group, Luigi Boscolo and Gianfranco Cecchin, went in a less formulaic direction, well described here by Paul Rhodes (Chapter 31); the other two, Selvini Palazolli and Giuliana Prata, moved more toward the structural/strategic model (Piercy et al., 1996). We have also included in this section a chapter on Ericksonian therapy (Chapter 28), which is a model of its own as well as a considerable influence on these brief therapy models of family therapy.

References

Fisch, R., Ray, W., & Schlanger, K. (2009). *Focused problem resolution—Selected papers of the MRI Brief Therapy Center.* Phoenix, AZ: Zeig, Tucker, Theisan.

Piercy, F., Wetchler, J, Sprenkle, D., & Associates. (1996). *Family therapy sourcebook.* New York, NY: Guilford Press.

Additional Resources

Boscolo, L., Cecchin, G., Hoffman, L., & Penn, P. (1987). *Milan systemic family therapy: Conversations in theory and practice.* New York, NY: Basic Books.

De Shazer, S., & Dolan, Y. (2007). *More than miracles: The state of the art of solution-focused brief therapy.* New York, NY: Haworth Press.

Fisch, R., Weakland, J., & Segal, L. (1982). *Tactics of change: Doing therapy briefly.* San Francisco, CA: Jossey-Bass.

Ray, W., & de Shazer, S. (1999). *Evolving brief therapies: In honor of John Weakland.* Iowa City, IA: Geist & Russell.

Yalom, V., & Rubin, B. (2003). Interview with Insoo Kim Berg on solution-focused therapy. Retrieved from https://psychotherapy.net/interview/insoo-kim-berg

28

HYPNOSIS AND BRIEF FAMILY THERAPY

Douglas Flemons

Many family therapists would be surprised to learn the extent to which hypnosis has influenced the theory and practice of our field. The primary source of this influence can be found in the work of the psychiatrist Milton H. Erickson (1901–1980), the most innovative clinical hypnotist of his time. Erickson used formal hypnosis only in about a fifth of the cases he worked on (Beahrs, 1971; cited in Zeig, 1985, p. 5); however, the techniques and logic of hypnosis (Flemons, 2002) are evident throughout his psychotherapeutic approach.

Erickson's methods made their way into the realm of family therapy initially and primarily by way of Gregory Bateson and his research assistants, Jay Haley and John Weakland.[1] Their Palo Alto research group spent 10 years (from 1952 to 1962) studying the role of paradox in human communication. Along the way, they became interested in both hypnosis and schizophrenia, and Bateson contacted Erickson to help them examine the formal similarities between the two phenomena (Zeig & Geary, 2000, pp. 58–59). In 1953, Bateson arranged for Haley to attend one of Erickson's seminars on the medical uses of hypnosis. Within a few years, Haley and Weakland were learning hypnosis and psychotherapy from Erickson, regularly traveling to his home in Phoenix to meet with him.[2] By 1956, Haley was working part-time in private practice, using hypnosis in brief psychotherapy (Zeig & Geary, 2000, p. 69), and Weakland was effectively practicing and demonstrating it (Haley, 1999, p. 78).

Neither Haley nor Weakland made careers as clinical hypnotists. Rather, they brought their understanding of hypnosis—refracted through their study of Erickson's methods and the interactional/contextual ideas invented and refined during the Bateson research project—into the family therapy approaches they each developed. Haley's strategic therapy model and Weakland and his MRI colleagues' brief therapy model both instantiate core principles of hypnosis, and, in the years since they first articulated Erickson's methods and the ideas and techniques they derived from him (e.g., Fisch, Weakland, & Segal, 1982; Haley, 1976; Watzlawick, Weakland, & Fisch, 1974), they have inspired and influenced many thousands of family therapists, including those who have gone on to develop their own models. Steve de Shazer, for example, said that his solution-focused ideas were "historically rooted in a tradition that starts with Milton H. Erickson and flows through Gregory Bateson and the group of therapists-thinkers at the Mental Research Institute" (1982, p. ix).[3]

To appreciate the tradition that Erickson started and Bateson and his associates brought into focus, it is necessary to understand a little about the phenomenon of hypnosis and how it can be used to effect therapeutic change. As a means of developing this understanding, let's look at what might happen if a hypnotist such as I were to invite a client such as Mary (the wife and mother in this book's central case) into hypnosis to treat her headaches.

Hypnosis

In her regular making-it-through-the-day mode of conscious awareness, Mary, like all of us, consciously distinguishes herself from those around her, but she also consciously distinguishes a conscious self being conscious. Aware of being aware, she has perceptions, thoughts, and feelings about her perceptions, thoughts, and feelings. Such reflexive awareness spins a sense of herself being separate from her own experience, as if her conscious self were a distinct homunculus within herself, seemingly in charge of noticing what the rest of the self is up to (e.g., "Note to self—headache starting behind the eyes") and seemingly capable of issuing commands to get things done (e.g., "Hey! Headache! Scram!"). But this experience of a separated homuncular self—a "distinguished I"—is simply an artifact of the reflexive nature of consciousness. It is, as Michael Crichton (2008) wryly put it, a "user's illusion." And the experience of the headache as an intractable entity, as a *thing,* is also an illusion. Both the distinguished I and the headache are *continuities*—they persist through time as a function of ongoing patterns of change. This is where hypnosis comes in.

My first task as a hypnotist is to facilitate a change in how Mary is distinguishing herself from me. If I'm successful in establishing rapport, then rather than viewing me as an outsider, she can feel comfortable with my gaining an insider's grasp of her experience. My second task is to facilitate a change in how Mary has been relating to herself and her experience, including her problem and her efforts to solve it. This change will make it possible for nonvolitional hypnotic phenomena to manifest and for the problem to begin shifting in spontaneous, unpredictable ways. And my third task is to invite change in the pattern of the problem itself. For the sake of explanation, I will describe each task separately, but in practice they intermingle considerably. They don't constitute stages to be passed through so much as threads or sinews to be interwoven.

Task 1: I will connect with Mary in such a way that, for the duration of our hypnotic interaction, the differences between us, and the division she usually draws between inside and outside experience, or between self (her) and other (me), will, for her, become to some degree irrelevant, unnecessary for maintaining her safety or integrity. This rapport-building process will begin immediately, long before we move into formal hypnosis. As I listen to Mary's descriptions of her pain, I will empathize with her, reflecting back a characterization of her situation that resonates for her. What she is telling me and what she is hearing back from me will be in accord, and this will, for her, render the boundary between us less and less noticeable and thus the differences between us less and less relevant.

As I formally invite Mary into hypnosis, I will talk in time with her breath so that her experience of my words is rhythmically connected to the automatic movement of her body, further entraining us. I will also pay close attention to whatever outside or inside distractions (e.g., noises, harsh light, worried thoughts, discomfort, etc.) are standing in the way of our developing connection so that I can accommodate them into what's unfolding between us (e.g., "Just as that siren out there sends a signal to the other vehicles on the road to create a space for freedom of movement and the efficient delivery of assistance, so too signals can be sent and received within your body that assist in the opening of the necessary space for you to quickly and efficiently relax all the way into trance. That opening into trance may be preceded or followed by a closing of your eyes, however briefly. That's right. It can all begin in the blink of an eye.") Erickson referred to such accommodation of ongoing experiences as "utilization," which Zeig (1992) defined as the "readiness of the therapist to respond strategically to any and all aspects of the patient or the environment" (p. 256).

It wouldn't be unusual for Mary to lose track of my voice for periods of time during our hypnosis together. As I continue helping her find it unnecessary to distinguish herself from me, my words will naturally dissolve into, and thus to some degree become indistinguishable from, her experience.

Task 2: The movement into hypnosis is marked by the therapist's invitation and the client's noticing of one or more nonvolitional changes in experience. I will make this possible with Mary by offering possibilities for her to become in sync with, rather than separate from, her experience, thereby blurring the usual conscious division between her distinguished I and the rest of her self. As we continue, she might notice her arms feeling too heavy to move or a hand that feels so light it lifts up off her lap; flashes of color or images or spontaneous dreams; a feeling of floating to the side or above her body; a distortion of time; and/or the ability to see or hear something that isn't there or not see or hear something that is. Because her distinguished I won't be set apart as a stand-alone entity, it won't feel itself to be responsible or in control of what is happening, and thus the experiences Mary has will feel spontaneous and outside of conscious control, as if they are happening on their own.

As part of this hypnotic connecting of Mary to her experience (thereby allowing her distinctive I to become an indistinctive I, a distributed I), I might ask her if she can generate a headache in my office. This will head her in the opposite direction from her usual coping strategy. Instead of recoiling from the pain, trying to escape or contain it, she will be approaching it with curiosity and the spirit of discovery, effectively dissolving the boundary between her and the sensations that constitute the headache.

Such an invitation can be understood as another instance of utilization—an engagement that is relevant not only to the process of inviting hypnosis, but also to inviting problems to shift. Gilligan (2002, p. xi) considered the principle of utilization to be Erickson's "great contribution to psychotherapy. Erickson brilliantly showed how the person's problem or symptoms could be accepted and used as the basis for creative solutions."

Task 3: My third task is to approach the problem as a pattern, rather than a thing. If Mary is able to bring on a headache, or if she has come into the session with one already in place, I will explore its location, qualities, dimensions, variations, associated perceptions (colors, etc.), intensity, and so on. Together in our explorations, we will pay close attention to the particularities of what is happening in the moment, which will have the effect of teasing the headache into component strands. This will make it possible for us to discover how one or more of these strands can begin or has already begun some small shift on its own, with ripples from that shift ramifying throughout other strands, resulting, over the course of the hypnosis, in a significant alteration in the overall experience of the headache.

Simply put, hypnosis creates an intimate connection between the therapist and the client and between the client and his or her experience, including the experience of the problem. This connective context alters the client's mind-body and self-problem relationships, opening the way for the therapeutic utilization of spontaneous variations in the component strands of the problem.

Hypnosis and Brief Family Therapy

When I am working with couples and families as a brief therapist, I bring my hypnosis sensibility along for the ride; however, the focus of my efforts is expanded, as there are typically more people in the room, and my interventions are generally offered as experiments to be conducted between sessions, rather than to be experienced within the context of a trance. When, for example, Mary, Fred, Bess, and Johnny all come to see me to address Johnny's truancy, my goals will be isomorphic to those I engaged in during my hypnotic work with Mary.

First, I will strive to empathically connect with everyone in the family. My appreciation of their situation from their perspective will allow them to experience me as an experiential insider, rendering unimportant (for them) the experiential boundaries separating them from me. Second, I will attempt to foster a connection between the clients and their problem. One way to do that will be to invite each of them to devote a week or two to paying close attention to, and gathering detailed information about, how he or she is currently dealing with the truancy. The curiosity they bring to the task will alter their relationship to something they've been trying to control or eradicate. And third, I will engage with the truancy not as a thing, but as a pattern of intrapersonal and interpersonal interactions, unfolding through time. Recognizing that a small change in some component or contextual strand of these interactions will ramify through the others, I will look forward to discovering what happens to Johnny's school involvement if one of the adults introduces a small, unpredictable difference into their usual way of relating to Johnny and/or to each other. Or discovering what happens if Johnny's not going to school is contextualized differently—as an act, say, of dignity or boredom, rather than of anxiety or rebellion.

Regardless of whether I'm offering in-office trance for an individual client or suggesting between-session experiments for a family, I remain committed to connecting with my clients and to inviting connections between them and their experience (Flemons, 2002). Such connections help alter the clients' problematic problem-solving attempts and facilitate the utilization of one or more of the strands that have been constituting or contextualizing the pattern of the problem. In these connections and in the nonvolitional, spontaneously developing shifts in the clients' experience, it is possible to recognize the hypnotic inspiration of brief-therapy methods.

Notes

1. Bateson had known Erickson since 1942, when Erickson attended the first of the Macy conferences, a series of meetings that established the field of cybernetics.
2. Haley and Weakland taped their conversations with Erickson as part of their research responsibilities with the Bateson project. Haley later drew on transcriptions of these interviews when writing about Erickson and his work (e.g., Haley, 1973).
3. Indeed, de Shazer (1988, p. 113) continued to define his solution-focused work as hypnotic long after he stopped using formal hypnosis during sessions. Many other prominent family therapists are historically linked to Haley and Weakland. For example, Salvador Minuchin (2001, p. 4), who worked with Haley for 10 years, said that over time Jay's indirect techniques became a staple of his own structural approach to therapy. In the 1970s, Harry Goolishian and Harlene Anderson were drawn to the work of the MRI (Hoffman, 2002, p. 135). Lynn Hoffman (2002) wrote her first book with Haley and was originally influenced by his strategic approach. The Milan team were intrigued by Bateson, Haley, and Weakland's theoretical work, and they drew inspiration from Paul Watzlawick, a psychologist who worked for many years with Weakland at the MRI. Other family therapists, such as Bill O'Hanlon, Jeffrey Zeig, Steve Lankton, Michele Ritterman, Gene Coombs, and Jill Freeman, had direct ties to Erickson.

References

Crichton, M. (2008). *Prey.* New York, NY: Harper.
De Shazer, S. (1982). *Patterns of brief family therapy: An ecosystemic approach.* New York, NY: Guilford.
De Shazer, S. (1988). Utilization: The foundation of solutions. In J. K. Zeig & S. R. Lankton (Eds.), *Developing Ericksonian therapy* (pp. 112–124). Bristol, PA: Brunner/Mazel.

Fisch, R., Weakland, J. H., & Segal, L. (1982). *The tactics of change: Doing therapy briefly.* San Francisco, CA: Jossey-Bass.

Flemons, D. (2002). *Of one mind.* New York, NY: Norton.

Gilligan, S. (2002). *The legacy of Milton H. Erickson: The selected papers of Stephen Gilligan.* Phoenix, AZ: Zeig, Tucker, & Theisen.

Haley, J. (1973). *Uncommon therapy: The psychiatric techniques of Milton H. Erickson, M.D.* New York, NY: Norton.

Haley, J. (1976). *Problem-solving therapy: New strategies for effective family therapy.* San Francisco, CA: Jossey-Bass.

Haley, J. (1999). John Weakland: A personal note. In W. A. Ray & S. de Shazer (Eds.), *Evolving brief therapies* (pp. 78–80). Iowa City, IA: Geist & Russell.

Hoffman, L. (2002). *Family therapy: An intimate history.* New York, NY: Norton.

Minuchin, S. (2001). Walking with Jay. In J. K. Zeig (Ed.), *Changing directives: The strategic therapy of Jay Haley.* Phoenix, AZ: Milton H. Erickson Foundation Press.

Watzlawick, P., Weakland, J. H., & Fisch, R. (1974). *Change: Principles of problem formation and problem resolution.* New York, NY: Norton.

Zeig, J. K. (1985). *Experiencing Erickson: An introduction to the man and his work.* New York, NY: Brunner/Mazel.

Zeig, J. K. (1992). The virtues of our faults: A key concept of Ericksonian psychotherapy. In J. K. Zeig (Ed.), *The evolution of psychotherapy: The second conference* (pp. 252–269). New York, NY: Brunner/Mazel.

Zeig, J. K., & Geary, B. (Eds.). (2000). *The letters of Milton H. Erickson.* Phoenix, AZ: Zeig, Tucker & Theisen.

29

MRI BRIEF THERAPY

Monte Bobele

According to the MRI, problems are formed as the result of the mishandling of ordinary, everyday difficulties in living. In talking about problem origination, Weakland is reputed to have modified Edna St. Vincent Millay's pessimistic quote: "Life isn't one damn thing after another. It's the same damn thing again and again" to "Life is one damn thing after another; problems are the same damned thing over and over again." So life consists of endless challenges, large and small, that everyone finds a way of handling. When faced with a challenge, we look into the storehouse of problem-solving tools that we have acquired over a lifetime and apply the tool that seems most appropriate for the problem at hand. If our solution doesn't work, we often try over and over again—harder, longer, or louder—in an effort to get our problem solved. This over-and-over trying leads to a positive feedback loop—a key notion in MRI therapy.

As an MRI therapist, I look for the interactional feedback loops that are maintaining the ongoing problematic behavior. Problems develop and are maintained by positive feedback loops. Essentially, a positive feedback loop occurs when people's interactions with another are characterized by an escalation of each other's behavior. In the everyday world, we see instances of positive feedback in collegiate rivalries where each school tries to outdo the other. The U.S./Soviet arms race is also an excellent example of a positive feedback loop. Each side increased its arms production as a response to the increase arms production (and perceived threat) of the other side.

In this case, there are several potential interactions to explore: Fred/Mary, Fred/Johnny, Mary/Johnny, Bess/Mary, and so on. An axiom of systemic therapy is that changes at any point in the system ripple throughout the system. Accordingly, I would look for the most accessible interactions in which to intervene. I would begin with whoever showed up for the first session.

A point of entry may be the interactions between Mary and Fred. It is not unusual for parents to occasionally take differing positions on child-rearing issues. These multiple points of view may develop into an escalating positive feedback loop. We might find that when Johnny began ordinary everyday teenager experimentation, Mary saw this as the result of a lack of nurturing on the part of the school and herself and her husband, his parents. Her response was to increase her nurturing behaviors. For example, she may have tried to have more heart-to-heart talks with Johnny. Fred, who sees Johnny's behavior as the result of a lack of discipline that needs to be corrected by punishment, may have countered each of his wife's nurturing responses with time out, withdrawal of privileges, and so on. Ultimately, the two parents may become locked in an interactional struggle to save Johnny from teenagehood, each trying to undo the effects of the other spouse's "misguided" interventions. It is no surprise that intimacy has been put on the back burner while Mary and Fred continue to wrestle with the challenge of raising a teenager.

Bess's relationship with her daughter and son-in-law is also critical. While her grandson's situation continues to get out of hand, she becomes increasingly alarmed and tries to help. She calls to give advice to her daughter. Her advice reinforces Mary's position. Bess's encouragement may give Mary the courage to stand more firmly in her nurturing position and serve to increase the intractability of the feedback loop she is in with Fred. For example, Bess may call frequently to inquire about the situation with Johnny. When she hears reports of Johnny's increasing rebelliousness and Fred's continued lack of understanding of his son's needs for nurturing, she encourages Mary to be firm. Mary may find herself trying harder to undo the effects of Fred's punishment by becoming more nurturing. Fred, for his part, may see himself as increasingly isolated from his wife and mother-in-law because he does not share their point of view. He may see himself in a struggle with both women, who are soft and lack the ability to take a stern position with Johnny. He may respond with increased efforts at punishment.

It is important to remember that everyone involved is doing precisely the things expected of them. Teenagers are expected to begin to move toward independence. Parents are expected to be protective and nurturing of their teenagers, and parents are expected to set limits as well.

After assessing the family's previous solution attempts, I would select one of the loops to intervene into. Perhaps the most accessible loop would be the parents' interaction. As you will remember, each of them is trying to convince the other of the correctness of their own position. One way they do this is to apply their solution to the problem with Johnny in the hopes that it will be successful and thereby demonstrate to their spouse that they had been right all along. So the continued lack of success in helping their son leads them to increasingly unsuccessful attempts to solve their problem. Seen in this way, the intricacies of the multiple feedback loops operating simultaneously are apparent.

I can imagine having reached a point in the conversation with the family such that I could say, "It appears to me that both you, Fred, and you, Mary, have some excellent ideas about what needs to happen for Johnny to get back on track with school. Fred, you know your son in ways that a mother never could. You know that sometimes boys need a strict disciplinarian to help them along the way. And, Mary, you know that a child needs to be nurtured, at home and at school. I know that you disagree about which of these two approaches is the right one to take with Johnny. And you both feel strongly that your position is the correct one. I am inclined to agree that he needs the best both of you have to offer. Fred, you have some expertise in discipline and know that punishment applied correctly can work miracles with young men. And, Mary, your nurturance of Johnny has been very important to him. God knows how much worse this situation would have been if the two of you had not been providing your individual expertise to this problem from the beginning.

"I suspect, however, that occasionally you waiver in your resolve to do what is right for Johnny. I suspect that you both wonder sometimes if your spouse's point of view has some merit and you back off from your position some, hold back some from what your gut tells you to do. I'd like to say that it seems to me that Johnny has the best of all possible worlds for parents. He has two people who are able to teach him something about the way the real world operates. When he gets older and moves on to having a life of his own, he is going to encounter all sorts of people. People who will want to nurture him as a way of guiding him. People who will see rewards and punishments as the way to help him become an adult. He is going to have to learn to deal with all sorts of people in life. Some will be nurturing and may try to guide him by appealing to that side of him. Others may be less interested in his feelings and demand that he respond to a system of rewards and consequences. [This idea would be slowly developed and elaborated for them.] He is lucky to have two teachers who can be of tremendous service to him. If both of you saw eye to eye on this, Johnny would not learn some important lessons in life. So, I want to ask each of you to remain firm in your convictions, for the time being."

In this way, the parents could relax from their stuck solution behavior of trying to agree, each trying to convince the other. Difference would be reframed as positive. My hope would be that by enlisting their cooperation in this manner, they would begin to decelerate the escalating, competitive positive feedback loop.

In order to address Bess's involvement with Mary, a number of ideas come to mind. If it were established that Mary thought that Bess was helpful, I might encourage Fred to remind Mary to call Bess for advice early on the day that she was to be in charge of Johnny. My hope would be that this would change the struggle Fred was in with his wife about his mother-in-law's involvement. It would provide a structured way for him to reestablish a good relationship with Bess. Furthermore, Mary is calling Bess, not the other way around. That would also be different.

In intervening with Johnny, there are a number of ideas that come to mind. Johnny may not be a customer for change. He is the least motivated member of the system. With him, it might be helpful to reframe his skipping school as beneficent attempts to help his parents learn how to be better parents and adjust to the day when he will be permanently gone from the home. I can imagine saying something like, "Johnny, I wonder if you are trying to help your parents learn to be better parents by making it challenging for them. For instance, if you were to go to school and continue making good grades like you used to, your parents would get lazy and figure that they had nothing to offer you. Nothing to teach you. If, on the other hand, you continued to find creative ways to challenge their parenting skills, they might appreciate your efforts."

But, at the end of the first session, I might do nothing more with Johnny than a standard MRI intervention: "Between now and the next time we meet, Johnny, don't change anything you are doing. I need to get a good baseline on the effects your parents' efforts make." Johnny may not be a customer for change. I would prefer to aim my interventions at the part of the system that appears most eager and motivated to change. In this case, the parents appear to be the most interested and willing to do something different to change the situation.

I expect that this case would take two to five sessions. In the second session, I would continue to refine and expand the helping frames I had initiated in the original session. I would help the parents continue to find creative ways to enact their differences cooperatively. I might move the focus to Johnny in the second or third session. If the parents were beginning to make some progress in this area, I would return to the idea that Johnny was unknowingly helping his parents to be better parents. I would ask him if he could find some small ways to challenge the recent acquired teamwork his parents were demonstrating.

In all these interventions, I am working from the assumption that these are caring, competent people who just became stuck in their solution behavior—and, once unstuck, will be creative enough to move on with their lives.

Resources

Fisch, R., Weakland, J. H., & Segal, L. (1982). *The tactics of change: Doing therapy briefly.* San Francisco, CA: Jossey-Bass.

Watzlawick, P., Weakland, J., & Fisch, R. (1974). *Change: Principles of problem formation and problem resolution.* New York, NY: W. W. Norton.

Watzlawick, P., Weakland, J. H., & Mental Research Institute. (1977). *The interactional view: Studies at the Mental Research Institute, Palo Alto, 1965–1974* (1st ed.). New York, NY: Norton.

Weakland, J. H., & Fisch, R. (1992). Brief therapy—MRI style. In S. H. Budman, M. F. Hoyt, & S. Friedman (Eds.), *First session in brief therapy* (pp. 306–323). New York, NY: Guilford Press.

Weakland, J., Fisch, R., Watzlawick, P., & Bodin, A. (1974). Brief therapy: Focused problem resolution. *Family Process, 13,* 1–28.

Weakland, J. H., & Ray, W. A. (1995). *Propagations: Thirty years of influence from the Mental Research Institute.* New York, NY: Haworth Press.

30

SOLUTION-FOCUSED BRIEF THERAPY

Lee Shilts

The following common case will be viewed through a brief solution-focused therapy lens and will offer the author's perspective on how to conduct a session utilizing the theory and technique of such a model. In preparing to answer the case questions, a good brief solution-focused therapist needs to address the situation from at least two different perspectives. One must consider the technical pieces of the model: that is, the miracle question, exceptions, scaling, and so forth. The utilization and timing of the techniques are essential with any case. However, beyond the technical ideas is the need to incorporate the human element in therapy and skillfully weave these questions into the process. I believe I can best explain these ideas with personal examples as I consider the case questions.

The case is a family referred to counseling. The reporting main concern appears to center around the teenage son who is described as failing in school and displaying defiant behavior toward his parents. The parents report marital difficulties that result in inconsistent parenting with the son. A mother-in-law is also in the picture, which appears to cause even further anxiety between the parents.

I typically neither require nor solicit a vast amount of information previous to my initial meeting with the client family. I may ask for some demographic information such as ages of clients, schools attended, job situations, and so forth. If the client wants to talk about their reason for seeking therapy, I will certainly listen with an open ear. However, my primary rule is to begin the process of therapy when I have the family physically in front of me in my office. Working from the assumption that the family possesses a lot of expertise with their situation, I often ask the family who they think should attend therapy. I tend to tell the family that I am usually comfortable working with a wide variety and number of people in my sessions. It has been my experience over the years that the family is usually a great resource for helping me decide who should attend therapy. I often state that the family should bring whoever they think is important to the process. I once had a family bring their next-door neighbor.

In the first session, I would typically ask the miracle question, one or more scaling questions, and exception questions to the presenting concerns. The first to be asked would be the miracle question, in which each family member would be asked if a miracle occurred overnight, and the problem disappeared, how would they know? This focuses each person on the absence of the problem, as well as on the interactional context of the problem. Scaling questions invite each participant to describe their level of concern, usually from 1 to 10. This opens up space for exceptions: if 10 is an extremely urgent situation, and the problem is at an 8, why is it not a 10? Exception questions are fundamental to solution-focused therapy as they ask about the absence of the problem: When is Johnny doing well in school? When do the parents agree, or cheerfully agree to disagree? What else is happening in their lives—besides the all-too hypnotic influence of the designated problem?

The next step would be to establish goals in therapy. Useful goals should have certain qualities that help clients (and therapists) realize what they are trying to accomplish in therapy. Goals should be concrete, easy to do or accomplish, within the realm of the client and family, and involve hard work. For a solution-focused therapist, the first step toward the goal is asking the miracle question, as noted earlier. This question will very nicely guide the client and therapist to a goal that should put the client in a better place. The miracle question will further allow the goal to be solely the client's goal and thus allow his or her own personal owner-ship in the overall therapy process.

As a solution-focused brief therapist, I would say that I have no exclusive ownership of the change process during therapy. It has been my experience that change occurs through a collaborative process between the therapist and client family. Often, I tend to take a position where I see the family as the major change amplifier in the overall process. I may help facilitate the process, but I certainly do not own exclusive rights when it comes to change.

In summation, as a solution-focused therapist, I often follow this outline when working with clients during my initial session:

> Develop fit with the clients. This is the socializing part where I begin to ac-cess the strengths and resources of the family.
>
> Seek the concerns that bring the client to therapy. Contrary to what some people believe, a good solution-focused therapist does want to hear at least a little about the problems that bring a family to therapy. Logic would dictate the fact that we can better seek solutions if we know the problem side to those potential solutions; this is the MRI piece of solution-focused therapy, avoiding solutions that have already been tried and failed.
>
> Attempt to elicit current exceptions to the concerns or problems. This is an essential piece of the solution-focused model.
>
> Introduce the miracle question. As previously stated, this question will nicely guide the family (and therapist) to well-formed goals.

After the miracle is stated, I would ask the client to simplify his or her responses to the miracle question. By simplifying the miracle, we can crystallize the goals down to one or two doable items.

After a goal is established, I often use that as a task for the client family between sessions. Depending on the goal, it may be a doing goal, an observation goal, or possibly a combination of the two

Hopefully, I have provided somewhat of an overlay of how to work with this case study utilizing a solution-focused approach. Every case is different, but the model is a constant.

Resources

De Shazer, S. (1985). *Keys to solution in brief therapy.* New York, NY: W. W. Norton.

De Shazer, S. (1988). *Clues: Investigating solutions in brief therapy.* New York, NY: W. W. Norton.

De Shazer. S. (1994). *Words were originally magic.* New York, NY: W. W. Norton.

Lipchik, E. (2011). *Beyond technique in solution-focused therapy: Working with emotions and the therapeutic relations.* New York, NY: Guilford Press.

31

POST-MILAN SYSTEMIC THERAPY

Paul Rhodes

The main focus of Milan systemic family therapy is on patterns of interaction. The presenting problem, most often exhibited by a child, is considered to be one step in such a pattern, one that has become stuck and can often escalate over time. Families often become stuck because they find it hard to adapt to changing circumstances, be they life stressors or those related to the life cycle. The prefix *post* in the term post-Milan systemic therapy signals that unlike traditional Milan systemic therapy the post-Milan systemic therapist works collaboratively. In the past, systemic therapists were accused, with others, of taking on an expert role and thinking they could work on the family like a mechanic works on a car. We now aim to join more closely with the family, helping them to see things for themselves and find new ways of interpreting the intentions that can lie behind problematic interactions. In our lives, we sometimes do things to push others away or hurt them. Our intentions are often different. We may be seeking support, asking for boundaries, wanting space, and so on. Opening up these meanings with the family can often make the difference.

The first thing the Milan systemic therapist would do with Johnny's family would be to prepare for the session carefully. I always take 15 minutes before each new session to draw up a genogram and think about possible interactions and relationships. This process, known as hypothesizing, helps me to become more aware of my biases and prevents me from focusing on simple conceptualizations of the problem. I will brainstorm until I reach a degree of empathy for each individual and until I have three or four themes concerning interactions. The aim is to prime my curiosity for the session. Here are three examples of hypotheses for Johnny's family.

1. While Johnny is causing his parents much stress, his behavior is his way of seeking a sense of belonging that he feels he is missing at home. He is trying to alert his family to the tension that exists and do something serious enough for it to be resolved.
2. Johnny's behavior is his way of inviting firm boundaries and guidance from his parents. It can be seen as a way of inviting both of his parents to come

together as a team, one that does not necessarily involve the direct input of his well-meaning grandmother Bess.

3. Johnny's behavior is his way of reaching out to his parents to let them know of the academic difficulties he is having at school.

Each of my hypotheses are usually framed in this way, starting with a positive connotation of the child's behavior. It is also important, however, to positively connote the behavior of each family member, to prevent any blaming or pathologizing. The father's wish to punish his son, therefore, can be seen more as the product of frustration with the mother and feeling isolated due to the close connection she has with her own mother. In turn, the mother's interaction with her own mother and her softer approach to Johnny might serve as a product of the exhaustion she feels from protecting Johnny from his father's harsher discipline. If the behavior of each family member is hypothesized as an understandable product of someone else's, no one can be at fault and systemic empathy has been achieved.

The aim of the interview is now to discount, develop, or confirm these hypotheses.

I would normally book two hours for the first session with a new family. I call them beforehand to request that all they all attend, in this case including Bess, given her possible role in interactions. I start the session by explaining how it will work. I tell them that the interview will take 90 minutes followed by a short 5-minute break. I will then return to give them my impressions. If they feel my feedback fits with them, then I will continue to see them fortnightly. If it does not, then I will respect their decision and wish them well.

I continue by getting to know each family member, starting with the parents, then Bess and then Johnny. I ask about what each person does during the day, including work, home duties, and school, and explore each person's hobbies or interests. The aim is to establish a connection with each person, setting the stage for the gradual establishment of the therapeutic relationship.

I then follow a similar order in asking about each person's concerns. I am careful to explore concrete details about behaviors, but I also ask, "What is it about Johnny's behavior that concerns you the most?" I also ask each person, "Do you have any other concerns for the family, apart from Johnny's behavior?" My aim is make room for interactive and relational information, which eventually allows the possibility for change. Sometimes the young person is reluctant to speak at first. I would use a circular question in this instance, asking his father, for example, "If Johnny did have concerns that were really worrying him, what do you think he would say if he felt more comfortable?" I would continue interviewing the father until Johnny reacted in some way, be it angrily if the father gets it wrong or more openly if his father is reading him correctly. I would then turn to Johnny and say, "How does what your father is saying fit with you?"

Next would come a detailed exploration of the onset of the presenting problem. Little was mentioned in the referral information concerning onset, but it could be the beginning of adolescence and/or one or more life stressors. I would ask the family when the behavior first started and why they think it started then rather than some other time. Once the onset event(s) are isolated, I would conduct a detailed exploration of their effects on family members. This would be done using circular questions, thus facilitating mutual understanding about what each person has been through. Depending on the events, this can be a moving part of the session, one where the family comes to understand the affective states that have been hidden but expressed less directly through interactions. Let us imagine, for example, that the onset of Johnny's behavior coincided with Bess moving into the household after the death of her husband two years ago. Johnny may be reacting to the fact that his mother has been less emotionally available to him due to her grief at her father's passing and the extra demands of caring for her mother. Fred may have felt as stressed as Mary at this time due to the changes in the household and their financial implications. A brief period of unemployment compounded the problem.

This would normally mark the halfway point of the interview, with 45 minutes to go. I would ask the family to tell me about a recent incident, one that they can all remember and that was serious enough to be representative of the problem. I would ask them to recall it, step by step, slowly enough for me to pick up the detail of interactions, checking with multiple family members to maximize the credibility of the account. The aim would be for me to discover a pattern in these interactions, a sequence that might be repeated during other incidents. It is important that the interviewer explores events well before the peak of the behavior and well after to ensure that all steps in this pattern can be seen. Once a pattern begins to emerge, I would ask the family questions to check that I am on the right track. In particular, I would ask circular questions about the effects of one step in the pattern on another family member to make more sense of the pattern and test it against some of the hypotheses I developed earlier. This can be challenging but sometimes allows the family to observe themselves in interaction, an important precursor to change. In this case, let us imagine that the mother's softer approach to Johnny's behavior frustrates the father and makes him react angrily, which in turn makes the mother feel protective of the son. Bess then joins in to criticize the father, due in part from her worry for her daughter, angering him further and making Johnny feel like staying away from the family home more.

Last comes the exploration of relationships. This is left to last because it is potentially the most challenging topic of discussion and one that requires more developed therapeutic relationships. The aim would be to ask a number of circular questions, asking one person about the relationship between two others—in the present, before onset, and how they might see things in the future.

Once the interview is complete, I will leave the family in the therapy room while I take a 5-minute break. In the literature, therapists often consult with a reflecting team at this point, who have been watching behind a two-way screen. Sometimes the team will instead swap rooms with the family and discuss their ideas while they watch. This is a luxury for many therapists, but taking a short break to gather your thoughts can also be effective. During this break I will revisit my hypotheses and try and piece the whole interview together. I will try and make direct links between the onset events and the sequence, wondering how the family came to be stuck in their interactions with each other and how improvements in relationships may be possible. When I return, I will order my thoughts in a structured way as follows: (1) affirm each family member, (2) describe concerns, (3) synthesize onset, sequence, and relationships, (4) positively connote the presenting problem, and (5) prescribe a systemic task.

Thank you for waiting, I would like to give you my impressions from the session.

First, I would like to say how impressed I have been by you as a family. Mary, I was really struck by your concern for Johnny. You are obviously a very committed and loving mother who wants to know how to get him back on track again. Same for you, Fred. You are both so clearly united in your worry for him, he is lucky to have two great parents who are seeking answers for their son. Bess, thank you so much for coming too. Your wise and thoughtful comments were much appreciated, and I hope you feel that you can attend again to continue contributing. Johnny, I know it was tough to be here, but from your responses I feel I may come to know a mature young man if your family chooses to return.

Mary and Fred, it sounds like your biggest concern is how Johnny seems to have changed in the past couple of years. You told me how he skips school frequently to be with his friends and are worried that he is drinking, smoking, and possibly worse while he is with them. Fred, you are particularly worried about hard drugs, given the state he is sometimes in when he comes home. Mary, you are worried about what he will turn out like in the future without a proper education. I share these very serious concerns. Bess, it sounds like you are also worried about your daughter, Mary. You worry about her headaches and her health and all the terrible stress the family is under.

Johnny, it seems like your biggest worry is all the fighting at home. You mentioned how everybody always seems to be fighting and how it is sometimes easier just to go out with your friends. Although you were slow to acknowledge it, you also expressed a tiny bit of concern about where all of this might lead.

It seems to me that while Johnny has gotten off track in his life, the family has also been jolted by a host of distressing and difficult events. Two years ago you all described a time of turmoil after the loss of Johnny's grandfather and the temporary loss of Fred's job. You each had a lot to deal with. Mary, you lost your father, and Bess, your husband. Fred, you struggled financially at this time and had to focus on finding and then keeping a new job. Johnny, it seems like you also lost a great deal, not just the relationship you had with your mother, with whom you had always been close, but also the chance to play ball and connect with your father, something that you told us you would really like to happen.

The big question, however, is how to get Johnny back on track. While his behavior may be his way reaching out to you both to reconnect, a lot more might be involved if his long-term safety is to be guaranteed. I can't help but wonder if, in a strange way, he is also asking for some boundaries to be drawn, those that are tough enough to ensure that he does have a future he can be proud of. At 15, there may only be a short time left to make sure this happens.

I would like to suggest some homework for the next two weeks. I'd like you, Fred and Mary, simply to send Johnny a text every two hours when he is out until we next meet. Simply write, "We both love you and want you to come home. Mom and Dad."

Once the feedback has been given, the therapist must wrap up the interview very quickly. I ask each family member to briefly describe one thing that interested them the most before scheduling the next meeting. This prevents them from returning to old habits in their conversation with you and leaves them to ponder the feedback at home without interruption.

The feedback would then be written up as a letter and sent to the family.

Resources

Hoffman, L. (1985). Beyond power and control: Toward a "second order" family systems therapy. *Family Systems Medicine, 3*(4), 381–396.

Jones, E. (1993) *Family systems therapy: Developments in the Milan-systemic therapies.* Chichester: Wiley.

MacKinnon, L., & James, K. (1987). Theory and practice of the Milan systemic approach. *Australian and New Zealand Journal of Family Therapy, 8*(2), 89–98.

Tomm, K. (1984). One perspective on the Milan systemic approach: Part II. Description of session format, interviewing style and interventions. *Journal of Marital and Family Therapy, 10*(3), 253–271.

32

PRACTITIONER'S PERSPECTIVE

MRI Brief Therapy Today

Wendel A. Ray

Founded in 1958, the Mental Research Institute is the birthplace of numerous contributions to communication theory and innovations in the application of these ideas to the practice of family and brief therapy. In 1965, when Richard Fisch, John Weakland, and Paul Watzlawick created the MRI Brief Therapy Center (BTC), they were determined to break away from an almost exclusive focus on individual pathology that then dominated psychotherapy. Inspired by Don Jackson (1961), Milton Erickson (1967), and Jay Haley (1963), the model is based on the communication theory created by the Bateson Research Team (Fisch, Ray, & Schlanger, 2009; Ray, 2005, 2009; Ray & Nardone, 2009). Discarding presuppositions not useful in the actual practice of effective brief therapy, BTC researchers created a nonpathological/nonnormative brief therapy approach explicitly focused on making therapy more effective and efficient. Pioneering numerous conceptual and intervention strategies that have permeated virtually all other models of brief therapy practice and training, some of the BTC's noteworthy contributions include the following: the first routine use of therapy teams, recording of all sessions to encourage analysis and to enhance effectiveness, use of one-way mirrors, telephone and in-session breaks for consultation with a team of observers, and limiting the number of sessions (10 with an actual average of 6.5) to encourage accountability on the part of client and therapist.

BTC researchers have always underscored the importance of discerning who is the most motivated person in a family or other interactional nexus. Most of the therapeutic work is then done with that person. Brief therapy involves experimenting with various methods of persuasion to influence clients to take action that is different from what they have tried previously (i.e., to desist from problem-maintaining behavior). The BTC team pioneered recognition that how one goes about motivating someone requires knowing who it is you are trying to motivate—in other words, helping people change requires inquiring into and learning the client's worldview, frame of reference, and situational/contextual circumstances—what the BTC term *client position.*

Embracing an uncompromisingly *nonpathological, nonnormative* (i.e., explicitly nonblaming) way to view and engage the client, effective MRI-oriented brief therapy involves knowing when, how, and with whom to inquire to make plain the problem definition as clearly and specifically as possible, and in concrete terms (i.e., for whom the problem is a problem, in what way it is a problem). Effective brief therapy interrupts problem–maintaining attempted solutions more than attempting to resolve problems (Fisch, Weakland, & Segal, 1982; Watzlawick, Beavin & Jackson, 1967; Watzlawick, Weakland, & Fisch, 1974; Weakland & Ray, 1995).

This same kind of careful analysis of interaction pioneered at the BTC is also done by the closely related approach of solution-focused brief therapy (SFBT). The central or organizing premises of SFBT derive from MRI brief therapy. (In fact, the cofounders of solution-focused therapy, Steve de Shazer and Insoo Kim Berg, met while training with John Weakland at MRI.) The Milan approach to family therapy was also heavily influenced by MRI; Paul Watzlawick consulted the original Milan team, and their focus on observing patterns around solutions is clearly MRI influenced.

The MRI brief therapy problem-formation and problem-resolution approach is elegant in its simplicity. It is less the problem itself, but rather the efforts being made to solve it, that inadvertently perpetuate and exacerbate the problem. Successfully interrupt the unsuccessful attempted solutions and the problem usually dissipates without need for further intervention. As simple as this framework is, the *practice* of therapy based on this conception to problem formation and problem resolution is not as easy as it sounds.

Grounded in 60 years of research that intentionally *does not rely* on conventional, individually oriented theories of human behavior, the BTC approach focuses on making sense of complaints and symptomatic behavior in terms of how it fits within the relational contexts (family and social) of which it is a part. The data of the orientation is the *actual behavior* of the complainant and those with whom he/she interacts. *How* is the problem behavior a problem, in *what way* is it a problem, and *to whom* is it a problem described in concrete behavioral terms? The model of causality used to comprehend complaints or problems is *cybernetic*— understanding and explaining all behavior in terms of its place in a wider, ongoing, organized system of behavior involving feedback and recursive reinforcement. Problem behavior is understood *not* in terms of deficits or abnormality, but rather as adaptive within the broader context.

MRI brief therapy seeks to promote the *minimum change* necessary to resolve the presenting problem, rather than trying to restructure the whole family system. Problems persist only if efforts to solve it are ineffective. Once clear understanding of the problem is achieved, primary attention is given to how the people involved are attempting to solve the problem. Attempts made to solve the problem are inadvertently perpetuating the problem. When the clients' efforts to solve the problem are successfully interrupted, the problem quickly resolves itself.

As one of, if not *the,* first social constructivist orientations, MRI brief therapy takes seriously the second order cybernetic position that ideas and premises held by the therapist about the nature of problems and treatment strongly influence what is focused on, whom is seen in treatment, what is said and done, and, equally, what is not said and done when working with the client. The therapist's presuppositions can facilitate change *or* contribute to maintenance of the problem. *Transparency,* congruency between theory and practice, and outcome—*effectiveness* of therapy—are the measures used by BTC researchers to shape the evolution of the approach. BTC researchers developed coherent, consistent, effective, *learnable,* and *teachable* skills to promote constructive change, and in so doing created a time-proven basic framework for effectively treating the widest range of emotional and behavioral problems. MRI brief therapy is among the most influential and effective treatment approaches in the brief therapy discipline. For more information about MRI brief therapy, please visit www.mri.org. While solution-focused therapy has grown to have its own organization (www.sfbta.org) and independent credentialing in Canada, MRI therapy is very much alive and well and practiced worldwide. Training is available in Spanish and Mandarin, and therapists travel from all over the world to study at MRI.

References

Fisch, R., Ray, W., & Schlanger, K. (2009). *Focused brief therapy–Selected papers of the MRI Brief Therapy Center.* Phoenix, AZ: Zeig, Tucker, & Theisan.

Fisch, R., Weakland, J., & Segal, L. (1982). *The tactics of change—Doing therapy briefly.* San Francisco, CA: Jossey-Bass.

Ray, W. (Ed.). (2005). *Don D. Jackson—Selected essays at the dawn of an era.* Phoenix, AZ: Zeig, Tucker, & Theisan.

Ray, W. (Ed.). (2009). *Don D. Jackson—Interactional theory in the practice of psychotherapy.* Phoenix, AZ: Zeig, Tucker, & Theisan.

Ray, W., & Nardone, G. (Eds.). (2009). *Paul Watzlawick—Insight may cause blindness and other essays.* Phoenix, AZ: Zeig, Tucker, Theisan.

Watzlawick, P., Beavin-Bavelas, J., & Jackson, D. (1967). *Pragmatics of human communication.* New York, NY: W. W. Norton.

Watzlawick, P., Weakland, J., & Fisch, R. (1974). *Change.* New York, NY: W. W. Norton.

Weakland, J., & Ray, W. (Eds.). (1995). *Propagations—Thirty years of influence from the Mental Research Institute.* New York, NY: Haworth.

33

COMPARE AND CONTRAST

Brief Therapy Models

Anne Rambo, Charles West, AnnaLynn Schooley, and Tommie V. Boyd

All the models in this section are influenced by both Erickson and Bateson. However, they balance that influence in different ways. MRI therapists put considerable emphasis on embracing the client's reality (Chapter 29) and see that embrace as in itself therapeutic. It is from within that reality that the MRI therapist suggests a qualitatively different type of solution behavior. From the perspective of SFBT, the therapist is comfortable shifting the client's reality from the presence of the problem to the absence of the problem (Chapter 30). The therapist then builds on the patterns of behavior that sustain the absence of the problem (the exception). The Milan therapist makes overt the ways in which the supposed problem is actually a solution and plays with that different perspective, traditionally through a message from the team or, less traditionally, as in Rhodes's chapter for this book, with a playful intervention (Chapter 31). While these differences in approach are important, it is also important to note what the models in this group share. In this respect, it is illustrative to note the influence of hypnotherapy on all these models (Chapter 28).

It may also be instructive to consider what therapists working from these brief therapy models would *not* do. None of these therapists attempted to get the parents to agree or to restore hierarchy in the family; none attempted to increase insight into past generations, or indeed anything other than find a way out of the present stuck situation. As Furman and Ahola (1994) note, the brief therapy models all share a pragmatic orientation toward action rather than insight, the future rather than the past, and new ways of being effective with clients rather than traditional ideas of assessment and diagnosis. As the sign over the door at MRI's Brief Therapy Institute reads, "Life is just one damn thing after another"—in other words, clients are no more pathological or troubled than any of the rest of us, they are just temporarily stuck, as we might all be from time to time. This is a nonpathologizing, nonnormative approach. In terms of underlying theoretical influences, these models are clearly influenced by Batesonian cybernetics, along with the ideas of Milton Erickson. Bateson's ideas are a natural fit with some aspects of social constructionist theory, so there is an influence of social constructionist theory as well (Hoyt, 1994).

Again, it can be instructive to look at what is absent as well as what is present. There is little to no influence from attachment theory, natural systems theory, or general systems theory. MRI (Chapter 29) and SFBT (Chapter 30) therapists in particular often see individuals and would have no particular imperative to see all members of a family except to gain additional information. This is a difference from the structural/strategic (IIC) models.

However, the brief therapy models, like the structural/strategic (IIC) models, are action oriented and directive, and this is a difference from the psychoanalytic/experiential models (IIA) and the intergenerational models (IIB). Brief therapists often feel at home with narrative and collaborative therapists (Furman & Ahola, 1994) as they share with practitioners of these models a nonnormative, nonpathologizing approach and an interest in social constructionism. Narrative models are more focused on meaning and issues of personal identity, though, and collaborative models are much less directive (Anderson, 2011). In terms of theory, brief therapy practitioners have more in common with narrative (IIE) and collaborative (IIF) practitioners, but in terms of practice, brief therapy practitioners focus on doing, as opposed to thinking or feeling, just as do those working from structural/strategic (IIC) models. So there is an interesting dichotomy of commonalities between these brief therapy models and their nearest allies.

In terms of the common factors to which we have been referring throughout (Sprenkle, Davis, & Lebow, 2009), brief therapy models conceptualize in terms of interactions, rather than specific family systems; they intervene indirectly by interrupting what is not working or promoting what is already working in clients' solution behaviors; and they expand the therapeutic system by joining with clients' multiple individual realities.

In terms of differences between these related models, one should also note the difference in acceptance, especially in the United States. MRI therapy is still an influence on the field both in the United States and worldwide (Chapter 32). However, SFBT has become more widely accepted, especially within the United States, as it is such a natural fit with the positive language, brief therapy orientation, and specific outcomes preferred by managed care (Quick, 2008). This acceptance has been so widespread that the model has been viewed as pervasive in many contexts (Stalker, Levene, & Coady, 1999). In contrast, the paradoxical nature of Milan-style interventions—keep doing what you are doing as it serves the system—is a difficult sell to insurance companies; Milan-style family therapy has been slower to find acceptance in the United States (Boscolo, Cecchin, Hoffman, & Penn, 1987) and is more influential in other countries.

The Batesonian and social constructionist theoretical foundations of MRI (Chapter 29), SFBT (Chapter 30), and Milan (Chapter 31) initially led practitioners of all three models to define success in terms of client satisfaction, rather than attempting large-scale experimentally rigorous comparisons, as the structural/strategic (IIC) models have done. The decision was made, however, in SFBT circles, to proceed with such research in order to move toward the designation of SFBT as an evidence-based model (www.sfbta.org). While SFBT does not have the years of such research that other models (notably structural/strategic and, for couples therapy, emotionally focused couples therapy) have accumulated, initial results have been promising. SFBT is now classified as a promising model by the U.S. federal government (Office of Juvenile Justice and Drug Prevention, 2012).

References

Anderson, H. (2011). *Postmodern social constructionist therapies.* Retrieved from http://www.harleneanderson.org/writings/postmodernchapter.htm

Boscolo, L, Cecchin, G., Hoffman, L., & Penn, P. (1987). *Milan systemic family therapy: Conversations in theory and practice.* New York, NY: Basic Books.

Furman, B., & Ahola, T. (1994). Solution talk: The solution oriented way of talking about problems. In M. Hoyt (Ed.), *Constructive therapies* (Vol. 1, pp. 41–66). New York, NY: Guilford Press.

Hoyt, M. (1994). On the importance of keeping it simple and taking the patient seriously: A conversation with Steve de Shazer and John Weakland. In M. Hoyt (Ed.), *Constructive therapies* (Vol. 1, pp. 11–40). New York, NY: Guilford Press

Office of Juvenile Justice and Drug Prevention. (2012). *OJJDP model programs guide.* Retrieved from www.ojjdp.gov/mpg

Quick, E. (2008). *Doing what works in brief therapy: A strategic solution focused approach* (2nd ed.). Burlington, MA: Academic Press.

Sprenkle, D., Davis, S., & Lebow, J. (2009). *Common factors in couple and family therapy: The overlooked foundation for clinical practice.* New York, NY: Guilford Press.

Stalker, C, Levene, J., & Coady, N. (1999). Solution focused brief therapy—One model fits all? *Families in Society, 80*(5), 468–477.

PART E
NARRATIVE MODELS

34

A BRIEF HISTORY OF NARRATIVE MODELS

Anne Rambo, Charles West, AnnaLynn Schooley, and Tommie V. Boyd

These models, narrative and "just therapy," originated in Australia and New Zealand, respectively. They brought a fresh viewpoint to the family therapy field in the 1980s and spread worldwide in the 1990s.

Narrative therapy began in Australia. Michael White and his partner, Cheryl White, started the Dulwich Family Centre in Adelaide, Australia, in 1983, and Cheryl White began publishing the *Dulwich Centre Newsletter* in 1984. (Again, husband/wife teams are an interesting feature of family therapy history—note Iván Böszörményi-Nagy and Catherine Ducommun-Nagy [IIB], Jay Haley and Cloe Madanes [IIC], and Steve de Shazer and Insoo Kim Berg [IID] as other examples.) Michael White began working with David Epston, who now runs the Family Therapy Centre in Auckland, New Zealand. Their ideas about therapy were influenced by Gregory Bateson, Michel Foucault, social constructionism, and narrative ideas (Beels, 2009). Beels (2009) has identified conferences in Tulsa, Oklahoma, in 1991, and in Reston, Virginia, as pivotal turning points when White, Epston, and others present first tried out the term *narrative*, and when it was "settled on by a motley international group of Ericksonian hypnotherapists, brief therapists, family therapists, paradoxical and solution-focused therapists, and other mavericks who were trying to decide what to call themselves... It was clear at that early point that narrative work, although it came out of the experience of family therapy, was not just another way of working with families. It was a new way of consulting with clients in a variety of contexts, including their families and their communities. It was a new way of defining these relationships as naturally in search of collaboration, of common purpose." In keeping with Foucault's ideas, narrative therapy has always included the idea of community and of work toward social justice.

Independently, although along similar lines, just therapy was developed at the Family Centre in Wellington, New Zealand. The intention of just therapy, the name of which is a play on words, to include both the idea of simplicity (*just* as in "only") and social justice (*just* as in "having the quality of justice"), was to move therapy from the clinic to the community (Waldegrave, 2009). There was a heavy influence of Foucault as well. White and Epston were influenced by the just therapy team and were influences on them in turn (White, 2009). Just therapy is less well known outside the Australia/New Zealand area, but as the Chapter 36 in this book indicate, it is making its way worldwide and is of particular interests to those working with underserved populations.

References

Beels, C. (2009). Some historical conditions of narrative work. *Family Process, 48*(3), 363–378.

Waldegrave, C. (2009). Cultural, gender, and socio-economic contexts in therapeutic and social policy work. *Family Process,* 1, 85–101. White, C. (2009). *Where did it all begin? Reflecting on the collaborative work of Michael White and David Epston.* Retrieved from www.narrativefamilycentre.com

Additional Resources

Madigan, S. (2010). *Narrative therapy.* Washington, DC: American Psychological Association.

Waldegrave, C., Tamasese, K., Tuhaka, F., & Campbell, W. *Just Therapy—A journey: A collection of papers from the just therapy team, New Zealand.* Adelaide, Australia: Dulwich Centre Publications.

White, M. (2007). *Maps of narrative practice.* New York, NY: W. W. Norton.

White, M., & Epston, D. (1990). *Narrative means to therapeutic ends.* New York, NY: W. W. Norton.

35

NARRATIVE FAMILY THERAPY

Stephen Madigan

Narrative therapy practice is premised on the notion that people organize their lives through stories (thus the use of the narrative or text metaphor). When we experience a client family coming to talk with us in therapy, they usually relate a telling of their lives through stories (Madigan, 2011). They tell their stories by linking together their understanding of the problem, relationship, illness, and so on through a sequencing of life events and ideas through time (Bruner, 1990). People often speak about what brought them into therapy, what they believe the history of their situation is, and who or what is responsible.

Often when a family decides to come to therapy, there is usually one prevailing theory told. However—as in the case of Mary, Fred, and Johnny's family—there may be possible differences as to why they are in therapy and what the solution might be. From a narrative therapist's point of view, the premise of each theory on the problem told, by each separate member present, is thought to be quite limiting of the families' descriptions of themselves and situation. Narrative therapists involve themselves in the interview to broaden and thicken these family accounts leading to newly formed counterstories and use questions that offer a pathway to rich story development. This may involve an investigation of a family's/person's history and future of longstanding but underappreciated skills, abilities, and know-hows—often restrained by the problem's version of the person and their relationships.

I make a practice of conversing as little as possible with other professionals about the person/family arriving into therapy. Stories made available about the person/family are usually those told by other professionals (psychologists, lawyers, guidance counselors, etc.) and are often told within a decontextualized individualist approach to problems and written through professional files. I keep myself distant from individualist ideas, professional files, and expert evaluations about clients. My preference is to privilege the more local telling of the person/family story as the first telling told.

The dilemma that Mary, Fred, and Johnny present is quite common to a general therapy practice. At the outset, the narrative therapist would surmise the individual family members (mother/father/son) did not arrive at negative identity conclusions or their orientations regarding problems and/or solutions on their own. I would be curious as to what inspired the family's call to therapy at this particular time (hope, despair, etc.). I would ask each member of the family this question: How is it that you've come to see someone like me in therapy at this particular time? This question tracks and situates the temporal dimension (past, present, future) regarding why the family chose to come to therapy at this time and not six months ago or six weeks into the future. The question familiarizes the therapist with who in the family/community is talking about the problem and in what way (the family, Mary's mother, siblings, teachers, counselors, other parents, friends). The question opens space to closely investigate the language used to describe the problem and person and what dominant cultural ideas this language belongs to (i.e., tough love, the curse of perfect parenting, gateway drugs, etc.). The question also explores from what particular ideological positions the problem is being articulated. The question can lead the therapist to inquire about each member's statement of position on the problem, potential pathways to freedom, and preferred outcomes from therapy.

From these conversations, Mary, Fred, and Johnny would begin to discover their preferences for living. Narrative therapy practice is based on the idea that people make meaning in the world about who they are, who they may become, who they are in relation to others, and what constitutes proper actions for living—through a dialogic relationship that is considered shaped by the prevailing cultural group. In order to offer a more colorful snapshot of their lives, client stories introduce a range of characters and backstories—in just the same way any good author might. While people live and construct stories about themselves, these stories also live and construct people (Bakhtin, 1986; White, 2002).

The narrative therapist holds a firm belief that the person arriving into therapy is not solely responsible for creating the problem-centered deficit-identity conclusion that is often relayed by other professionals and parlayed by the client in the first session. For example, a mother experiencing a child viewed by the preschool as not quite fitting in (to what might be considered proper preschool behavior) may blame herself as unfit following in step with a predominance for mother-blaming ideas in our culture. Young girls struggling with strict specifications of the body, perfection, and anorexia may feel they have personally failed; a heterosexual corporate employee not able to spend more time with his or her children feels socially torn and inadequate; a gay or bi-curious high school student is entered into a fearful secrecy and feels a sense of individual shame; and so on.

The initial story often told in therapy is one that adheres to placing specific individual responsibility for "their problem" directly onto the problem-identified person's body. I observe this when encountering so-called problems involving youth (in this case Johnny) that are unfairly privatized directly onto their bodies in the form of a decontextualized, pathologized individualized category or name (for example, when dealing with the overdiagnosed issue of pseudo-ADD). These perplexing humanist descriptions of individual responsibility for the daily problems we collectively create, experience, and reproduce appears cut off from the relational context and influence of prevailing culture.

I am usually inclined to invite the family to the first session and any other primary interlocutors (to an upcoming session) who describe and bear witness to a version of the story told. The reason for these interlocutor inclusions is to find a membership of support and possibility. This membership would include whoever is talking about the problem, including the family, Mary's mother (Bess), siblings, teachers, counselors, coaches, other parents, and Johnny's friends. By organizing a community around the family and the problem, a more communal relational approach to the problem can be achieved. Narrative therapists are not concerned with behavior, as in categories of behavior or, in this case, trying to make meaning out of Johnny's school-refusing behavior. Instead, they turn their curiosity toward action and interaction—that is to say, the action and interaction of experience, response, and reflection of the client. Within the practice of narrative therapy, problems are viewed as relational, contextual, interpretive, and situated within dominant discourse, expression, response, and cultural norms. This interplay presents the backdrop to the narrative maxim *the person is the person and the problem is the problem*—they are not separate, but rather culturally, discursively, and relationally interwoven.

Reauthoring conversations (Epston & White, 1990; Madigan, 2011) are a key feature in the practice of narrative therapy. Reauthoring conversations invite clients to help flush out some of the more neglected areas and events of their lives (often covered over by the problem story being told). These may include achievements under duress, survival skills growing up, and qualities of themselves left out of their story, such as generosity, ethical stances, and kindness, and so forth. These are very often stories that could not have been predicted through a telling of the dominant problem story being told. These untold counterstories can be sadly neglected in the telling of the problem story—by both client and the professionals involved with the client's story (and community members are of great help in re-remembering these stores).

Neglected events in the client's life are viewed as exceptions or unique outcomes that are utilized as a beginning point for reauthoring conversations and the development of alternative storylines.[1] Often these conversations evoke a longer standing curiosity and appreciation about the counterstory the client finds him- or herself telling. The telling of these alternative and often preferred recollections of lives and relationships shapes newly formed stories that can be further broadened and enriched.

Narrative therapists ask questions as a way to expand on the counter or subordinate story by trafficking in what Jerome Bruner (1990) called the landscape of action and the landscape of identity. Landscape of action questions center on events that happened in a person's telling of his or her life and links these events through time—forming a plotline. These questions are organized through events, circumstance, sequence, time, and plot (Michael White, personal conversation,

1991, Adelaide, Australia). Landscape of identity questions are (in part) those that are asked regarding what the client might conclude about the action, sequences, and themes described in response to the landscape of action questions. Landscape of identity questions also bring forth relevant categories addressing cultural identities, intentional understandings, learnings, and realizations.

Everyday narrative therapy interviewing involves a process known as relative influence questioning, which is comprised of three sets of questions: (1) one set maps the influence of the problem on the person and losses experienced within this relationship; (2) another set encourages persons to map their own (and others') influence in the life of the problem (White, 1988); and (3) the third set begins to map out the unique outcomes or the occasions where the person experienced some influence in his or her life despite the discursive power of the problem.

Woven together, relative influence questions invite a retelling of the client story in such a way as to evoke a discursive means of understanding and performing aspects of the client's abilities and skills in the face of the problem. If the dialogue arose, I might expect to interview Johnny with some of the following questions.

1. What are the practices of life and ways of thinking about life that have helped you cause your parents to be so filled with worry about your relationship to yourself, your friends, and your school?
2. Is this a worry good thing or a not-so-good thing in your life?
3. Is this a problem for you or is this just a problem for your parents?
4. Are their certain requirements and ways that you live because of this particular way of thinking?
5. What are these ways of living (practices)? Where did you learn them? Why are they appealing?
6. How do these ways of living have you relating to yourself?
7. Does it bring you closer in or further away (to yourself, others)?
8. Are there any downsides to living with this way of thinking on your relationships with others? To yourself?

Note

1. Papers published through Dulwich Centre Publications. For a more in-depth discussion of Bruner's landscape of meaning, see selected Dulwich Centre publications.

References

Bakhtin, M. M. (1986). *Speech genres and other late essays.* Trans. by Vern McGee. Austin: University of Texas Press.
Bruner, J. (1990). *Acts of meaning.* Cambridge, MA: Harvard University Press.

Epston, D., & White, M. (1990). *Narrative means to therapeutic ends.* New York, NY: W. W. Norton

Madigan, S. (2011). *Narrative therapy—Theory and practice.* Chicago, IL: American Psychological Association Publications.

White, M. (2002). Addressing personal failure. *International Journal of Narrative Therapy and Community Work, 3,* 33–76.

36

"JUST THERAPY"

Mathis Kennington

Just therapy was developed at New Zealand's Family Centre as a critical response to Eurocentric family therapy, which often fails to consider the cultural impact of psychological and social health. Just therapy endeavors to evaluate the impact of marginalization on family interaction and liberate culturally marginalized families from the experience of Eurocentric mental health treatment (Tamasese & Waldegrave, 1994). The central aim of just therapy is to broaden the traditional scope of family therapy practice by creating new meaning that individuals and families can apply to their experiences of discrimination in the critical contexts of culture, gender, and socioeconomic status (Waldegrave, 2000). Just therapy was established out of a reflexive process in which therapists at New Zealand's Family Centre recognized that their traditional treatment was ineffective against the socioeconomic realities of their clientele. Subsequently, therapists were unable to treat the salient problems with which families presented. Indeed, as Tamasese and Waldegrave (1994) observe, traditional therapy cannot sufficiently handle the cultural impact of poverty and discrimination. Therapies that fail to address these issues lack the tools necessary to treat the deleterious impact of social inequity, cultural marginalization, and health disparities and often leave people "happy in poverty" (Waldegrave, 2005, p. 272). Family therapy that fails to assess these foundational issues subsequently labels symptomology (i.e., family stress, depression, etc.) as the presenting problem.

Essential Elements

Just therapy was developed in an effort to unfetter forms of knowledge that are often overlooked by scientific methods of anecdotal assessment and treatment (Waldegrave, 2000). Waldegrave contends that mental health practitioners such as psychologists, social workers, and family therapists have been taught under a largely modernist framework, which is an observation made by other family therapy contemporaries (Bott, 2001; Kleist & Thorngren, 2002; Mills & Sprenkle, 1995). Modern practice follows the scientific method, which aims to classify and categorize pathology in an effort to systematically treat pathology through various theoretical and practical approaches. Indeed, mental health research methods reflect the scientist-practitioner model through the gold standard approach of randomized clinical trials, which suppresses other forms of knowledge (Sexton, Kinser, & Hanes, 2008). Just therapy attempts to deconstruct categorical anecdotes in favor of understanding behavior in the light of critical contexts.

There are multiple therapeutic tools that just therapy practitioners use to accomplish these tasks. First, just therapy uses the strength of the socially constructed meaning to develop new understandings for cultural, gendered, and socioeconomic experiences. Attention to social construction and language has recently found a home in postmodern forms of therapy (White, 2007). The social sciences are a social construction for understanding behaviors. Just therapy employs the use of the socially constructed meaning both to deconstruct and to reconstruct marginalized experiences. Second, just therapy works out of an action/reflection stance in which individuals and families offer the meanings they have created out of problematic experiences. Therapists, then, reflect and offer their own meanings accompanied by the therapist's knowledge of the critical context. Just therapists pay close attention to issues of gender, for example, and how women are often marginalized as a result of patriarchal therapeutic practices, in which family therapy is rooted. In New Zealand, just therapy practitioners developed three cultural centers in which individuals and families from New Zealand cultural groups were treated. Pacific Islanders were treated by a team of therapists who shared their cultural heritage. Maori therapists treated Maori families and individuals.

In the United States, we have a similar dilemma. Although we have multiple ethnic populations represented, those populations bear the burden of disparity in almost every socioeconomic category. People of European descent enjoy better physical health, lower mortality rates, access to better education, less social exclusion and racial discrimination, better housing, and drastically lower rates of incarceration (Borrayo, 2007; Foster & Hagan, 2007; Frist, 2005; Hummer & Chinn, 2011; Medford, 2004; Pew Center on the States, 2009). It is for this reason that just therapy would be a good fit in the United States, because it emphasizes the value of overlooked cultural and communal knowledge. The knowledge of marginalized cultural groups such as individuals and families of African descent, Latino families, Native Americans, Asian and Pacific Islanders, and so forth would be emphasized. Clients of European descent would also be treated within the realm of their cultural knowledge. U.S.–based just therapy would be an effort to liberate the value of cultural knowledge to heal intrafamilial concerns and alleviate problems that result from social disparity.

Case Study

In the fictional case of Mary, Fred, and Johnny, I would open by assessing the family's cultural background, and I would see the family together. This would begin with a cultural genogram in an effort to discover the uncovered mores and beliefs that have been passed down through the family's previous generations. In the first session, I would be especially interested to know about the family's socioeconomic status (SES). I would also ask what meaning Mary and Fred give to Johnny's behaviors. Finally, I would want to know what meaning Mary and Fred give to Mary's mother's involvement in their lives. This family's cultural background is crucial to know how to progress with the issue of Mary's mother and her involvement with the family. If Mary and Fred are a couple who values autonomy over ancestry, my goal would be to help Mary and Fred differentiate from Mary's mother. Just therapy assessment is extremely important for this reason. If Mary and Fred are from a culture where ancestral connections are more highly valued than familial autonomy, then I would emphasize the connection between Mary and her mother, strengthen the relationship between Fred and Mary's mother, and invite other members of the family to weigh in on what can be done to help Johnny overcome his social and academic concerns.

The goals of just therapy would be established once the family culture was thoroughly explored. I would establish therapy goals with the family depending on what meaning the family gives to therapy. I would request that the family suggest three therapeutic goals. From these goals, I would reflect how I felt these goals needed to be modified or elaborated. Only with the family's permission and acceptance of those goals would we move forward. It is crucial to note that my reflection of the therapeutic goals is subject to the family and my cotherapists, to ensure that the goals are cocreated and not self-imposed.

Just therapy would be especially concerned with the family's SES. Mary and Fred might be experiencing the cultural marginalization that stems from poverty. To address this issue, I would consider Johnny's struggle at school as a condition of the family's struggle against poverty. Indeed, I would work alongside a team of two other therapists, at least one of whom was a female therapist, to congratulate this family on their ability to survive among such difficult circumstances. This reframe is necessary because poorer families experience multiproblem labels from practitioners who fail to assess their cultural knowledge or circumstances (Waldegrave, 2005). Mary, Fred, and Johnny's belief that they have been resilient will contribute to the therapeutic process. I would work with my therapeutic team to identify resources in the community that would meet the family's primary needs. In the case of Mary and Fred, this may mean identifying employment opportunities, assisting Mary and Fred with applications for government aid, working with extended family members to provide resources in times of distress, and discovering prosocial institutions such as churches, synagogues, humanist organizations, and so on to which Mary and Fred belong to facilitate community involvement.

Finally, a crucial method of change in just therapy is in the use of cocreating shared collective meaning. I would be interested in seeing how the family can create new meanings for Johnny's behaviors. I would have at least one session alone with Johnny to explore the meaning he gives to his behaviors. Then, I would encourage a process of shared meaning making between Johnny, his parents, and possibly other family members. This would involve applying new meaning to school attendance, good grades in school, and high-risk behaviors. It would also mean accessing positive family rituals such as discipline and rewards when these new meanings are discarded or inculcated, respectively. For example, Johnny might suggest that he finds these behaviors fun or that he doesn't see the point in going to school when he doesn't have to. In this case, I would work with Johnny to discover the value of school in Johnny's language. Then, I would encourage Johnny to share the meaning he has made about the value of school with his parents so that they can reinforce his positive experience of school rather than what they have created. In other words, where Mary and Fred are concerned about Johnny's grades, Johnny doesn't like to go to school because he is bullied. As a result, his behaviors become a statement of his distress. I would encourage Mary and Fred to recognize that struggle and develop a strategy for addressing Johnny's feelings of being bullied while creating a positive meaning for school attendance and work. The combination of attending to family stress brought on by poverty or cultural marginalization, accessing community resources, and creating new meaning around problem behaviors are central to the practice of just therapy.

References

Borrayo, E. A. (2007). Using a community readiness model to help overcome breast health disparities among U.S. Latinas. *Substance Use & Misuse, 42*(4), 603–619. doi:10.1080/10826080701202205

Bott, D. (2001). Towards a family-centred therapy: Postmodern developments in family therapy and the person-centered contribution. *Counselling Psychology Quarterly, 14*(2), 111–118. doi:10.1080/09515070110058549

Foster, H., & Hagan, J. (2007). Incarceration and intergenerational social exclusion. *Social Problems, 54*(4), 399–433. doi:10.1525/sp.2007.54.4.399

Frist, W. H. (2005). Overcoming disparities in U.S. health care. *Health Affairs (Project Hope), 24*(2), 445–451. doi:10.1377/hlthaff.24.2.445

Hummer, R. A., & Chinn, J. J. (2011). Race/ethnicity and U.S. adult mortality. *Du Bois Review: Social Science Research on Race, 8*(1), 5–24. doi:10.1017/S1742058X11000051

Kleist, D. M., & Thorngren, J. M. (2002). Multiple family group therapy: An interpersonal/ postmodern approach. *Family Journal, 10*(2), 167–176. doi:10.1177/1066480702102006

Medford, R. (2004). Housing discrimination in U.S. suburbs: A bibliography. *Journal of Planning Literature, 18*(4), 399–457. doi:10.1177/0885412204263509

Mills, S. D., & Sprenkle, D. H. (1995). Family therapy in the postmodern era. *Family Relations, 44*(4), 368–376.

Pew Center on the States. (2009). *One in 31: The long reach of American corrections.* Washington, DC: Pew Charitable Trusts.

Sexton, T. L., Kinser, J. C., & Hanes, C. W. (2008). Beyond a single standard: Levels of evidence approach for evaluating marriage and family therapy research and practice. *Journal of Family Therapy, 30*, 386–398.

Tamasese, K., & Waldegrave, C. (1994). Some central ideas in the "just therapy" approach. *Family Journal, 2*(2), 94–103. doi:10.1177/1066480794022002

Waldegrave, C. (2000). Just therapy with families and communities. In G. Burford & J. Hudson (Eds.), *Family group conferencing: New directions in community-centered child and family practice.* Hawthorne, NY: Aldine de Gruyter.

Waldegrave, C. (2005). "Just therapy" with families on low incomes. *Child Welfare, 84*(2), 265–276.

White, M. (2007). *Maps of narrative practice.* New York, NY: W. W. Norton.

37

PRACTITIONER'S PERSPECTIVE

Narrative Therapy as an Essential Tool in Conflict and Trauma Resolution

Cathie J. Witty

Positive peace is the absence of violence in all forms including the structural violence of oppression and restrictive dehumanizing policies, the restoration of relationships, and the creation of social systems that serve the need of the whole population and the whole person and manage conflict with respectful attention to the legitimate needs and interest of all.

In conflict work on an interpersonal or community level, personal healing of the physical and emotional symptoms of horror, loss, depression, and the persistent loss of hope individuals experience is essential. There is no movement to reconciliation, change, or hope for a future without resolving the fundamental issues of trauma, whether in Rwanda, the Congo, or American communities oppressed by racism, gangs, and related violence.

As a narrative therapy practitioner and veteran conflict analyst, my teaching and practice take me from villages of Kosovo working with disenfranchised families with children with disabilities, to gang violence survivors, to adults coping with the lingering effects of childhood abuse. All carry the burden of not being seen or heard in the public policy process, many areas of professional practice, and many nation- and peace-building efforts.

Narrative therapy techniques, questions, and strategies are easy to weave into community meetings and interest groups rather than practicing therapy in the traditional structured way. There are several reasons this indirect approach works well. First, in many cultures, telling your painful story to an outsider is not accepted, as people use networks of friends and family as mentors, guides, and "therapists" on a daily basis, often over coffee and a substantial number of cigarettes. These are the cultural norms of self-help and recovery for many peoples in the world. A professional therapist is not an affordable option and also represents the dangerous other in times of stress and anxiety, who people must avoid to protect the honor of the family, the threat of outside interference, and one's individual sense of dignity and saving face.

Second, narrative transformational conversations transfer easily to family-focused, high-context social systems as well as generalized group discussions of situational trauma (Hurricane Irene or recurring 9/11 memorials) in Western culture. In high-context settings, the conversational style blends seamlessly into group debates as long as some level of trust, group acknowledgment, and acceptance are present. Peace-building efforts often fail to establish the personal relationships and community acceptance on a group level to support this type of practice before plunging into structural community building. However, successful local programs such as trauma recovery in Rwanda, in the former Yugoslavia, in Australian aboriginal communities, and through programs like Latino Health Access in California are just a few current examples of narrative deconstruction and collaborative practices using narrative healing practices such as externalizing, rebuilding links between traditional culture and ritual and the present, and listening and witnessing the consequences of trauma.

Finally, through consultation and training of local healers and community builders, narrative therapy centers, institutes, and conflict practitioners plant permanent seeds of transformational healing for people and communities, sustained as local resources by programs that engage in group dialogue, narrative songwriting, expressive arts and journaling, letter writing, remembering and renewal ceremonies, and practices that link survivors to ancestors, lost family members, and the spiritual, cultural narratives of resilience and change. This is a necessary part of healing and cultural reconnection before beginning the journey toward a more positive future, both as individuals and members of a healing community.

Narrative skills and techniques can also be combined with body-focused psychomotor therapy; expressive arts such as puppet theater, art, and dance; and energy healing work such as emotionally focused therapy and Reiki and can be integrated into local healing practices in an expanding therapeutic process that is carried forward by local communities in whatever way suits their needs. The Balkan Trauma Recovery Project, the Centre for Ubuntu in South Africa, and the Coalition for Work with Psychotrauma and Peace in Vukovar, Croatia, are some excellent examples of this type of culturally integrated, ongoing program.

This type of narrative work is a critical component of sustainable peace because peace begins within individuals' resolution of their own hopes, fears, and prejudices; community participation, empathy, compassion, planning for the future, and peace building follow from that individual transformation. This work is not limited to clinical practice but is critical in peace and conflict work to move communities in the direction of positive peace in which people reshape their present trauma- and violence-saturated stories into recovery and hopeful action-based stories that heal and empower. In changing their stories, they change themselves and their communities, and that, to me, is the epistemological basis of narrative therapy. In global terms, we need more than an "Arab Spring," but rather a humanitarian spring that can begin the process of healing past injustices, inequities, and fears to give us all a chance to reclaim the human dignity found within the tenets of positive peace.

38

COMPARE AND CONTRAST

Narrative Models

Anne Rambo, Charles West, AnnaLynn Schooley, and Tommie V. Boyd

In terms of our thinking/feeling/doing triad, these approaches appear most interested in thinking; the therapist wishes to privilege the submerged voice, to change the way the client thinks about him- or herself. The models are clearly influenced both by Batesonian and social constructionist theories (Beels, 2009), but they are also primarily influenced by the ideas of Foucault, and that sets them apart from other models of family therapy. Narrative practitioners share with other family therapists an interest in context and relationship. The use of reflecting teams within narrative therapy in particular has been linked to the work of Tom Andersen (Chapter 41; Dulwich Centre Communications, 2012), and there are clear links to the collaborative models. However, narrative therapy is equally influenced by ideas of social constructionism, feminism, and social justice, especially 'again' the work of Foucault, and by contributions from indigenous Australian communities (Dulwich Centre Communications, 2012). The narrative models are never only or primarily about technique; the commitment to community and social justice is woven throughout their approach.

Thus, in terms of our shared family therapy common factors (Sprenkle, Davis, & Lebow, 2009), narrative therapists clearly conceptualize in terms of larger systems—communities and cultures as well as family systems. They intervene by attempting to change the story the client is telling about him- or herself and bear witness to that new story. They expand the therapeutic system by considering larger social and cultural factors.

As a group, narrative models can be said to play well with others. In their emphasis on meaning, narrative practitioners find common ground with intergenerational (Chapter 13) and psychoanalytic therapists (Chapter 7). In their emphasis on social constructionism, and embracing the client's reality rather than imposing an agenda, narrative therapists are a natural fit with practitioners of the brief therapy models (Chapter 27) and the collaborative models (Chapter 39). In particular, the SFBT therapist's focus on exceptions, times when the problem is not present, and the narrative therapist's interest in unique outcomes, also times of exception to the dominant discourse, can appear very similar (Rambo, 2003). However, narrative therapists are careful to note what they see as their unique focus on personal identity. Their interest is in how personal identity is formed by our stories about ourselves and others' stories about us, including history and culture; "narrative therapy focuses on the degree to which that socially constructed identity fits our lives" (Sween, 1998, p. 5). The criticism has been leveled that narrative family therapy is not really family therapy, that narrative practitioners see individuals and are not interested in the family as a system (Minuchin, 1998); the narrative response to this is to state that narrative therapists are interested in significant relationships, including the relationship of differing stories and ideas, and not just in family relationships (Hayward, 2009). In this respect, narrative therapy models are similar to brief therapy and collaborative therapy models. All three of these groups of models (narrative, brief, and collaborative) are *not* much influenced by general systems theory, unlike the psychoanalytic and structural/strategic groups of models. Lacking this influence from general systems theory, there really is no particular reason why seeing the entire family at one time is essential. Like brief and collaborative therapists, narrative therapists work with individuals in their relational contexts, not necessarily with families.

The intense influence of social constructionism has resulted in most narrative therapists measuring their success by their clients' perceptions, rather than by quantitative outcome assessments. This may be changing, however, as there is now some interest in obtaining evidence-based practice status for narrative therapy approaches. (www.dulwichcentre.com.au) Narrative therapy is widely practiced in Australia, New Zealand, and Canada and has been a major influence in Europe and the United States as well. While the more explicitly political aspects of just therapy in particular may be difficult to adapt to the U.S. context of managed health care, there are practitioners successfully integrating narrative ideas with brief therapy ideas in managed care contexts (Hoyt, 2000). It will be interesting to watch the future of these models as they continue to spread worldwide.

References

Beels, C. (2009). Some historical conditions of narrative work. *Family Process, 48*(3), 363–378.

Dulwich Centre Publications. (2012). Community questions about narrative approaches. Retrieved from http://www.dulwichcentre.com

Hayward, M. (2009). *Is narrative therapy systemic?* Retrieved from http://www.theinstituteof narrativetherapy.com

Hoyt, M. (2000). *Some stories are better than others: Doing what works in brief therapy and managed care.* New York, NY: Routledge.

Minuchin, S. (1998). Where is the family in narrative family therapy? *Journal of Marital and Family Therapy, 29*(4), 397–403.

Rambo, A. (2003). The collaborative language based models of family therapy: When less is more. In L. Hecker & J. Wetchler (Eds.), *An introduction to marriage and family therapy.* New York, NY: Haworth Press.

Sprenkle, D., Davis, S., & Lebow, J. (2009). *Common factors in couple and family therapy: An overlooked foundation for effective practice.* New York, NY: Guilford Press.

Sween, E. (1998). The one minute question: What is narrative therapy? *Gecko, 2,* 3–6.

PART F
COLLABORATIVE MODELS

39

A BRIEF HISTORY OF COLLABORATIVE MODELS

Anne Rambo, Charles West, AnnaLynn Schooley, and Tommie V. Boyd

In this section, we consider the collaborative family therapy model of the Houston Galveston Institute (HGI) and the reflecting team model, both grouped as collaborative models. The work of the Houston Galveston Institute goes back to the development of multiple impact therapy (MIT) at the University of Texas Medical Branch in Galveston, Texas (MacGregor et al., 1964). Harry Goolishian was involved in the creation of this influential early model and was soon joined by Harlene Anderson. MIT involved every member of the family being interviewed by his or her own therapist, with all voices coming together, therapists and family members alike, at the end of the day (MacGregor et al., 1964). This respect for individual voices influenced Goolishian, Anderson, George Pulliam, and other colleagues of what later became the Galveston Family Institute and is now the Houston Galveston Institute (www.talkhgi.com). In these early days, the team was also influenced by the brief therapy approaches, in particular MRI (Chapter 29), but as time went on, Goolishian and Anderson in particular began to deemphasize intervention and put more emphasis on joining with the reality of clients (Anderson, 2011). By the 1990s, collaborative therapy was clearly identified as a distinct model (Anderson, 1997). Lynn Hoffman also used the term to describe her model of therapy (Hoffman, 1993).

Meanwhile, Tom Andersen in Norway was going through a similar transition. Having been trained in Milan-style therapy, he had the idea one day to switch off the lights in the therapy room and on in the observation room, allowing the family to hear the reflections of the team, to become the observers rather than just the observed (Andersen, 1991). From there, he and his colleagues developed a radically collaborative approach to team therapy. Parallel to the process of the Houston Galveston team, they began over time to de-emphasize intervention, and substitute instead noninvasive, nonjudgmental reflecting. There has been mutual contact and influence between Andersen's reflecting team model and the collaborative model of Anderson and Goolishian (Anderson, 2011). Both these models are relatively new in the field, dating from the 1990s. However, their influence has been considerable. In part this is due to research on clinical efficacy suggesting that a collaborative relationship between therapist and client is critical to outcome (Duncan, Miller & Sparks, 2004). This finding has provided support for all approaches associated with social constructionism (IIC and IID), as well as for general joining skills with clients, applicable to all models, but of particular salience for collaborative approaches (IIE).

References

Anderson, H. (1997). *Conversation, language, and possibilities: A postmodern approach to therapy.* New York, NY: Basic Books.

Anderson, H. (2011). *Postmodern social constructionist therapies.* Retrieved from www.harleneanderson.org/writings/postmoderntherapieschapter.htm

Andersen, T. (1991). *The reflecting team: Dialogues and dialogues about the dialogues.* New York, NY: W. W. Norton.

Duncan, B., Miller, S., & Sparks. J. (2004). *The heroic client: A revolutionary way to improve effectiveness through client-directed, outcome-informed therapy.* San Francisco, CA: Jossey-Bass.

Hoffman, L. (1993). *Exchanging voices: A collaborative approach to family therapy.* London, England: Karnac Books.

MacGregor, R., Ritchie, A.M., Serrano, A.C., Schuster, F.P., McDanald, E.C., & Goolishian, H. A. (1964). *Multiple impact therapy with families.* New York, NY: McGraw-Hill.

Additional Resource

Anderson, H., Cooperrider, D., & Gergen, K. (2008). *The appreciative organization.* Taos, NM: Taos Institute Publications.

40

COLLABORATIVE THERAPY

Sylvia London With Reflection by Harlene Anderson

The basic principles of collaborative language systems are summarized elsewhere (Anderson, 1997); here, I (London) will present one image of how they might appear in practice. During the initial phone call with Mary, we talked about who would be important for her to include in the first meeting and why. As Mary talked, she indicated that she was struggling with a number of issues, some of which included her husband, others her mother, and most of them her son Johnny. As a therapist, I do not know which issue will be the most important for the client to choose as the topic for our first meeting; it is important for me that the client has the freedom to choose who she wants to invite to the first meeting, who the important participants in the conversation are. I do not assume that the family needs therapy, that therapy is the best way to address their particular problem, or that I am the best fit for the family.

First Meeting

To help the reader experience a sample of a possible conversation between a collaborative therapist and Mary, I will present a made-up conversation. Please keep in mind that this is only one of the possible conversations that could have happened between Mary and me. I'll pretend that Mary said she wasn't sure if she would come to the session alone or if Johnny's father or all three of them would come. I am prepared to meet with whoever comes, and I trust that Mary and the family know what is best.

Mary arrives to the session alone. After greeting her and having a short conversation to help us feel comfortable in this first encounter, I might tell her: "In our phone conversation you were worried about a number of issues and did not know which was the best way to begin to talk about them, and then you decided to come to this first session alone. Do you mind telling me how you made that decision?"

Mary: "After our conversation, I decided there were some ideas I had to clarify for myself before inviting Fred and Johnny, who were not very eager or happy to come here. I thought it would be easier to come by myself."

I might ask her: "What do you think will be important for me to know regarding your family in order to be able to help you think about your situation?" (As a collaborative therapist, I see myself as a visitor in my client's life; the client is the one who decides what is important for him or her to share in the session. At the same time, the client is a guest in my office, and my responsibility as a therapist is to create a space where the client feels safe and free to talk about what it is important for him or her. I see my work as a professional who creates the kind of conversations and relationships that invite all the participants, clients and therapist, to access their creativity and develop possibilities where none seem to exist before.) Mary said she had specific questions regarding therapy and how helpful therapy could be in a situation like the one in her house. She was worried about Johnny, and she shared those worries with her mother, who agreed with her. On the other hand, she did not think her husband was as worried about Johnny as she was, and she had been experiencing severe headaches. She wanted to sort out by herself the best option before she invited her husband to join in. She did not know what to do about Johnny and was not sure he would agree to come. At this point in the conversation, I did not know where Mary wanted to go or how she wanted to use the time. We had been talking about three topics, and I asked her: "So far, we have been talking about your worries regarding Johnny, your roles and differences as parents, and your headaches. Which one of these subjects would you like to continue to address?" (Following a collaborative philosophical stance, I do not know what is important for the client to talk about, and I ask them to make sure we are using the session the way the client wants to use it and we are talking about the issues that are important for the client.) Mary tells me that she is confused, that she thinks the three issues are related to each other, and that she does not know how to proceed; she is very worried about Johnny, but she also feels stuck in her conversations with Fred regarding their ideas about the best way to parent Johnny now that he is a teenager. She is not sure if Johnny has a problem or if the problem is related to the difference they are encountering; some days she believes Johnny will get into a lot of trouble, and other days she thinks that she might be exaggerating and the only thing they need to do as parents is to be firm and set limits, but she is not sure how to do it. She thinks Fred might be too strict, and she is afraid he might hurt Johnny's feelings.

I found Mary's description of the situation somewhat confusing; I was interested in knowing some more about Fred's and Johnny's positions regarding the situation, and I asked her about that. Mary said she thinks Fred might say she is exaggerating when she says there is nothing wrong with Johnny—"he is just being a typical teenager who needs limits, and we as parents are having a hard time and are afraid to set limits on him." She goes on to say: "He would say that we do not need to be wasting our time in therapy talking about something that is very simple to solve by just punishing the boy and that he will learn right from wrong if there are consequences to his behavior. He might also add that I am making everything complicated by my fears of losing Johnny and the fights that are happening between us because we cannot agree."

"Mary, when you listen to yourself talk from Fred's perspective, what do you hear?"

"I hear that he has some clarity I do not have, and I hate to acknowledge it, but on the other hand, I am afraid that by punishing Johnny he will resent us and move away from us, or that he might become even more rebellious...so Fred could be right and have good intentions in the way he would like to parent Johnny, but I am afraid and do not know what is the best thing to do in a situation like this." At this point, I am curious to know more about the relationship and the interactions between Mary and Fred when they try to discipline Johnny. The curiosity comes from Mary's description and questions about what to do, and I ask her: "What do you tell Fred?"

"I usually try to stop him from setting limits because I am afraid he will be too harsh on Johnny."

"What happens to Fred when you stop him?"

"He gets very angry at me; we end up arguing and fighting instead of being able to talk about our differences."

"And Johnny?"

"Johnny goes to his room or leaves the house; he hates to see us fighting. I am thinking that it might be a good idea to invite Fred to join me in a conversation here with you; you might help us have a different kind of conversation. This could be more useful to us than bringing Johnny to therapy." During the conversation, Mary thinks about the kind of conversation that could be more useful for her in the situation, and together we can look at the next possible step.

I ask her, "What makes you think that inviting Fred to the conversation can be useful?"

"The kinds of questions you have asked me today have helped me think about the differences between us—my confusion and his clarity. I realize we have only been arguing about our differences and not discussing them; maybe that is what we need to do."

"Do you think you can have that conversation at home?"

"I am not sure. I am afraid that I will go back to blame him for being too harsh."

"Do you think he will accept the invitation to come to a therapy session? How would you invite him?"

"Fred knows I came today to see you. He did not want to come but he had no problem with me coming. I can talk with him about what happened in the session and tell him I thought it would be a good idea to come together. I really think it would be important for us to talk about our different styles."

"So, the next step would be to invite Fred."

"Yes."

Opening possibilities: This pretend session and dialogue helps me illustrate one of the possible conversations Mary and I could have, given the number of issues she was interested in talking about. From a collaborative perspective, I try to be respectful of the topics the clients choose and at the same time allow space for my questions as a way to express my curiosities—this helps me learn more about the client and his or her situation and at the same time may help the client listen to his or her own story in a different way. In this particular situation, the conversation helped Mary look at Fred's parenting style from a different perspective. This new understanding could create the possibilities for a different kind of conversation between them. The conversation itself evolved to the idea of inviting Fred.

Harlene Anderson's Reflections

"How can our practices have relevance for people's everyday lives in our fast-changing world, what is this relevance, and who determines it?" is a persistent question for me in my work with clients, whether in a therapy room, classroom, or boardroom. My response to this question has evolved over the years through a reflexive process of theory and practice. My current work, referred to as collaborative practice, is one among similar therapy approaches referred to as conversational, dialogue, open dialogue, reflecting, and postmodern therapies—all largely based on the ideas of philosophers such as Bakhtin and Wittgenstein about language and dialogue.

Distinctive to collaborative practice is the philosophical stance and its principles, which serve as action-orienting sensitivities (Anderson, 2011) for the therapist. This suggests that collaborative practice is not an approach populated by techniques and strategies but is informed by a way of being with another. As Lynn Hoffman and John Shotter suggest, it is a withness rather than an aboutness approach to practice.

Sylvia's hypothetical and pretend phone call and first session illustrate one way that a collaborative therapist prepares and meets with clients in a manner characterized by a natural and spontaneous way of responding in the moment rather than being guided by, for instance, formulaic prestructured steps and questions. Preparing and meeting refers to being poised to respond in the moment. Her responses stay respectfully close to the mother's utterances, eliciting and honoring the mother's expertise on her situation and its unique needs. Sylvia connects and constructs with the mother through engagement with her in a collaborative relationship and dialogic conversation, referring to the metaphorical space and the polyphonic process in which transformation is generated. In other words, transformation occurs in the dynamics of the relationship and the conversation. The direction of the conversations, and the newness in meanings, understandings, and actions that come to be, cannot be predetermined ahead of time.

References

Anderson, H. (1997). *Conversation, language and possibilities: A postmodern approach to psychotherapy*. New York, NY: Basic Books.

Anderson, H. (2011). *The philosophical stance: The heart and spirit of collaborative practice*. Plenary paper presented at the World Psychotherapy Congress, August 26, 2011, Sydney, Australia.

Additional Resources

Anderson, Harlene. Personal website. http://www.harleneanderson.org

Anderson, H., & Gehart, D. (2007). *Collaborative therapy: Relationships and conversations that make a difference.* New York, NY: Routledge.

Anderson, H., & Goolishian, H. A. (1988). Human systems as linguistic systems. Preliminary and evolving ideas about the implications for clinical theory. *Family Process,* 27(4): 371–393.

Houston Galveston Institute. http://www.talkhgi.org

International Certificate in Collaborative Practices. http://www.collaborativecertificate.org

International Journal of Collaborative Practices. http://www.collaborative-practices.com

41

A SEA OF IDEAS ON THE REFLECTING PROCESS

Reflective Techniques in Community Engagement: A Collaborative Recovery Model

Susan E. Swim, Angela Priest, and Tomomi Mikawa

This brief chapter focuses on the use of the reflecting team at Now I See a Person Institute. Angela, Tomomi, and Susan thought it would be appropriate for us to present our chapter by reflecting on our thoughts. Angela took the first step. Susan's reflections are next, followed by Tomomi's. We see reflections as the focal point of all collaborative conversations and meaningful change. Our work may include the formal process of reflections or the sea of meaning that occurs in reflective dialogue.

Angela's Reflections

In my experience, the reflecting team is an opportunity to open up the dialogue among various members of a system. This includes a reflection upon both the inner and outer dialogues that we all engage in as human beings (Andersen, 1995). We use these dialogues to create meaning in our interactions and relationships with others. The reflecting team approach uses these premises to provide space for inner and outer dialogues to be reflected upon and reworked as well as the cocreation of new meanings and new interpretations in novel ways. Because it is a nonconfrontational method of presenting new options, clients are given the opportunity to reflect and respond to different ideas without feeling an obligation to take them on as solutions (Friedman, 1997). They have the ability to take it or leave it without feeling pressured to conform to cultural norms or the goals of the therapist; because ideas are presented in an indirect fashion, clients are freed to respond in a manner that is appropriate for their family without feeling that they are in conflict with the therapist's thoughts or ideas. In many ways, the reflecting team appears to equalize the therapeutic relationship; tentative contemplation of the dialogue and ideas are presented with reservation, rather than as statements.

In my work, the reflecting team may take many forms, from a formal configuration of a group of therapists listening to the clients' therapeutic dialogue and the clients listening to the therapists' dialogue during appointed times in session to a less formal configuration in which I may utilize the clients themselves as the reflecting team, asking various people to reflect on what others have said throughout the therapeutic dialogue (Andersen, 1991; Friedman, 1997). Regardless of which approach is used, I find that the most important element is that there are distinct opportunities within the session for listening and reflecting upon the spoken words and that the reflective, nonauthoritative stance is maintained throughout (Friedman, 1997). As a therapist, my role is to witness the clients' journey and provide the opportunity for them to engage in the cocreation of change; my role is not to force my interpretations upon them.

Angela's Thoughts on the Case

In the case of Mary, Fred, Johnny, and Bess, ideally, I would like to invite all four family members (parents, child, and grandmother) to be involved in the therapeutic dialogue. Prior to beginning therapy, I might ask the family who else they've spoken with regularly about the problem and invite those people; they, too, are part of creating meaning around the problem. Since the problem appears to be centered around school behaviors, I might also invite Johnny's teachers or school administrators to be part of the dialogue. All of these people may be involved in speaking about the problem and through their dialogue developing and maintaining the problem. To deconstruct this problem dialogue, I might find it beneficial to have all members of the dialogue present so that they can each be involved, creating and witnessing the change through reinterpretation. In this way, all members of the dialogue buy in to the change process, becoming invested in the outcome, and in so doing support long-term change.

During the first session, I might ask questions related to each person's interpretation of the problem, allowing the space for each person to add or reflect upon the thoughts and interpretations of the others involved. I might ask questions of each member of the system, things like, "Do you think Johnny might be doing or saying this because . . . or do you think it might be something else?" I might speculate about the interpretations of each individual and the collective system, tentatively posing questions related to the meanings behind the words. I might use words such as, "Do you think . . . " or "I wonder . . . " or "I don't know, but . . . "; in my opinion, words such as these maintain my nonauthoritative stance within the room and support a reciprocation of reflective dialogue from clients, allowing them to engage in a re-creation of meaning by opening possibilities for a new type of dialogue, which is the ultimate goal of the reflective approach.

Susan's Reflections

Nice ideas, Angela. When I think about the reflecting team, my thoughts draw upon the past and what is happening currently at Now I See a Person Institute.

At the institute, we use the reflecting team often as a teaching opportunity as well as to provide clinical proficiency. Since the early 1980s, I was fortunate to learn from Tom Andersen as he fine-tuned the reflecting process. At first we were in a room and the lights were turned out so the clients could not see us but we could see them. Then one or two brave souls would leave our safe sanctuary to offer reflections based on what the team talked about behind the one-way mirror throughout the session. Then Tom would take these ideas and tentatively offer them to the clients. I always wished to be the clever student and then faculty member, for it was hard for me to grasp the sacredness of this process of reflections (Andersen, 2001a, 2001b; Gergen, 2001; Swim, St. George, & Wulff, 2001).

Then the lights came on for the clients and the therapist team to look and see each other. The security of our small room rose to bright lights, and the clients saw us speaking. As the rooms with the clients and the therapists became transparent to each other's voices, with the team and the family/couple clients being able to see each other and the dialogues ensuing, there was more openness among the team players and less of the prejudice that Tom often alluded to. Then, as the reflecting progressed, as do all clinical/theoretical venues, much to my anxiety, we were in the room with the clients with our reflections. We no longer were separated from the clients. It was here that I learned not to be clever; it was here that I learned to honor the voices and reflect on the immediate discourse devoid of the prejudices of prior theories, personal experience, clinical assessment, or what I felt was right or wrong for the client; and it was here that I learned to embrace the reflecting team when seeing and hearing clients, trainees and interns, graduate students, and organizational development (Swim, 1995).

Angela, just writing this brings such a rush of emotions. I feel so fortunate to be able to carry on this process with you and our students. Now I See a Person Institute reflects the works of Tom Andersen and Harry Goolishian as well as a host of others. We use what we call at the institute community engagement: a collaborative recovery model. In our recovery model of community-based work, we work within the entire client system. It is a reflective venue where the clients are the expert in their treatment and are aides in directing the course of therapeutic change. The therapist's position is to reflect the clients' dialogue back to them in a different enough manner that new possibilities arise. In this manner, the dialogue evolves in a way that is not too unusual for the clients to hear. During the reflection, the therapist alters the discussion through slight changes (similar to the differences between waves on the sea), and, through these slight changes, the clients are able to steer a new course.

In our experience, any participation with clients must derive from authentic collaboration. In all our work, we embrace the idea that severe mental illness and addictions are often symptoms that make a person be seen as deficit. Often, all that is seen are symptoms and not the person, the context, nor the relationships—or potential relationships—in the community. We think that most of the people we work with have the possibility of recovering their own agency, deciding for themselves the best "solutions of their own situation," and empowering themselves to design their possibilities to live in a better way. Therapist, psychiatrist, social workers, client, and community support are all team players on the client's team. Our clients see themselves as the directors of their services, for if services are not self-tailored to the needs of the individual in community, then these plans are for services that only serve ourselves! Clients wish and need to be in charge of their treatment and lives; we wish to create an environment where no one feels judged but, rather, are allowed a conversational space where the client leads the team to what is important to talk about. Clients need the freedom to express their thoughts in a manner that respects and hears their ideas for change. We talk in the clients' language. We work with severe and chronic mental health illnesses in this manner on the premise that no one wishes to be talked to, but rather talked with. These ideas reflect the works of the Houston Galveston Institute; Kanankil Institute; Now I See a Person Institute; Miller, Duncan, and Hubble (1997); Jaakoo Seikkula in Finland; the Rhizome Way of Christopher Kinman; and Lynn Hoffman. In our research on community engagement and the reflecting process, we have found that 80% found successful change.

How do we do this? We work through relationships and reflections. As Tom's ideas and the ideas of those mentioned earlier have changed through the course of our lives, so has our participation in the reflecting process at our institute. One thing that has never changed is the reverence that we must embrace when working in this manner. We talk about the immediate discourse that all members are invested in. Because we work with such large numbers at one time, we have a sea of conversations that ebb and flow in the most amazing of directions and create such novel and proficient self-tailored possibilities and solutions.

Tomomi's Reflections

Compared to other models of family therapy, reflective techniques may appear harder to explain in words, and those who are new to this method may find it a bit difficult to fully grasp its concepts. However, not having a structured treatment manual gives therapists freedom to engage in dialogical conversations spontaneously, let clients self-tailor their own treatment plan, and accompany them on their journey to healing and recovery in their own environment. We recommend that adequate hands-on training and experience be gained in mastering this model of family therapy.

References

Anderson, H. (2001). Ethics and uncertainty: Brief unfinished thoughts. *Journal of Systemic Therapies, 20*(4), 3–6.

Andersen, T. (1991). *The reflecting team: Dialogues and dialogues about the dialogues.* New York, NY: Norton.

Andersen, T. (1995). Reflecting processes: Acts of informing and forming. In S. Friedman (Ed.), *The reflecting team in action: Collaborative practice in family therapy* (pp. 11–37). New York, NY: Guilford Press.

Andersen, T. (2001). Ethics before ontology: A few words. *Journal of Systemic Therapies, 20*(4), 11–13.

Friedman, S. (1997). *The reflecting team in action.* New York, NY: Guilford Press.

Gergen, K. (2001). Relational process for ethical outcomes. *Journal of Systemic Therapies, 20*(4), 7–10.

Miller, S. D., Duncan, B. L., & Hubble, M. A. (1997). *Escape from Babel.* New York, NY: W. W. Norton.

Swim, S. (1995). Reflective and collaborative voices in the school. In S. Friedman (Ed.), *The reflecting team in action: Collaborative practice in family therapy* (pp. 100–118). New York, NY: Guilford Press.

Swim, S., St. George, S. A., & Wulff, D. P. (2001). Process ethics: A collaborative partnership. *Journal of Systemic Therapies, 20*(4), 14–24.

Additional Resources

Anderson, H., & Swim, S. (1995). Supervision as collaborative conversation: Connecting the voices of supervisor and supervisee. *Journal of Systemic Therapies, 14*(2), 1–13.

Paré, D., & Larner, G. (Eds.). (2004). *Collaborative practice in psychology and therapy.* New York, NY: Haworth Press.

Shilts, L., Rudes, J., & Madigan, S. (1993). The use of a solution-focused interview with a reflecting team format: Evolving thoughts from clinical practice. *Journal of Systemic Therapies, 12*(1), 1–10.

Taos Institute. (2011). *Manuscripts for downloading.* Retrieved from http://www.taosinstitute.net/manuscripts-for-downloading

42

PRACTITIONER'S PERSPECTIVE

HGI and Beyond

Sue Levin and Sylvia London

The use of the term *collaboration* is widespread in the world today. There are fields of collaborative law, medicine, therapy, research, leadership, and others. In the non-profit and funding world, *collaboration* has become a buzzword for finding ways to work together to reduce costs and eliminate duplication of services. It has been a surprise to find how popular this term has become and how differently it is being used. At Houston Galveston Institute (HGI) we think of collaboration as a post-modern, philosophical stance that guides the processes we use in therapy, in train-ing (as in collaborative learning communities), in administration and management, and in consultation and research.

In our experience, community collaborations refer to the joining of organiza-tions or individuals who have a mutual interest or service for a particular purpose. The group or individual who initiates the process sets or directs the structure for the process and outlines the roles each partner will play. When HGI approaches collaborative projects, we invite people to help construct the structure, roles, and expected outcomes. Peter Block's book *Community* (2008) discusses community work using similar values and processes as we do at HGI. Our philosophical stance that values collaboration and the inclusion of all participants' voices takes time at the beginning of the relationship to set goals and working styles. This sometimes leads to frustration from those who expect more direction and focus. They view the initial process as wasting time and lacking direction. They have entered the process with different expectations; therefore, it is vital for us to distinguish our way of collaborating from others.

In spite of the initial confusion and occasional withdrawal from participation by some people, these collaborations (meetings/projects) have been highly valued and successful. They have resulted in long-term relationships between HGI and many community partners and requests for HGI to lead initiatives in various are-nas including disaster mental health, work in schools, leadership, and child abuse prevention and intervention.

Like many who do supervision and training from a postmodern perspective, HGI views the trainee as the expert on his or her experience as a learner. HGI honors the learner's perspective by having him or her take the lead in supervision—and the supervisor, as a life-long learner, joins to explore the questions, challenges, and issues that are brought to supervision. This framework creates interesting challenges as training occurs in a context that includes the following: legal and licensing requirements, university policies and procedures, and the organization and all of its routines, paperwork, and reporting requirements. All options are not available for our trainees. HGI trainees, just like our clinical staff, operate in a dual reality, one that is highly collaborative and postmodern and the other that is legalistic, hierarchical, linear, and modernist. Learning to manage this dualism is one of the opportunities of being at HGI.

Conversations and relationships have been at the heart of collaborative practices, and there has been a long history of traveling and presenting the ideas in different parts of the world. Harry Goolishian and Harlene Anderson pioneered these efforts and engaged others and shared collaborative practices worldwide at conferences and institutes and by hosting visiting colleagues through study programs and conferences organized by HGI. These traveling conversations and relationships generate new ideas and new practices and nourish the ongoing evolution of our work. Following the death of Harry in 1991, Harlene continued the International Summer Institute (ISI) in Houston. ISI then expanded in collaboration with Grupo Campos Elíseos, to be held in different parts of Mexico, most recently in Playa del Carmen.

ISI is an international bilingual multicultural learning community that has served as an important platform to exchange ideas and foster international collaborations regarding collaborative practices in different cultures and settings. Many participants return year after year to reconnect to a special spirit of connection that is created in these meetings based on these values and practices. A recent ISI attracted approximately 100 participants. In our conversations at ISI, we became aware of the need to have a space online to share the projects that were being developed in different countries and institutes around the world. This led to the creation of the *International Journal of Collaborative Practices,* a free bilingual online journal (www.collaborative-practices.com) where collaborative practitioners can publish their work.

During the last year, HGI, with the support of the Taos Institute (TI), has developed the International Certificate in Collaborative Practices (ICCP; see www.collaborativecertificate.org) This project invites institutes and other academic institutions around the world that have a long history of relationship with collaborative practices to offer certificate programs. The project is a response to the demand of students and teachers to have a network of collegial supports and available resources to help them teach collaborative practices in a way that is congruent with the philosophical stance and at the same time attentive to the needs of each institute and culture.

As we speak we have certificate programs in these locations: Mexico City, Mexico (Grupo Campos Elíseos); Merida, Mexico (Instituto Kanankil); Bogota, Colombia (Sistemas Humanos); São Paulo, Brazil (Interfaci); Brno, Czech Republic (Narrativ); Texas, United States (HGI); and California, United States (Now I See a Person). Each institute offers a training program that suits its individual needs within an overall framework that fits the requirements of HGI and TI.

The practice of collaborative therapy is becoming widespread and familiar around the world. As these ideas spread and collaboration becomes part of common language, its meaning expands and transforms. This creates the possibility of new applications and practices as well as a wider definition of what collaboration is. The network of collaborative practitioners grows as interest in these practices grows. This web of relationships allows us to continue on the path of life-long learning and the generation of new and meaningful ways to continue working with people in therapeutic ways.

43

COMPARE AND CONTRAST

Collaborative Approaches

Anne Rambo, Charles West, AnnaLynn Schooley, and Tommie V. Boyd

At the authors' request, we refer to collaborative approaches, not models. At first glance, these approaches may seem to have much in common with other groups of models heavily influenced by social constructionist theory, specifically the brief therapy (IID) and the narrative (IIE) models. But it is instructive to consider what collaborative practitioners do *not* do. Collaborative therapy is at heart a philosophical position, rather than a set of techniques or a model (Anderson, 2011); it reflects a particular stance toward the client. This open, not-knowing stance precludes attempts to direct the conversation in a particular, predetermined manner, whether that be in the direction of exceptions (SFBT, see Chapter 30) or a particular story about the client's life (narrative, see Chapter 35). Collaborative therapists do not attempt to bring about change in any area, so our triad of change in thinking/feeling/doing—the common factors of effective therapy—will not work here. The collaborative therapist focuses on being with a client, on relationship. The influence of the work of Carl Rogers is evident, as well as that of social constructionism (Anderson, 2011). Collaborative therapists would also resist thinking of their work in terms of the common factors of conceptualizing systemically, intervening in pattern, and expanding the therapeutic system (Sprenkle, Davis & Lebow, 2009). While one could conjecture how the experience of feeling completely heard and understood might reverberate in terms of systemic change, to discuss this approach in those terms would be presumptuous of us, as these are not terms they would accept.

The focus on relationship can at times strike a chord with other therapists influenced by psychoanalytic ideas (see Flaskas, Chapter 8). However, collaborative family therapy itself is not psychoanalytic. The influence of social constructionism makes collaborative approaches somewhat similar to brief therapy (IID) and narrative (IIE) approaches, but again one must note that collaborative therapists are far less directive and willing to intervene than other approaches (Anderson,

2011). Differences between these approaches and more directive models such as structural and strategic should be obvious.

Research on efficacy has tended to be anecdotal or qualitative (Anderson, 2011); quantitative research comparing outcomes would not fit with the stance of these approaches. While collaborative models have been an influence on the field as a whole, they are more influential in Europe, as these approaches are difficult to reconcile with the United States' imperatives of measurable goals, brought about by managed care. However, there has been much interest within the United States in collaborative approaches to organizational consulting, training, and coaching (see Chapter 42). The reflecting team approach has been used creatively in academic training programs for family therapists (Prest, Darden, & Keller, 1990). While it is often too expensive in agency settings, it has great application in training settings of all kinds, and, as Swim, Priest, and Mikawa's chapter for our book (Chapter 41) indicates, it can be successfully used in a private practice or clinic setting.

References

Anderson, H. (2011). *Postmodern social constructionist therapies.* Retrieved from www. harleneanderson.org/writings/postmoderntherapieschapter.html

Prest, L., Darden, E., & Keller, J. (1990). The "fly on the wall" reflecting team. *Journal of Marital and Family Therapy, 16*(3), 265–273.

Sprenkle, D., Davis, S., & Lebow, J. (2009). *Common factors in couple and family therapy: An overlooked foundation for effective practice.* New York, NY: Basic Books.

PART G
INTEGRATIVE MODELS

44

A BRIEF HISTORY OF INTEGRATIVE MODELS

Anne Rambo, Charles West, AnnaLynn Schooley, and Tommie V. Boyd

The integrative models discussed here, narrative solutions and internal family systems, came to prominence in the 1990s. They represent very different, yet equally thoughtful and creative, approaches to integrative practice. For this section, we will omit our usual historical introduction and compare/contrast sections. Instead, we recommend a review of the history and foundational concepts of the models these models integrate and the following reflections on the nature of integrative practice.

In a sense, all models are integrative—they all draw on what came before and evolve out of their practitioner's prior training and experience with clients. Nonetheless, once a particular model or approach is developed, the impression in the field has tended to be that being eclectic, going from one model to another randomly, is confusing to clients and may indicate a lack of knowledge or seriousness on the part of the therapist (Corey, 2009). Being integrative, however, is seen more positively—with integration, the therapist chooses related aspects of different models to combine into his or her own unique hybrid. When such an integration is both sufficiently distinctive and appealing to other practitioners, it then becomes a model of its own. This is true of the following two models: narrative solutions therapy, which integrates narrative therapy, SFBT, and MRI; and internal family systems, which integrates psychoanalytic ideas, structural ideas, intergenerational therapy, and narrative therapy. Integration can combine the most useful aspects of individual models into a synergistic new whole that offers more than the sum of its parts.

Reference

Corey, G. (2009). *The art of integrative counseling.* New York, NY: Brooks/Cole.

Additional Resources

Eron, J., & Lund, T. (1998). *Narrative solutions in brief therapy.* New York, NY: Guilford Press.

Lebow, J. (1987). Developing a personal integration in family therapy: Principles of model construction and practice. *Journal of Marital and Family Therapy, 13*(1), 1–14.

Schwartz, R. (1997). *Internal family systems therapy.* New York, NY: Guilford Press.

45

THE NARRATIVE SOLUTIONS APPROACH

Maelouise Tennant

Editors' Note: The narrative solutions approach integrates narrative therapy, SFBT, and MRI therapy.

The cornerstone of narrative solutions is that people have strong preferences for how they like to see themselves, how they like to act, and how they like to be seen by others (Eron & Lund, 2002). The approach uses the term *preferred view* to refer to this constellation of ideas about self. The narrative solutions approach stresses the importance of holding helpful conversations with clients. In order to do so, it is important to understand how problems are constructed.

Seven Assumptions of Problem Construction

According to narrative solutions, problem construction evolves from and is maintained by seven basic assumptions (Eron & Lund, 1996). The first assumption is that the way people feel and act in a situation depends on how they construe the situation (i.e., what meaning they assign to the situation). Second, a person's construction of an event or a situation, and consequently how the person feels and acts, depends on one's view of the other and one's view of the other's view of him/her. This includes a construction of the other person's motivations and intentions. Third, one of the key elements motivating behavior has to do with a person's preferred view. Fourth, people experience emotional distress when they behave, see themselves, and/or imagine that others see them in ways that are discrepant with preferred views. Troubled relationships revolve around *disjunctions,* or gaps, between how people would like to be viewed and how they think significant others do view them. Fifth, problematic interactions often emerge as one or more people begin to see others seeing them in ways discrepant with how they prefer to be seen. This often happens at times of family transition, when views of self and others are changing, fluid, and unsettled. Sixth, as problem cycles evolve, views of self and others become more fixed and actions more restricted.

Repetitions of the cycle reinforce disjunctive attributions, escalate negative emotions, and promote more-of-the-same behavior. The seventh assumption is that as problematic interactions come to dominate family life, family members become more convinced that a problem really exists and locate its cause in perceived deficiencies of the self and others.

Basic Principles

Narrative solutions assumes that people can change, that they have the resources within themselves to alter their life circumstances and resolve problems. Therapy is more likely to help people change their behavior when the conversation focuses on clients strengths, not on what is wrong with them, and on what the clients would like for themselves. Mapping how people became fixed on problematic views of self and other leads to an understanding of how to affect change (Eron & Lund, 2002).

Narrative Solutions Approach Applied to the Common Case

Therapy using this approach does not require presession information. Since a narrative solutions therapist sees family distress as being fueled by one or more of its members experiencing a perceptual disjunction, learning the preferred views of Mary, Fred, and Johnny would be useful. Thus, it would be preferable to have them all attend the therapy sessions. Managing helpful conversations begins with the therapist maintaining a position of interest in the clients' preferences and hopes. At the same time, the therapist pays attention to life events or stories that reflect how each family member prefers to see himself/herself and prefers to be seen by significant others.

Assessment Using Narrative Solutions

The therapist's interpretation of preferred view is inferred from the answers a person gives to a host of *preference* questions. Such questions come from categories about how people feel about themselves when they behave in a particular way, or how they think the others involved feel about them, or by asking questions about how people view themselves in their various activities at home, school, or with friends. Keen attention is paid for evidence of not only the ways each prefers to see himself/herself or have others see him/her, but also for how the person sees his/her behavior as not consistent with his/her preferred view. For example, Johnny may be asked the following: When are you at your best—feeling your best—at home, school, with friends, and so forth? Who notices (e.g., family, friends, teachers)? What do they notice about you at these times? When you look into the future and are the person you would like to be, what do you envision? Johnny may also be asked how it is for him when his grades slip. How do his parents and teachers react? How does he imagine that they see him? How does he feel about that?

Narrative solutions views life transitions (e.g., the transition to teenage years) as being unsettling to people and that such events can awaken a search for new meaning as people reconsider how they see themselves and how other people see them. In this charged emotional climate, people may view their own behavior and/or imagine that others see them in ways that clash with their preferred views of self. For example, the therapist may explore with the family what life was like before the problem began. Was there a time in the preproblem past when Johnny liked school and saw himself as a competent, capable student? Was there a time when Johnny's parents also saw him that way? This process of identifying the transitional context surrounding the emergence of the problem has a motivational component. It injects hope, often helping family members see that the problem is not a permanent property of the person or the family. This process may also help mom identify the stressful underpinnings of her headaches (although this should in no way rule out the pursuit of further medical evaluation and intervention for these symptoms).

Assessment also includes looking for more-of-the-same problem cycles. The focus on these cycles is not just on behavior, but also on what people think about their problems. In Johnny's case, the therapeutic assessment could unearth that when his grades started to decline, his parents, teachers, and others (motivated by their own preferred views of themselves as helpful, knowledgeable, responsible, or so forth) began reminding him every day that he would never get into college or achieve anything worthwhile if he did not make good grades. Because of their reaction, Johnny could have begun to suspect that they saw him as a failure. As he began to doubt himself, Johnny might have sought out other students who were earning similar grades. The more time he spent with these underachievers and the more accepted he felt, the less Johnny was able to see himself as a competent person in the eyes of his parents and teachers. Repetitions of this cycle would reinforce negative attributions Johnny had of himself and would promote more of the same behavior. With the pattern becoming embedded, Johnny (along with his teachers and parents) might become more convinced that a problem actually exists and begin to locate its source in perceived deficiencies of himself. Johnny and others involved in the escalating cycle might begin to lose sight of his problem's evolution from a transitional life event and might not have any idea that they were constructing its shape and course.

Therapeutic Interventions in Narrative Solutions

Problems dissolve when family members see the event, the ideas, and the actions of others as consistent with their preferred ways of being and acting (Eron & Lund, 1993). This is accomplished by helping people clarify their preferred views of self and providing an atmosphere in which people experience the therapist seeing them in ways that align with their preferred view. When clients see their therapists seeing them in preferred ways, they are apt to speak more openly about their difficulties and feel invigorated to consider alternative solutions (Eron & Lund, 2002). Thus, the cycle of problem-maintaining behavior is interrupted and creative solutions emerge (Dagirmanjian, Eron, & Lund, 2007). Once this process is accomplished, a narrative solutions therapist would address any identified disjunctions by using a combination of reframing from the MRI model and restorying from narrative therapy (Dagirmanjian et al., 2007). Effective therapeutic conversations address meaning and action, and, by so doing, help resolve problems (Eron & Lund, 1996). With the case of Johnny, he may have recently accomplished several complicated tasks on his own initiative outside the classroom and grades environment. He may not have seen these actions as demonstrations of his competence. A narrative solutions therapist could easily reframe these actions as just that. Furthermore, Johnny's actions could be seen as an extension of all the things he did while successfully achieving good marks in previous years and thus similar to what he previously saw as acts of competence.

The therapist explores how people see the effects of their behavior on themselves and others (e.g., What happened when you did X or did not do Y? or How was that for you? A good thing? A bad thing?). These *effects* questions externalize the problem, separate the person from the problem, and allow room for discussion of the problem without the client feeling blamed, labeled, or judged. The therapist points out past and present stories that are in line with the client's preferences and contradict problem-maintaining behavior. Progress toward change occurs as the therapist focuses the discussion on what the future will look like when the problem is resolved. For example, Mary could be asked: When Johnny is doing well in school again, and you no longer have frequent headaches, what will you be doing? How will that be?

A final therapeutic intervention involves conversations between the client and significant others (Dagirmanjian et al., 2007). With Johnny, once he becomes clearer about who he would like to be and how he would like to be seen by his parents and teachers, he may be encouraged to speak up about his preferences with those around him. Fred and Mary may also be encouraged to think of ways that might engage Johnny's preferred view of self and help him stay on course with living his preferred view. They may also be invited to consider how to get back to the relationship they once enjoyed before the problem began—to return to a less stressful, less headache-prone version of family life. These helpful conversations help to consolidate narrative solutions.

References

Dagirmanjian, S., Eron, J., & Lund, T. (2007). Narrative solutions: An integration of self and systems perspectives in motivating change. *Journal of Psychotherapy Integration,* 17(1), 70–92.

Eron, J. B., & Lund, T. W. (1993). How problems evolve and dissolve: Integrating narrative and strategic concepts. *Family Process, 32,* 291–309.

Eron, J. B., & Lund, T. W. (1996). *Narrative solutions in brief therapy.* New York, NY: Guilford Press.

Eron, J. B., & Lund, T. W. (2002). Narrative solutions: Toward understanding the art of helpful conversation. In J. D. Raskin & S. K. Bridges (Eds.), *Studies in meaning: Exploring constructivist psychology* (pp. 63–97). Memphis, TN: Pace University Press.

Additional Resource

Eron, J. B., & Lund, T. W. (1998). Narrative solutions in couple therapy. In F. M. Dattilio (Ed.), *Case studies in couple and family therapy* (pp. 371–400). New York, NY: Guilford Press.

46

INTERNAL FAMILY SYSTEMS

Richard Schwartz

Internal family systems (IFS) is an integrative model developed out of client experience. In its emphasis on subsystems and their necessary hierarchy, it is influenced by structural family therapy. The calm and centered experience of leading from the self, which IFS promotes, is similar to the experience of differentiation in Bowenian family therapy. While not explicitly Ericksonian, there are hypnotic elements in the model's focus on mindfulness and shifts in conscious awareness. Like narrative therapy, the IFS model considers multiple realities and alternative narratives about the self. IFS is a profoundly strength-based model in that the assumption is made that every person, no matter how disturbed, has access to an inner self that is both calm and confident. While these are all influences, the model's biggest influence has been what clients themselves tell us about their lived experience. The author's knowledge of meditation and spiritual practices has also been important. The process of IFS is a growth enhancing one, for the therapist as well as for the client.

IFS was originally developed when the author was working with a population of at-risk youth, many of whom had absent or unavailable families. Unlike many other family systems models, IFS can be applied with individuals, with the focus being on the internal relationships within the client's mental system. It is equally applicable to couples and families.

About the Case

Given the case presented, the IFS therapist would begin by seeing Johnny individually. Johnny would be encouraged to talk about the situation as he sees it, with the therapist listening closely. As Johnny talks, it is likely he will make a comment that opens the door for a discussion of other parts. For example, Johnny might say, "I know I should go to school, but I really don't want to." This would allow the therapist to follow up by asking, "What part of you thinks you should go to school? And what part of you doesn't want to?" Should Johnny refer to parts of himself as *sides* or *voices* or in some other way, his language would be used by the therapist. Gently, the therapist would begin to introduce the idea of multiple voices within Johnny's mind. The therapist would expect to find four types of voices: the authentic voice of the self; the voice of a manager, controlling and often critical, charged with keeping unwanted emotions buried; the voice of exiled parts of Johnny's experiences, strong feelings from experiences Johnny prefers not to remember; and the voice of the firefighter, a part of Johnny's mind that swings into action when he is flooded with intense feelings from exiled experiences. The firefighter emerges when the exiled experiences flood Johnny with strong feelings. The firefighter then attempts to distract with strong stimulation and protect through anger, until the strong feelings subside. This internal turmoil is exacerbated in those who have experienced extreme stress and trauma. IFS takes a step beyond just accepting parts and actually helps them heal by having clients interact lovingly with the exiles and hearing their stories of pain and shame, which then frees the protectors from their roles. A visualization exercise might be used, for example, asking Johnny to climb onto a mountaintop with his self, and view the manager, exile, and firefighter parts of himself from that mountaintop perspective, as they reside down in the valley. Over time, the goal would be for Johnny to be able to spend more time with his self in a leadership position: to appreciate the contributions of the manager but not be led by it; to view the exile feelings and experiences with compassion, as from a distance; and to rely less on the firefighter.

Before seeing Mary and Fred, the therapist would ask Johnny for his permission. The IFS therapist would not see Mary and Fred unless it was acceptable to Johnny. Assuming that it was, the IFS therapist would then ask both Mary and Fred what parts of themselves typically respond to Johnny and would guide them toward calmer, less emotionally reactive interactions with him. In this process, the therapist might find himself triggered by some aspect of the clients' responses— for example, an angry diatribe from Mary, or a sudden change of topic from Fred. The practice of IFS therapy also requires the therapist to be constantly aware of his or her own reactions and processing them from the perspective of the therapist's self. Thus, difficult clients can be a growth experience for the therapist.

Marital sessions with Fred and Mary would also center around their ability to heal their own inner parts and thus respond to one another with less defensiveness and more open understanding. This process, once begun in the family, has ripple effects on parent-child and couple relationships alike. While this case does not involve young children, it is worth noting that even very young children can participate in IFS therapy through the medium of play therapy (Krause, 2011).

Once you are attuned with your client, sessions begin to flow, and there's an almost effortless quality to the work, as if something magical were unfolding, almost by itself. Often, as an experienced IFS therapist, when I reach this point, I don't even think about what I am going to say—the right words just come out as if something were speaking through me. Afterwards, I am full of energy, as if I'd been meditating for an hour rather than doing hard, demanding clinical work. In a sense, of course, I've been in a state of meditation—a state of deep mindfulness, centered awareness, and inner calm. And even after all these years, I still have the sense of being witness to something awe-inspiring, as if the client and I were connected to something beyond us, much bigger than we are.

Training and Research

IFS training is available through www.selfleadership.org. Interested therapists may become certified as certified internal family systems practitioners or therapists. An internal family systems scale has been developed, and research is ongoing. At present, the evidence for the model's efficacy is anecdotal, but the new scale is part of a planned long-term research project to develop evidence-based outcomes research on the model.

Reference

Krause, P. (2011). *Child counseling with internal family systems therapy*. Retrieved from http://www.selfleadership.org

Additional Resources

Earley, J. (2009). *Self-therapy: A step-by-step guide to creating wholeness and healing your inner child using IFS, a new cutting edge therapy.* Minneapolis, MN: Mill City Press.
Goulding, R. A., & Schwartz, R. (2002). *The mosaic mind: Empowering the tormented selves of child abuse survivors.* Oak Park, CA: Trailheads Publications.
Schwartz, R. (1995). *Internal family systems therapy.* New York, NY: Guilford Press.
Schwartz, R. (2008). *You are the one you've been waiting for: Bringing courageous love to intimate relationships.* Chicago, IL: Center for Self Leadership.

PART H

PSYCHOEDUCATIONAL FAMILY THERAPY

47

A BRIEF HISTORY OF PSYCHOEDUCATIONAL FAMILY THERAPY

Anne Rambo, Charles West, AnnaLynn Schooley, and Tommie V. Boyd

The provision of information to families is not in and of itself systemic or relational and need not be the province of family therapists. Yet as it is family therapists who most often have direct contact with family members of those suffering from addictions or major mental health diagnoses, family therapists are often asked to convey information from other professionals to the family and are often asked by the family to give them information about how the system works or what their options are. Family therapists in schools have a similar experience.

The history of psychoeducation is beyond the scope of this book, as it predates family therapy and indeed all forms of psychotherapy. Therefore, we will omit our usual historical introduction. Comparison and contrast between psychoeducational and other models would not be useful either, as in most cases psychoeducational work will be an addition, not a substitution. Psychoeducation can be used along with whatever other type of family therapy the practitioner may be providing. How information is offered to the family will differ depending on the orientation of the therapist. A structural therapist may want to empower parents to become experts themselves on options within the school system, rather than providing information in a way that displaces the parent as the expert. A narrative therapist may offer information about the same options with an emphasis on parental rights and privileged versus subjugated voices within the system. For all family therapists, the issue of how and when to provide information, and what type of information to provide, is a delicate one, and one that directly relates to larger social justice issues.

Resources

Anderson, C., Reiss, D., & Hogarty, G. (1986). *Schizophrenia and the family.* New York, NY: Guilford Press.

Levant, R. (Ed.). (1986). *Psychoeducational approaches to family therapy and counseling.* New York, NY: Springer.

McGoldrick, M., & Hardy, K. V. (2008). *Re-visioning family therapy: Race, culture, and gender in clinical practice* (2nd ed.). New York, NY: Guilford Press.

Metcalf, L. (2003). *Teaching towards solutions: Improving student behavior, grades, parental support, and staff morale.* New York, NY: Springer.

48

PSYCHOEDUCATION IN FAMILY THERAPY

Marlene F. Watson

Psychoeducation is at the heart of everything that I do when working with families. Since a major goal of mine is to empower the family through knowledge, psychoeducation is a natural part of what I do. In general, the purpose of psychoeducation is to help the family better understand and manage problems. Likewise, my aim is to enhance the family's understanding of the problem by helping the family think about the problem from multiple perspectives: individual, extended family, societal, sociocultural, and political. As well, I seek to increase the family's coping ability through identification of personal resources and support from the larger system. Toward this end, I pursue the family's religion/spirituality and connectedness to the wider system (including extended family and community) and make specific recommendations (e.g., groups, books, films, referrals, etc.). All in all, I am looking to uncover family strengths and to expand the family's range of possibilities.

The family genogram is a great psychoeducational tool. It helps put things into perspective while educating clients about their problems and learned ways of dealing with them. In addition, the family genogram helps normalize or destigmatize problems, which may help to lower defenses and/or remove barriers. Thus, a multicontextual genogram (McGoldrick, Carter, & Garcia-Preto, 2011) is critical in my work.

I fervently believe that individual, couple, and family development are influenced by the larger sociocultural context along with the political landscape of the time. Our past and present histories are comprised of a social hierarchy primarily based on race, gender, ethnicity, class, religion, ability, and sexual orientation. Accordingly, families may be faced with the same or similar issues, but their perceptions may vary on the basis of social location and power and privilege. Frequently, social location determines power and privilege, and power and privilege, in turn, determine access to resources. Because all human problems and solutions are constructed within the framework of the family's past, present tasks/challenges, and hopes for the future (McGoldrick, Carter, & Garcia-Preto, 2011), it behooves us as family therapists to not only understand the sociopolitical matrix that affects the family's functioning but also to educate the family about it. Like us, many of the families that we work with tend to be oblivious or blind to the sociocultural and political forces that construct our past, impinge on our present, and sometimes block our future. For example, the same-sex marriage debate is not so different from the interracial marriage debate of the not-so-distant past when we think about it from the perspective of discrimination, social hierarchy, and injustice. The subtext in the interracial marriage debate was imposed white racial superiority. In the current same-sex marriage debate, it is imposed heterosexual superiority. Unless educated, we may not connect the dots between the sociopolitical context and individual, couple, and family development.

Families must be positioned to be their own best advocates. Through education and awareness, we can help them to help themselves. I grew up hearing the saying, "If you give a man a fish, he'll eat for a day, but if you teach him how to fish, he'll eat for a lifetime." Hence I strive to educate families about the larger forces influencing their lives, often without their conscious awareness and critical appraisal. When families understand how as a whole and as individuals they are organized by the larger sociocultural environment and their specific history, it seems to free them to be more compassionate and forgiving. Sequentially, they seem better able to work toward the common good.

Given the hypothetical case, I would need additional information about race, ethnicity, sexual orientation, class, and religion/spirituality in order to effectively work with the family. I do not buy into the notion that all families are the same. Nor do I believe having evidence for a model means it will be unconditionally effective across all families and locations. Though it may be true that all families deal with life's universal struggles in some form or fashion, they do not all have the same support, resources, and protection when coming face to face with these struggles.

I would want to see Mary, Fred, Johnny, Mary's mother, and any other person(s) with a stake in the presenting problem, including siblings. Seeing all who have a stake in the presenting problem can spark strengths, wisdom, and support from the wider system.

Also, inclusion rather than exclusion of those with an interest in the presenting problem may help to prevent sabotage and/or premature termination. Moreover, an extended family member, such as a grandparent, may occupy an invisible seat of power in the family. Sibling relationships are paramount in families. However, scant attention has been given to them in the family therapy literature and in the broader field of mental health. Siblings often have a powerful influence on one another and may develop in opposition to each other or in likeness. Significantly, culture and gender dictate a lot of sibling expectations and behavior. Parental expectations and demands on children may be related to dreams, disappointments, sexism, and/or hopes for other siblings or even the parents' own siblings. Hence, we need to question parents about their expectations so no one child is unjustly burdened (whether intentionally or unintentionally) or totally responsible in a family (McGoldrick & Watson, 2011). Also, sibling relationships are particularly important in adolescence. Since adolescence is a crucial time for the development of self-identity, including racial, ethnic, gender, and sexual identity, adolescents are very vulnerable to societal devaluation. Sibling relationships therefore matter because they could either positively or negatively affect the adolescent's self-esteem. For instance, gay, lesbian, and bisexual adolescents may experience school bullying and social isolation in general that may be mediated by a supportive sibling network (McGoldrick & Watson, 2011).

I would begin my work with this family by focusing on these elements:

- What is the presenting problem and who is affected by it or who might contribute to an understanding of the problem and/or possible solution?
- Why now? Are there any specific events, losses, trauma, abuse, violence, learning challenges, changes (including health status), fears, and so on that could shed light on the presenting problem or why the family is seeking treatment now? Is the family being mandated to seek treatment due to truancy laws or other legal issues?
- What is the family's view of contextual variables (race, class, gender, ethnicity, sexual orientation, religion/spirituality, etc.), and how they might affect the problem, solution, and/or dreams of the future?

Since I believe in the importance of building community, I would endeavor to help the family (all those with a stake in the problem) to see the connection between all their concerns/views/solutions regardless of how divergent they may appear. Rather than reinforce the family's either/or split, I would attempt to educate the family about a both/and approach. In doing so, hopefully the family would discharge the emotional tension around right and wrong, freeing the family to consider the problem from all angles and to collectively reach a unified goal. I would not stop at the family system level, however.

As the therapist, I would aspire to educate the family toward understanding the connection that exists between what happens at the individual, family, community, and societal levels. As such, I would use the multicontextual genogram to generate the family's understanding of itself within its sociopolitical context and past history. In addition, special emphasis would be placed on the period of adolescence, including revisiting and rethinking learned ways of dealing with adolescent issues. Further, the family would be guided or coached toward understanding unique issues to adolescents of color, low-income adolescents, and/or to adolescent males or females. Films and/or books could be used to heighten the family's awareness and sensitivity to such issues. Exploration of educational and/or family policies that may be helpful to the family in dealing with the adolescent's educational needs would be encouraged. Connecting the family to teachers at the adolescent's school and/or helping the family to identify mentorship programs or religiously affiliated youth programs would be important along with strengthening the family's own natural resources.

At the end of the day, I see my therapeutic efforts as elucidating contextual variables and sociopolitical processes that affect families, validating connection, highlighting family and other social resources, promoting justice, and empowering families. Furthermore, I view my therapeutic efforts as leading families to more informed options, growth, and change.

References

McGoldrick, M., Carter, B., & Garcia-Preto, N. (2011). *The expanded family life cycle: Individual, family, and social perspectives* (4th ed.). Boston, MA: Allyn & Bacon.

McGoldrick, M., & Watson, M. F. (2011). Siblings and the life cycle. In M. McGoldrick, B. Carter, & N. Garcia-Preto (Eds.), *The expanded family life cycle: Individual, family, and social perspectives* (4th ed., pp. 149–162). Boston, MA: Allyn & Bacon.

Additional Resources

Adams, M., Blumenfeld, W. J., Castaneda, C., Hackman, H. W., Peters, M. L., & Zuniga, X. (2010). *Readings for diversity and social justice* (2nd ed.). New York, NY: Routledge.

McGoldrick, M. (2011). *The genogram journey: Reconnecting with your family.* New York, NY: W. W. Norton.

McGoldrick, M., & Hardy, K. V. (2008). *Re-visioning family therapy: Race, culture, and gender in clinical practice* (2nd ed). New York, NY: Guilford Press.

Rothenberg, P. S. (2011). *White privilege: Essential readings on the other side of racism* (4th ed.). New York, NY: Worth Publishers.

Section III

COUPLES THERAPY, SEPARATELY CONSIDERED

49

COUPLES VERSUS FAMILY THERAPY

Is There Such a Dichotomy?

Martha Gonzalez Marquez

As responsible and ethical practitioners and educators, it is important to keep abreast of the most current research and literature in the field. What we define as our field determines where we look for the latest information and will eventually shape what we know as couple and family therapists. Being wedded to only certain journals or books in our field may exclude valuable information from other sources. In our field, we have journals and books regarding couples therapy as a subset of family therapy and others that consider couples therapy as its own specialty. This chapter proposes that there exists an underlying tension regarding couples therapy and discusses whether or not it is a unique specialization. Some argue (Doherty, 2002; Jacobsen & Addis, 1993) that, indeed, working with couples inherently has specific idiosyncratic elements and dynamics that differ entirely from individual and family dynamics. It would then follow that supervisors should be specifically experienced in couples therapy in order to offer competent supervision to those conducting couples therapy (Doherty, 2002). Others consider that individual, couple, and family issues are inextricably linked and thus the same model of therapy should be applied in differing case situations, whether individual, couple, or family (Lindblad-Goldner, Igle, & Simms, 2011; Nelson & Thomas, 2007). In this chapter, both sides of this controversy will be presented.

Terminology

Although our field is known by the term "marriage and family therapy" as per licensure and our main organizations, it is important to note that many have opted to alter it to be "couples and family therapy" in part to reflect, acknowledge, and respect that many couples we work with are often not married at all. They may be in a premarital phase, they may be divorced, or they simply may be unable to wed legally due to the continued homophobia that exists in many states. Another rationale for adopting the term "couples and family therapy" is so that we include some of the models that are exclusively designed and developed for use with couples, aka intimate partners. These include emotionally focused couples therapy (EFCT), behavioral couples therapy, and the Gottman method (Chapters 51, 52, and 53). As noted earlier in this book, some models of family therapy work with larger systems such as organizations and with individuals, just as easily as with family systems (brief therapy, especially solution focused, Chapter 30; narrative therapy, Chapter 35; and collaborative therapy, Chapter 40). In view of this, some in the field eschew the couples and family designation altogether and refer to themselves as "systems therapists," referencing our origins as a field and including larger systems such as organizations as well as couples and families. For the purposes of this chapter, the author chose to utilize the term "systems therapist" to refer to those therapists who practice a systemic model that works with individuals, couples, and families, and "couples therapist" to refer to a therapist who practices a model specific to couples.

Working With Couples as an Extension of Other Systemic Models

In the systemic family therapy models considered earlier in this book (IIA–G), content is of less importance, and interactional process is the focus. Therapists focus on patterns developed between people. Many of these models include ample discussion about specific work with couples. But the focus on pattern and process remains the same.

Couples Therapy as a Unique Specialization

In recent years, we have seen the emergence of specific couple therapies. These models stress that factors in an intimate relationship, that is, between two individuals who are involved romantically, are qualitatively different than factors in a nonintimate relationship. Even much of the literature on the neuroscience of relationships supports the notion that our brains, and bodies, create and emit different neurotransmitters and hormones in intimate relationships. The argument has been made that parent–child relationships are also intimate; however, parent–child relationships do not typically deal with physical intimacy issues, nor with resolving power differentials between two equal adults. Couples therapists also note that couples therapy sessions may be particularly intense. A room with two adult intimate partners can spark heated conversations, especially when children, who are often somewhat shielded from that intensity, are excluded from the sessions. Many couples will lower their guard in a session with their therapist since children and outside distractions, which also serve to regulate the intensity, are not present. Add to that many times the strong pull from each partner to win over the therapist. Models that are used primarily with couples often deal directly with this intensity and with the regulation of emotions.

Content Versus Process Versus Processing Content

At the heart of the matter is whether our focus as therapists working with couples is processing the dynamics that have been created or processing the content. This is essentially what differentiates the systemic therapist from the nonsystemic therapist. When it comes to working with couples, as a systems therapist, the content is less relevant. We examine and learn the dynamics and intervene at the process level. Therefore, when a couple presents with issues such as coping with an extramarital affair, the systemic therapist focuses on the pattern, the intervention that disrupts the pattern, finding solutions, and so on.

On the other hand, as those who identify specifically as couples therapists see it, these distinct couples content issues are exactly what should be studied, taught, and learned about in order to competently help couples. Much has been written especially about distinct content issues such as surviving affairs, blended families, sex, separation, divorce, and more. In addition, specific assessments have been developed for use with couples, including both marital and premarital measures and scales.

Alternative Framework: What Fits Best for Each Therapist

The burgeoning research on common factors identifies common elements that contribute to the success of therapy (Sprenkle, Davis & Lebow, 2009). One finding from this research is that the therapist's own embracing, believing, and integrating of a chosen approach is supportive of positive outcome. Thus, perhaps we should support the notion that therapists evaluate what fits for them. We can thus legitimately extrapolate that whether therapists embrace the content or the process model, as long as they are trained and believe in what they do, they will have an equal chance of being helpful to couples.

The Current Culture of Couples Therapy

We should consider as well the political landscape and its impact on couples therapy. We cannot overlook the fact that much of couples therapy is cash paid. Since insurance companies still only cover couples therapy when one partner has DMS-IV TR symptoms and diagnosis, many couples don't meet the criteria, and many refuse to use insurance at all. Working with couples may actually thus become a trendy cash haven for those clinicians reluctant to deal with managed care; at the same time, couples therapy may be more free to develop apart from the constraints of managed care.

A Call for Training: Spending Our Energy Where It Counts

Given the cash nature of much marital counseling, and the lack of involvement of managed care, perhaps instead of arguing about process versus content, systems therapist and couples therapists alike should consider the question of credentialing. What about mental health practitioners who take workshops in a distinct couples model with no systemic training? Systemic training is not a prerequisite to becoming certified in any premarital or enrichment program. Practitioners may claim to have a specialty in couples' therapy after attending only a handful of workshops at most. One need not look far to see so-called relationship experts (an unregulated title) on talk shows, news interviews, and the like. A view into their training often reveals little more than a course or workshop in couples work, if anything at all. If we are to expend energy engaging in a debate about anything in reference to whether or not couples therapy is its own specialization, those energies could be much better spent identifying the needed training to call oneself qualified to work with couples. Perhaps our focus should shift to developing standards or protocols, much as has been done with family therapy. Many of us immersed in the practice of couples therapy have done more reparative work and damage repair with couples who have had negligent, even traumatic experiences with so-called couples therapists. This should alarm our ethical core and move us into action.

A Final Note

The models discussed in the preceding section of this book (Chapters 7–48) are all used with couples, as well as with individuals and families. The models now to be discussed (Chapters 50–55) are all designed specifically to be used with couples. The common case has been adapted in this section to reflect this reality.

References

Doherty, W. (2002, November/December). Bad couples therapy: Betting past the myth of therapist neutrality. *Psychotherapy Networker, 26*–33.

Jacobsen, N., & Addis, M. (1993). Research on couples and couple therapy: What do we know? Where are we going? *Journal of Clinical and Consulting Psychology, 61*(1), 85–93.

Lindblad-Goldberg, M., Igles, E., & Simms, S. (2011). Ecosystemic structural therapy with couples. In D. Carson & M. Casado-Kehoe (Eds.), *Case studies in couples therapy: Theory based approaches.* New York, NY: Routledge.

Nelson, T., & Thomas, F. (2007). *Handbook of solution-focused brief therapy: Clinical applications.* New York, NY: Haworth.

Sprenkle, D., Davis, S., & Lebow, J. (2009). *Common factors in couple and family therapy: An overlooked foundation for effective practice.* New York, NY: Basic Books.

Additional Resources

Carson, D., & Casado-Kehoe, M. (Eds.). (2011). *Case studies in couples therapy: Theory based approaches.* New York, NY: Routledge.

Gottman, J. (1999). *The marriage clinic: A scientifically based marital therapy.* New York, NY: W. W. Norton.

Gurman, A. (Ed.). (2008). *Clinical handbook of couple therapy* (4th ed.). New York, NY: Guilford Press.

50

EMOTIONALLY FOCUSED COUPLES THERAPY

Brent Bradley

"I've tried everything I can think of with this boy," Mary says with despair. "He needs more support. He needs teachers who understand him."

"He needs parents who will hold him accountable!" Fred says with emphasis.

"That's all I ever get from him," Mary says to the therapist. "It's always 'be more strict' or 'stop babying him.'"

Knowing this couple came in for couple therapy to "get back their intimacy," the therapist responds with empathy while keying in on the adult love relationship between Mary and Fred—which is the core focus for longstanding change in emotionally focused therapy (EFT). "You guys have really been going through it with your son. You care about him or you wouldn't be seeking help and working this hard on it. I bet it leaves you mentally and physically exhausted."

Both parents take deep sighs and nod their heads in agreement. The therapist continues, "But at the same time, I can't help but wonder what kind of havoc this has wreaked on your relationship—the one between you two—how you find each other, and how you help take care of each other. Can you begin to tell me where you two are as a couple?"

Early Session Goals: Genuine Empathy and Emotional Connection

From the onset of therapy, the EFT therapist reflects with intensive *empathy*. He invites in the desperation of the couple's situation, lets it resonate in his own body and seeks to connect with the couple *from* a genuine place *within himself* (Fosha, 2006; Siegel, 2010). Learning to be effective in this approach is less about the steps, stages, and interventions and more about learning to be emotionally open, vulnerable, and present—*as a therapist*—moment by moment with human beings in a powerfully experiential way (Bradley, 2011). The EFT therapist is trying to feel *in* herself what it must be like to be in the couple's situation right now within an attachment, love, and intimacy context (Lewis, Amini, & Lannon, 2000). It's much less about head knowledge and much more about heart knowledge.

The body is a powerful emotional indicator, with nerves throughout internal organs sending lightning-fast messages to our brains telling us what is important and what is needed—both in couple partners and therapists themselves (Siegel, 2010). The heart actually does ache, for example, and it sends that message to the brain. This low road of processing is not controlled by cognitions, which follow more slowly in different parts of the brain. We now know that these immediate bodily sensations affect and color the ensuing cognitions—they set the stage for our thoughts. These powerful and immediate bodily sensations most often occur outside of our awareness. Contemporary experiential therapy anchors itself in this prethought, out-of-awareness arena (Greenberg, 2010). The research is clear: high levels of primary emotional experiencing within a safe and caring in-session environment are what lead to lasting change in this approach (Johnson & Greenberg, 1988). Without this therapeutic emotional openness to oneself and couples throughout the therapy process, little else matters.

Mary and Fred describe how they have become sort of like enemies in dealing with their son's acting-out behavior. Fred thinks whatever he suggests is shot down or ignored altogether, while Mary thinks Fred sees her as a marshmallow melting atop a cup of hot cocoa, incapable of making informed and tough actions. The result is a pattern of Fred withdrawing from Mary—both as a father to his son and as a husband to her. Yes, he is there financially and carries out his home duties to her expectations, but when it comes to supporting her, hearing her fears and pains—he is AWOL. And yes, she is there as a mother to her son and wife to him in many ways, but hearing his sense of exclusion and inadequacy hidden under his gruff exterior is not on the menu.

While the therapist tracks and reflects the couple's negative behavioral pattern, she is in fact more curious about and interested in accessing the emotions underlying their arguments. As the couple explains their cycle, the therapist listens for the inevitable perturbations of primary, underlying emotions that bubble up and break through even the best of defenses (Greenberg, 2010). These primary emotions show themselves through watering in the eyes, breaks in voices, abrupt silences, and long looks down or away from the other's contact.

> M: He doesn't care about what I say or think concerning our son anymore. He just looks at me with contempt and thinks I am a big softie who is ruining our son. (The therapist notes that her voice cracks at the end and that she looks down.)
>
> T: Hmm. You said, "He looks at me with contempt" and your voice cracked, and you looked down...
>
> M: (Nods in agreement, still looking down.)
>
> T: And now your foot is wiggling quickly. What's going on inside of you right now as you hear yourself say this? You say, "He looks at me with contempt," and it sets off all of these reactions in you. What's happening inside?

(The therapist points out bodily reactions because these are so often tied to immediate emotional experiencing. By having clients pay attention to bodily reactions, they begin to become more aware of what their bodies are saying, rather than ignoring it.)

M: (Takes a deep breath.) I am just realizing how little he thinks of me as a person anymore.

T: (Allows silence.) Stay with it.... Let it happen.... Tell me more about this, please, when you are ready.

(The therapist uses himself to be present with the client and encourage her to stay connected to her emerging affect.)

M: (Softly.) He just thinks I am stupid. Naive. A pushover.

T: Hmm. Those are strong words. Do you feel those in your body right now?

M: Yes. My chest feels tight ... and it feels like there is something in my throat.

T: Right. Keep paying attention to these things. I wonder.... What is it like for you to believe that he sees you as stupid. Naive. A push over?

M: It's awful. (Silence.)

T: Yeah. I am trying to feel in myself how this must be for you. It feels heavy, you know? Kind of like, "I am trying so hard, and yet it means nothing to you." And he's your husband, the *last* person you want to hear this from. As I say this I myself begin to feel kind of... desperate... lonely too, maybe?

(The therapist uses himself to try to resonate with the client's emotional experience and reflect this in a tentative manner.)

M: I feel very lonely. (Tears.)

(Seven seconds of silence—the therapist allows respectful silence as the client integrates previously unacknowledged bodily felt sensations and emotions into awareness. As this "integration" occurs [Siegel, 2010], the therapist helps the client receive the meaning associated with it.)

M: All alone.

T: What's it like to share this in here with me, with your husband right here listening?

M: It's kind of scary, you know? I mean, I don't really talk like this with him.

T: Yeah, kind of scary. I bet it's kind of risky, too. (Fred nods yes.) I appreciate you sharing this with me in here. And I hear you that it's *really* scary to share this with him in here. He means a lot more to you than I do. You opened up, showed vulnerability. That's not easy. Shows me you care about this relationship.

Right From the Start: Working With Emotions Inside and In Between

A central aspect of working relationally is always being aware of how what you say to one partner is simultaneously having an impact on the other listening partner. In the segment here, the therapist intentionally highlights and validates the *risk* Mary took in being this *vulnerable* and followed with an attachment reframe ("Shows me you care about this *relationship*"). The idea is to give Fred every chance to be affected and moved by the emotions revealed. Intimacy-oriented emotions *pull* for comfort from a loved one. The therapist works to access and reflect primary emotion with Mary and now pivots *within that emotional atmosphere* to address Fred.

> T: Fred, Mary really risked being vulnerable just now. She opened up and took a real risk by sharing this with you in here. What was it like for you to hear how *lonely* she gets, and how *scary* it is for her to reveal that to you?
> (Once again, the therapist leads with Mary's vulnerable emotions and as-sociated fears, which invites Fred in to comfort her.)
>
> F: It's really new to me. I don't get this from her at home.
>
> T: She doesn't show this part of herself to you often? The part that feels alone and scared to open up to you?
>
> F: No, she doesn't. All I usually see is her ignoring me or acting as if I have nothing to offer.
>
> T: Right. So what's it like now for you inside as she risks opening up to you some, right here in this first session?
>
> F: It's different. (Five seconds of silence.) It really is a different side of her.
>
> T: How do you feel *toward* her now as you see this vulnerable part of her?
> (The therapist has a laser-like focus on *intimacy-related emotions* that have strong potential to pull the couple toward each other. She also tries to stay in the *present tense* of experiencing.)
>
> F: Well, I don't want her to feel alone. I don't want her to be afraid. I feel some of these same things.

This is a very good early indicator in EFT. Fred was indeed affected by Mary's more vulnerable emotions and was *moved* to clearly say that he didn't want her feeling alone and afraid. Furthermore, he revealed that he feels these emotions as well. This, in turn, should affect Mary. At this point, the therapist would similarly begin to walk with Fred by showing genuine empathy and accessing his underly-ing emotion around his attachment, love, and intimacy desires/goals with Mary. The couple is stuck in a pattern of behavior fueled by secondary, reactive emo-tions that squeeze out any chance of risking being vulnerable with each other. In fact, in many cases the cycle has *become their relationship*. The opposite of that cycle is already beginning to take place in the first session.

Summary

De-escalating the negative cycle is the goal of stage 1 of EFT. EFT is based on the belief that secure adult attachment, intimacy, and love are healthy and integral keys to holistic adult love relationships. This chapter pinpointed key therapeutic elements in a typical first session of EFT. Change in EFT comes through repeated deep and focused emotional experiencing in session, which typically begins in session 1. Therapists new to EFT may overemphasize teaching couples about attachment, or helping couples cognitively understand their cycle, or teaching couples about each partner's attachment style, and so on. Adult attachment theory is a base of EFT. It provides a map of what is important to specifically focus on with couples, and it provides answers to many developmental questions. But be it session number 1 or session number 10, high levels of primary emotional experiencing within a safe and empathic in-session environment are what lead to lasting change in this approach.

Moving Forward

EFT is one of only two couple therapies recognized as an empirically supported treatment (Lebow, Chambers, Christensen, & Johnson, 2011). There is ample literature available describing in detail the nine steps, three stages, and interventions of EFT, which are beyond the scope of this chapter. The following are references and resources recommended not only to learn EFT, but also to learn to effectively work with emotion and get updated on empirically supported couple therapy treatments.

References

Bradley, B. (2011). New insights into change in emotionally focused couple therapy. In J. Furrow, S., Johnson, & B. Bradley (Eds.), *The emotionally focused casebook* (pp. 59–83). New York, NY: Routledge.

Fosha, D. (2006). Quantum transformation in trauma and treatment: Traversing the crisis of healing change. *Journal of Clinical Psychology, 62*, 569–583.

Greenberg, L. S. (2010). *Emotion-focused therapy.* Washington, DC: American Psychological Association.

Johnson, S. M., & Greenberg, L. S. (1988). Relating process to outcome in marital therapy. *Journal of Marital and Family Therapy, 14,*175–183.

Lebow, J. L., Chambers, A. L., Christensen, A., & Johnson, S. M. (2012). Research on the treatment of couple distress. *Journal of Marital and Family Therapy, 38*(1), 145–168.

Lewis, T., Amini, F., & Lannon, R. (2000). *A general theory of love.* New York, NY: Random House.

Siegel, D. J. (2010). *Mindsight: The new science of personal transformation.* New York, NY: Bantam Books.

Additional Resource

Johnson, S. M. (2004). *The practice of emotionally focused couple therapy: Creating connection* (2nd ed.). New York, NY: Routledge.

51

COGNITIVE BEHAVIORAL COUPLES THERAPY

Charles West

This chapter will cover both traditional (first- and second-wave) cognitive behavioral couples therapy and introduce the newer third-wave approaches, which will be discussed in more detail in the Chapter 52. Please refer to sources cited at the end of this chapter for more information.

In this particular case, a therapist using cognitive behavioral couples therapy (CBCT) would work with Mary and Fred to turn their vague couple complaints (e.g., lack of intimacy) into specific, targetable behaviors, creating a pathway for change. In order to accomplish this, a CBCT therapist would conduct an assessment to include individual, family, and contextual factors, the couple's positive and negative exchanges, and any repeating behavioral patterns (such as demand/withdraw). The assessor would also look for broad themes (including "we have lost interest in each other," in this case) relevant to the couple's functioning. In addition, the CBCT therapist would evaluate if these patterns are affected by skills deficits, unsuccessful or maladaptive attempts to get personal needs met, failure to adapt to changes in the family life cycle, mounting environmental stress, the presence of psychopathology, reciprocally reinforcing response patterns, and other relevant factors (Baucom et al., 2008).

In Mary and Fred's case, this could include gathering relevant relationship history (such as looking for a time when things were better, assessing for relationship themes based on past relationships, and so on) that could provide context for current issues, including communication problems (e.g., do Mary and Fred lack communication skills, or are they not using skills they possess?). This history would be utilized to invite Mary and Fred to begin noticing the positives in their relationship. Additional concerns to be evaluated include, but are not limited to, the following: Does the couple need some parent education? What is the role of in-laws in their difficulties? What are Mary and Fred's attributions of each other's behavior? What standards and expectations do they hold of themselves and the other as mates and parents? What are common interaction patterns? (i.e., What happens next after Mary does this? What happens after that?) However, it is important to note that regardless of what contributed to this couple's difficulties, the primary focus of therapy is on how these difficulties are maintained behaviorally, cognitively, and emotionally (Baucom et al., 2008). An important premise of CBCT work is the idea that couple dysfunction is influenced by distorted or extreme cognitive appraisals, as well as unreasonable expectations of partners or of the relationship (Baucom et al., 2008).

The first session would primarily be an assessment session, so information-gathering questions would focus on what Fred and Mary view as the important issues of their relationship, as well as identifying common attributions and assessing common interaction patterns. Once the initial evaluation of Mary and Fred as individuals and as a couple was completed, the therapist would conduct a feedback session, outlining the therapist's formulation of the couple's difficulties. The therapist would work with Mary and Fred to establish agreed-upon treatment goals and methods. The CBCT approach assumes that changes in emotions and behavior follow changes in cognition, so an important therapy goal is to assist each partner to become more aware of thoughts as well as behaviors (Baucom et al., 2008). Another important goal is to decrease destructive interaction patterns and increase more positive interactions, increasing safety and motivation (Baucom et al., 2008).

Once Mary and Fred's general complaints have been become more specific (behaviorally, emotionally, cognitively, and pattern identified), specific methods can be utilized. Such methods often include in-session and between-session activities. Specific interventions might focus on behavior, such as assigning "caring days" or more specifically targeted behavior changes that address a couple's needs, or communication skills training to address a deficit in either skills or skill performance (Baucom et al., 2008). Other interventions might focus on cognitions, addressing attributions, standards, assumptions, and so on (Baucom et al., 2008). Therapy might also focus on emotions, primarily to increase expression of emotions or limit overexpression of negative emotions. In general, the therapist would take an active role in therapy, teaching, coaching, refereeing, and supporting the couple to reach the goals of therapy. This would include teaching communication skills, problem-solving skills, and increased insight into common interaction patterns (Epstein & Baucom, 2002). Thus, traditional (first- and second-wave) CBT couples therapy relies on both teaching new behaviors and increasing insight into cognitions, leading to change in cognitions as well.

Traditional behavioral couples therapy enjoys the highest level of demonstrated research effectiveness for the treatment of couples; it is the only marital therapy currently categorized as both "efficacious and specific" (Jacobsen, Christensen, Prince, Cordova, & Eldridge, 2000). However, leading cognitive behavioral researchers and clinicians themselves have sought in recent years to expand the ground of cognitive behavioral couples therapy by including not only change in behaviors and cognitions, but acceptance/reframing of existing behaviors as well (Jacobsen et al., 2000).

Hayes (2004) describes early behavior therapy as first-wave therapy focusing on specific symptom relief, skills training, and first-order change. Hayes then argues this first wave has been followed by a second wave, cognitive behavioral therapy, which added a focus on addressing and changing cognitions in a direct manner. More specifically, CBT has included the examination of core cognitive schema, the disputing of automatic thoughts, and the use of behavioral experiments. Hayes argues second-wave CBT generally has an "eliminative agenda," attempting to change or get rid of targeted negative thoughts and emotions. Finally, Hayes proposes there is now a third wave of behavioral and cognitive therapy, a wave that includes such models as acceptance and commitment therapy (ACT) and dialectical behavior therapy (DBT). What distinguishes third-wave CBT treatment models is a reduced emphasis on eliminating negative feelings and thoughts and an increased focus on awareness and acceptance of these thoughts and feelings. An integration between all three waves, integrative behavioral couples therapy, was proposed by the noted cognitive-behavioral clinician and researcher Neil Jacobsen shortly before his untimely death (Jacobsen et al., 2000). The third-wave option will be discussed in Chapter 52.

References

Baucom, D., Epstein, N., LaTaillade, J., & Kirby, J. (2008). Cognitive behavioral couple therapy. In A. Gurman (Ed.), *Clinical Handbook of Couple Therapy* (4th ed.) (pp. 31–72). New York, NY: Guilford Press.

Epstein, N., & Baucom, D. (2002). *Enhanced cognitive-behavioral therapy for couples: A contextual approach.* Washington, DC: American Psychological Association.

Hayes, S. C. (2004). Acceptance and commitment therapy, relational frame theory, and the third wave of behavior therapy." *Behavior Therapy 35,* 639–665.

Jacobsen, N., Christensen, A., Prince, S., Cordova, J., & Eldridge, K. (2000). Integrative behavioral couple therapy: An acceptance based, promising new treatment for couple discord. *Journal of Consulting and Clinical Psychology, 68* (2), 351–355.

Additional Resources

Datillo, F. (2010). *Cognitive-behavioral therapy with couples and families: A comprehensive guide for clinicians.* New York, NY: Guilford Press.

Dobson, K. (Ed.). (2010). *Handbook of cognitive-behavioral therapies* (3rd ed.). New York, NY: Guilford Press.

Harway, M. (Ed.). (2005). *Handbook of couples therapy.* Hoboken, NJ: Wiley and Sons.

Kirby, J., & Baucom, D. (2007). Treating emotional dysregulation in a couples context: A pilot study of a couples skills group intervention. *Journal of Marital and Family Therapy, 33*(3), 375–391.

52

BEHAVIORAL MARITAL THERAPY, THIRD WAVE

Charles West

As discussed in the Chapter 51, what distinguishes third-wave CBT treatment models is a reduced emphasis on eliminating negative feelings and thoughts and an increased focus on awareness and acceptance of these thoughts and feelings. This awareness and acceptance can lead to a state called mindfulness. Researchers like Barnes, Brown, Krusemark, Campbell, and Rogge (2007) have found that mindfulness may contribute to relationship satisfaction.

Bishop and colleagues (2004) defined mindfulness as "the direction of attention toward one's ongoing experience, in a manner that is characterized by openness and acceptance." Mindfulness may help individuals and couples better monitor and communicate about the emotional climate of their relationship to each other and themselves, be less likely to become overwhelmed by their own or their partner's emotions, decrease the likelihood they may engage in relationship-destructive strategies to avoid negative feelings, and invite them to be more comfortable with the ambiguity that inhabits our lives (Fruzzetti & Iverson, 2004; Barnes et al. 2007; Wilson and DuFrene, 2008).

Two of the most important third-wave CBT models are dialectical behavior therapy (DBT; Linehan, 1993a) and acceptance and commitment therapy (ACT, which is pronounced "act"; Hayes, Strosahl, & Wilson, 1999). At the heart of the DBT and ACT treatment models are arguably systemic principles. For example, DBT is based on a "dialectical world view," which includes the ideas of inter-relatedness and polarity followed by integration (Linehan, 1993a, p. 33). Linehan argued the tension between opposing forces in a system ("positive and negative, good and bad, children and parents, patient and therapist, person and environment, etc.") creates change. In addition to these principles, it is arguably systemic to believe that an invalidating environment feeds emotional dysregulation and, therefore, disconnection from one's self and others (Fruzzetti & Iverson, 2004; Kirby & Baucom, 2007).

One of the primary principles of ACT, functional contextualism, is also arguably systemic (Hayes, 2004; Hayes, Strosahl, & Wilson, 1999). Functional contextualism proposes that any psychological event (behavior, thinking, etc.) must be viewed as part of a "whole event" and has a function in a particular context. Hayes (2004) proposes that a therapist working with a client gains understanding of the function of an event by engaging in "an ever-widening examination of context.... What once was context becomes content, and more context needs to be sought."

A key concept common to both DBT and ACT is that of emotional dysregulation. When individuals experience high levels of negative arousal, their tendency is to become psychologically inflexible, fail to "accept, be aware of, tolerate an emotional experience" (Fruzzetti & Iverson, 2004), and begin to focus very narrowly on escaping physically, emotionally, cognitively, and/or relationally from the aversive state (Wilson & DuFrene, 2008). Once an individual's orientation is to escape, he or she is "out of control" or emotionally dysregulated (Fruzzetti, 2007). Fruzzetti (2007) proposes that couples attempting to escape aversive states may settle into some common conflict patterns: (1) mutual avoidance of conflict, where both partners sense conflict and seek to escape emotionally aversive states by avoiding each other or particular topics; in this pattern, conflict may be rare but so is connection; (2) destructive engagement, where there is significant conflict and emotional dysregulation; often both behave poorly, both have regrets, but both have little changes; and (3) an engage/distance pattern, when one partner typically tries to avoid conflict by leaving, but the other person pursues, both in an attempt to avoid an aversive negative state; in this pattern, negative emotions are often increased over time.

Working With Mary and Fred Within an Integrated Third-Wave CBT-Influenced Model

Much of what follows is an integrated model that borrows a great deal from both the ACT and DBT treatment models. One of the early goals of a third-wave CBT-informed couples therapy would be to assess Mary and Fred as a couple and as individuals, including a brief assessment of their families of origin and relationship history and a detailed assessment of their common, often entrenched conflict patterns (both emotional and behavioral) and the contexts that invite disconnection. These patterns of disconnection are both intrapersonal patterns (e.g., Mary experiences stress and anxiety, responds by overfunctioning, which leads to feelings of failure, followed by angry feelings directed at Fred, which leads to increased feelings of disconnection from her own needs and wishes, which leads to more stress...) and interpersonal patterns (e.g., Mary has headaches and feels depressed, son feels neglected and acts out, Mary overfunctions in an attempt to feel connected while Fred underfunctions to avoid anxiety, Mary and Fred argue and invalidate each other's thoughts and feelings, both become emotionally dysregulated and further disconnected, Mary calls mother to feel better but actually ends up feeling more depressed while Fred isolates himself, Mary has headaches and feels depressed, son feels neglected and acts out...).

In addition, the therapist would assess their vulnerability to negative emotions as individuals and as a couple, including their level of sensitivity to the behavior of others, level of reactiveness, and ability as individuals and as a couple to return to calmer emotional states quickly. Finally, the therapist working with Mary and Fred would assess how each may be contributing to an invalidating environment where one or both member's expression of personal thoughts and feelings is experienced as rejected, condemned, or wrong. Fruzzetti (2007) describes this as "soiling their nest." Similar to many systemic models (e.g., Minuchin, Nichols, & Lee, 2007), it is also important to challenge the idea that the problem is located inside an identified patient and to seek to validate the couple's thoughts, feelings, and responses.

If it became apparent that chronic or intense emotional dysregulation was common for either Fred or Mary (or both), it may be necessary to provide some individual sessions focusing on "emotion management" before working with Fred and Mary as a couple (Kirby & Baucom, 2007). Otherwise, therapy would primarily occur as a couple.

After a discussion of the assessment and agreed-upon goals derived from the assessment, the therapist would work with Mary and Fred to overtly establish their values and commitments—their chosen life directions lived out in the current moment (Wilson & Murrell, 2004). Wilson and Murrell (2004) propose the following question to help clarify values: "In a world where you could choose to have your life be about something, what would you choose?" which could be modified to the following question: "In a world where you could choose to have your marriage to be about something, what would you choose?" Wilson and Murrell (2004) also propose that these values tend to fall in 10 domains: family, couple/intimate relations, parenting, friendship, work, education, recreation, spirituality, citizenship, and physical self-care. Clarifying values can provide both direction and motivation for couples (Wilson & Murrell, 2004). In Mary and Fred's case, they have identified a value (intimacy) and a commitment (redeveloping their intimacy). When obstacles to living out chosen values present themselves (e.g., disagreements about parenting, disagreements about separateness and togetherness, and so forth), the values and commitments would be revisited.

Once some initial potential patterns and values have been identified (these typically evolve through the course of therapy), the next goal would be to increase each individual's self-control within the context of the relationship, which includes becoming more mindful of relational events and triggers, an increased ability to respond differently, practicing self- and other-validation, and becoming more mindful of positive emotions. Questions a third-wave CBT therapist might ask Mary and Fred may include, but are not limited to, the following: How does this depression and anxiety appear in your life? What purpose does this worry about your son serve? How is this overfunctioning and underfunctioning working for you? What is it like to be aware of this interactional pattern as it inhabits your relationship? What shows up for you as we talk about this pattern? Can you observe this emotion without getting into a struggle with it? Is it possible to have that thought, recognize it as a thought, and yet do something different?

As this therapeutic conversation progressed, it would be important to keep in mind the therapist's mindfulness as well. Hicks (2008) proposes that mindfulness is an important therapist skill, "a way of paying attention with empathy, presence, and deep listening that can be cultivated, sustained, and integrated into our work as therapists through the ongoing discipline of meditation practice . . . a shift from a 'doing mode' to a 'being mode.'"

In terms of working with clients, learning and practicing mindfulness skills are a first step to change. Asking Mary and Fred to commit to "stop making things worse" and commit to "being effective" has a foundation in their practicing awareness of their patterns, emotions, and thoughts and permits them to also practice "alternative reactions ahead of time until they become automatic" (Fruzzetti, 2006). This commitment includes thinking about the consequences of engaging in the old pattern, as well as how one's own behavior may be contributing to keeping a pattern intact (including how they may be contributing to an invalidating environment). This increased awareness of the steps in a pattern will hopefully lead to a decrease of the power of the pattern to overtake a relationship. For example, understanding how Mary's overfunctioning usually invites depression in herself and anxiety in Fred can allow the couple to notice the pattern and mindfully choose different, nondestructive practiced responses (e.g., relax and soothe yourself by focusing on breathing or sense of smell, vision, hearing, taste, touch; engage in self-validation; engage in self-distracting pleasurable activities such as paying attention to someone else, engaging in chores and tasks, creating a distraction plan, etc.; notice that a thought is just a thought and not automatically the truth; pay attention to how you are feeling without judgment of yourself or the other; look at one's own contribution to the pattern; recount valued commitments; accept things as they are, not as you want them to be; and so on; Beckerman and Sarracco, 2011; Fruzzetti, 2006; McKay, Wood, & Brantley, 2007). Fred and Mary may also benefit from some skills training in how to exit and reenter conflicts and effective relationship repair.

Another goal might be to help Mary and Fred recognize when either partner may be heading toward or already experiencing emotional dysregulation by (1) identification of triggers to common patterns that invite automatic responses and (2) taking steps toward "being 'together'" when they are with each other (Fruzzetti, 2006). Some couples become accustomed and comfortable with disconnection from themselves and each other, and that disconnection may invite Mary and Fred to be unaware of how their responses influence their interactions. Working with Mary and Fred to be more intentional in their responses may help them to enhance and maintain a more positive emotional connection with themselves and each other. This skills training would likely include practicing describing events, rather than judging these events (Fruzzetti, 2006; Linehan, 1993b). Describing events helps a couple to distinguish their "thinking selves" from their "feeling selves," work toward "wise mind" where logic and emotion are both present and balanced, and derail rising reactiveness and behavioral inflexibility (Fruzzetti, 2006).

Learning to describe may also increase awareness of when one is making "right or wrong" judgments about events that are more accurately categorized as unwanted (Fruzzetti, 2006). Individuals are constantly making judgments about others and themselves; it is something we do whether we wish to or not. As such, the goal of this increased awareness would not be to help Mary and Fred to become nonjudgmental (a goal like this would likely increase self-judgment), but rather to increase their awareness of these judgments so that they can practice viewing judgments as only judgments, not necessarily the truth, and therefore be less likely to engage in destructive self-righteousness, and so on. Other things Mary and Fred might do to "be together" are the following (Fruzzetti, 2006): (1) find a comfortable, dedicated place to spend time each day to "think about your partner mindfully, think about how important he or she is to you," a place to "recharge"; (2) help each to focus more on the things that are most important to them; (3) working on being "actively together" by working to "appreciate and enjoy each other's company" and engaging in mutually enjoyable activities; and (4) working to be together in the present moment, even in the face of conflict, "thinking about and experiencing yourself as partners, as part of a partnership, a team, not as opponents or adversaries."

In addition, the therapist may work with Mary and Fred on developing or reviving communication skills. An example of this might be some in-session "talking stick" exercises with Mary and Fred to slow down the interaction process and allow them to practice mindful responding and validation—acceptance and acknowledgement of their own and the other person's experience—as well as provide opportunities to revisit values and commitments. As a caveat, Fruzzetti (2006) proposed that judgments individuals or couples make about "themselves or others, or any behavior that degrades someone or treats someone as incompetent or unworthy" should not be validated.

The following references and resources are provided for someone interested in learning more about common third-wave CBT treatment models.

References

Barnes, S., Brown, K., Krusemark, E., Campbell, W., & Rogge, R. (2007). The role of mindfulness in romantic relationship satisfaction and responses to relationship stress. *Journal of Marital and Family Therapy, 33*(4), 482–500.

Beckerman, N., & Sarracco, M. (2011). Enhancing emotionally focused couple therapy through the practice of mindfulness: A case analysis. *Journal of Family Psychotherapy, 22*, 1–15.

Bishop, S., Lau, M., Shapiro, S., Carlson, L., Anderson, N., Carmody, J., ... Devins, G. (2004). Mindfulness: A proposed operational definition. *Clinical Psychology: Science and Practice, 11*, 230–242.

Fruzzetti, A. (2007). *The high-conflict couple: A dialectical behavior therapy guide to finding peace, intimacy, and validation.* Oakland, CA: New Harbinger Publications.

Fruzzetti, A., & Iverson, K. (2004). Mindfulness, acceptance, validation, and "individual" psychopathology in couples. In S. Hayes, V. Follette, & M. Linehan (Eds.), *Mindfulness and acceptance: Expanding the cognitive-behavioral tradition* (pp. 168–191). New York, NY: Guilford Press.

Hayes, S. (2004). Acceptance and commitment therapy and the new behavior therapies: Mindfulness, acceptance, and relationship. In S. Hayes, V. Follette, & M. Linehan (Eds.), *Mindfulness and acceptance: Expanding the cognitive-behavioral tradition.* New York, NY: Guilford Press.

Hayes, S., Strosahl, K., & Wilson, K. (1999). *Acceptance and commitment therapy: An experiential approach to behavior change.* New York, NY: Guilford Press.

Hicks, S. (2008). Cultivating therapeutic relationships: The role of mindfulness. In S. Hicks & T. Bien (Eds.), *Mindfulness and the therapeutic relationship.* New York, NY: Guilford Press.

Kirby, J., & Baucom, D. (2007). Treating emotional dysregulation in a couples context: A pilot study of a couples skills group intervention. *Journal of Marital and Family Therapy, 33*(3), 375–391.

Linehan, M. (1993a). *Cognitive-behavioral treatment of borderline personality disorder.* New York, NY: Guilford Press.

Linehan, M. (1993b). *Skills training manual for treating borderline personality disorder.* New York, NY: Guilford Press.

McKay, M., Wood, J., & Brantley, J. (2007). *The dialectical behavior therapy skills workbook: Practicing DBT exercises for learning mindfulness, interpersonal effectiveness, emotional regulation, and distress tolerance.* Oakland, CA: New Harbinger Publications.

Minuchin, S., Nichols, M., & Lee, W. (2007). *Assessing families and couples: From symptom to system.* Boston, MA: Pearson Education.

Wilson, K., & DuFrene, T. (2008). *Mindfulness for two: An acceptance and commitment approach to mindfulness in psychotherapy.* Oakland, CA: New Harbinger Publications.

Wilson, K., & Murrell, A. (2004). Values work in acceptance and commitment therapy: Setting a course for behavioral treatment. In S. Hayes, V. Follette, & M. Linehan (Eds.), *Mindfulness and acceptance: Expanding the cognitive-behavioral tradition.* New York, NY: Guilford Press.

Additional Resources

Hayes, S., Follette, V., & Linehan, M. (Eds.). (2004). *Mindfulness and acceptance: Expanding the cognitive-behavioral tradition.* New York, NY: Guilford Press.

Hayes, S., & Smith, S. (2005). *Get out of your mind and into your life: The new acceptance and commitment therapy.* Oakland, CA: New Harbinger Publications.

Hayes, S., & Strosahl, K. (Eds.). (2004). *A practical guide to acceptance and commitment therapy.* New York, NY: Springer Science + Business Media.

53

GOTTMAN COUPLES THERAPY

Virginia Boney

I would not need any additional information before considering taking on the case; however, I would want to have the couple complete a number of questionnaires as a part of the assessment process. The assessment process for couples counseling from a Gottman perspective consists of four sessions: an initial conjoint session, an individual session with each spouse, and a feedback session. It is important to be able to meet with each spouse individually to assess whether or not they have different commitments to therapy or different hopes/expectations for therapy. Another purpose for meeting with spouses individually is to assess the presence of violence, the existence of an ongoing extramarital relationship, spouses' personal goals, and possible individual psychopathology. Therapy is contraindicated if there is either an ongoing extramarital affair or violence.

At the first session, I would ask the following questions:

1. Tell me the story of what brings to you to therapy at this time.
2. What would you like to see happen in your relationship?
3. What issues would you like to deal with?

During the assessment phase of therapy, goals include assessing and understanding the concerns and emotions that the couple expresses, along with building a therapeutic alliance with the couple. Following the assessment sessions, the three goals for therapy are the following:

1. creating constructive ways of managing conflict that build intimacy and understanding from the conflict;
2. enhancing the couple's friendship, intimacy, and positive affect;
3. building and maintaining a system of shared meaning for the couple.

Facilitating change for this couple would focus primarily on (1) creating constructive ways to manage conflict and (2) enhancing the couple's friendship, intimacy, and positive affect.

From a Gottman perspective, parenting and in-law issues would be conceptualized as perpetual issues as opposed to resolvable issues. Therapy would focus on educating this couple in regard to the differences between resolvable and perpetual issues (i.e., not all conflict is the same). Change would be facilitated for this couple by focusing on the following in sessions:

- assist each spouse in understanding the other's point of view;
- eliminate the Four Horsemen (criticism, defensiveness, contempt, and stonewalling) and replace them with their antidotes to decrease escalation during arguments;
- move from gridlock to dialogue about the issue;
- develop six skills to constructively manage conflict:
  - ○ soften startup (bring up an issue as a complaint instead of a criticism);
  - ○ accept influence from your spouse;
  - ○ make effective repairs during conflict;
  - ○ de-escalate arguments;
  - ○ compromise;
  - ○ do physiological soothing of self and partner.
- process fights and "regrettable" incidents.

The loss of interest in each other that this couple identifies and their desire to redevelop intimacy are strongly related from a Gottman perspective. Maintaining a strong friendship with your spouse creates a sense of trust and emotional intimacy in a relationship, according to Gottman's research. As a result, a couple experiences their marriage as romantic and passionate, and their physical intimacy flourishes. Facilitating change for this couple in regard to their loss of interest in one another and loss of intimacy would focus on strengthening their friendship with one another with an emphasis on the following:

- building love maps
  - ○ This relates to how well a couple know one another and are interested in regularly updating their knowledge of their partner's inner psychological world (e.g., worries, joys, dreams, fears) and external world (e.g., stressors, responsibilities, people in their life). The primary means to strengthen love maps is by asking open-ended questions.
- building a culture of fondness and admiration
  - ○ This is a measure of how much affection and respect are present in a couple's relationship. The primary means to build fondness and admiration is by expressing respect and appreciation to one's partner through words, behavior, and physical touch.
- building their emotional bank accounts

o   Each individual's emotional bank accounts represent how connected they feel to their partner. Building emotional bank accounts refers to how well a couple uses small moments of everyday life to turn toward, turn away, or turn against a bid their partner makes for connection. A bid is a gesture (verbal or nonverbal) for some sort of positive connection. To strengthen turning toward, partners need to be aware of the other's bids to connect and turn toward them.

Couples find the feedback session, during which I discuss briefly the seven levels of Gottman's sound relationship house (SRH), to be extremely useful in understanding from a theoretical research-based perspective why they are so stuck in their relationship. Couples often feel a little overwhelmed by the amount of information that I am providing them with in the feedback session—Gottman's SRH theory and research, in addition to feedback regarding my assessment of their relationship strengths and vulnerabilities. As a result, I give couples a handout at the end of the first session to provide them with a brief description of the levels of Gottman's sound relationship house that I discussed in the feedback session, as it is a lot of information to absorb in one session. I do not give them a hard copy of my assessment, as I am not comfortable giving distressed couples information that could be used to harm the relationship further. I encourage couples to begin reading the texts listed on the handout to better understand Gottman's theory and research in more depth so that they can begin to understand what needs to change in their relationship and how to begin to implement change.

Resources

Gottman, J. (1999). *The marriage clinic: A scientifically based marital therapy.* New York, NY: W. W. Norton.

Gottman, J. (2002). *The relationship cure: A five step guide to strengthening your marriage, family, and friendships.* New York, NY: The Three Rivers Press

Gottman, J., & Gottman, J. (2008). *Level I: Bridging the couple chasm* [Seminar on DVD]. Seattle, WA: Three Rivers Press.

Gottman, J., & Silver, N. (2000). *The seven principles for making marriage work.* New York, NY: Three Rivers Press.

Schwartz Gottman, J. (Ed.). (2004). *The marriage clinic casebook.* New York, NY: W. W. Norton.

54

PRAGMATIC/EXPERIENTIAL THERAPY FOR COUPLES

Brent J. Atkinson

"Things changed almost immediately once Johnny came along," Fred explained. "Nothing I did was good enough. According to her, I was selfish and thought only about myself. At first I thought that maybe she was right, so I really tried to devote more attention to her. I called her during the day to say hi, and I got babysitters so we could have dates, but it wasn't enough. After a while, it became clear to me that I would never meet the mark with her."

Mary painted a different picture. "I can tell when a person's heart isn't into something," she said. "He isn't into our relationship, and I don't think he ever really was. He can get enthusiastic about all kinds of other things—his work, the kids, even our friends—but not with me."

In my initial sessions with them, it was clear that Mary and Fred each believed that the other was mostly to blame for the distance that had crept into their relationship. Fred believed that Mary was a negative, controlling person who was emotionally immature; Mary believed that Fred was self-centered and emotionally stunted. Like most people, Fred and Mary had no idea that their internal beliefs could paralyze their relationship, but the evidence is clear: beliefs that fuel feelings of contempt are highly toxic to relationships. Contempt arises when one believes him- or herself to be on a higher plane of maturity than one's partner. It is the single most potent predictor of negative relationship outcomes that has been identified to date. When contempt takes a foothold, relationships rarely survive. Studies suggest that even the most well-intentioned person cannot swim upstream against the current of his or her partner's contempt for long.

Fred came upon contempt innocently enough. His belief about Mary's relative culpability and his relative innocence was not a vicious maneuver intended to injure Mary. It was his best attempt to make sense of what had gone wrong. He had no idea that in adopting this belief, he had wandered into extremely dangerous territory. I knew that if Fred wanted Mary to treat him differently, he would need to find another way to make sense of what had happened in their relationship—one that didn't place Mary in the role of the villain. In my initial interviews with them, I found ample evidence suggesting that Mary wasn't the villain any more than Fred was. Both of them had habits that studies have been shown to be damaging to relationships.

Phase I: Getting Off the High Horse/Assuming Personal Responsibility

I began by simply letting Fred know about studies that have verified the destructive power of beliefs such as the one that he held about Mary. I summarized, "Of all the things that researchers found to be damaging to relationships, the mistaken belief that one's partner is 'the main problem' ranks near the top of the list. In most situations where one or both partners believe this, researchers have found that it isn't true. Usually, both partners have habits that are just as detrimental to their relationship. Misplaced overall blame is the first thing I look for when I begin working with a couple. It's clear that both you and Mary believe that the other person is the main problem. I believe that you are both biased, and this bias is no small thing. Beliefs about one's own relative innocence and one's partner's relative culpability, whether spoken out loud or silently held, paralyze relationships and prevent partners from letting down their guard with each other. I know that if I can't help each of you develop a more balanced understanding of your relative contributions to the depleted condition of your relationship, we'll probably be wasting our time."

These were strong words for Fred, and I'm sure that he would not have been able to receive them from me had he not sensed that I liked him, understood him, was not judging him, and wanted nothing more than for him to have his heart's desire. Fred was keenly aware of Mary's bad habits but relatively blind to his own. He listened intently as I cited examples of his problematic habits and contrasted them with those of people who know how to get their partners to treat them well. Fred was not aware that he had habits that were highly predictive of poor relationship outcomes. He had operated on the assumption that the person who commits the first offense in any given situation is the most culpable party. To him, Mary's criticism seemed to come out of the blue and was almost always unwarranted. I told Fred about evidence from relationship studies suggesting that sooner or later, all people in long-term intimate relationships do things that are unhealthy for their relationships, whether intentionally or not. I explained, "The question is not *if* your partner is going to engage in unhealthy relationship conduct, the question is *when* it is going to happen. Studies suggest that if you want to be treated well by your partner, you must have the ability to react effectively when your partner says or does things that are unhealthy. The ability to respond effectively is *not optional*. It's a requirement for anyone who hopes to have a partner who treats him or her well over the long haul."

I had a similar conversation with Mary, challenging her belief that the main problem was Fred's selfishness and helping her understand the harmfulness of some of her own habits. As I had with Fred, I assured Mary that I wasn't telling her what to believe—I was just giving her information that I believed could be important for her to have, and I would respect her need to decide for herself if the information applied to her (in pragmatic/experiential therapy [PET-C], the therapist proposes goals but is careful to avoid imposing them).

The first phase of PET-C always involves a concerted attempt to help partners come down off their high horses. As each partner gains a better understanding of how his or her own habits have contributed to the depleted condition of the relationship, the therapist helps each accept mutual responsibility while in the presence of the other. Old wounds are healed as the therapist helps partners avoid blame and defensiveness while engaging in conversations about past hurts.

Phase II: Developing New Habits for the Respectful Negotiation of Differences

In the second phase of therapy with Mary and Fred, attention shifted from the past to the present. I assisted Fred in developing internal habits that enabled him to avoid hitting the panic button when Mary became critical, dismissive, closed-minded, or inflexible, and I helped Mary develop the ability to check her tendency to blindly accept the validity of her knee-jerk interpretations of Fred's actions. The process for developing new habits of thinking and reacting during emotionally charged situations is no different than the process required for acquiring any habit that is too complex to be consciously implemented in a linear fashion (such as the development of complex musical or athletic skills). Practice must be focused, repetitive, and intense. The person practicing must be well motivated to practice and clear about the specific internal and external processes that need to be practiced, and the practice must be state specific (i.e., new processes must be practiced when the client is in the emotional state that typically becomes active when upsets occur). Using a variety of practice methods, Fred developed the ability to remind himself that it was natural for Mary to favor her own opinions and preferences. Instead of making a big deal of it, he learned how to simply stand up for himself without a lot of fanfare and without thinking badly of Mary for her temporary inflexibility. Using the same methods, I helped Mary develop the ability to ask Fred to care about her wants and needs without punishing him emotionally when he seemed more occupied with his own.

Phase III: Increasing Emotional Connection

As Mary and Fred progressed through the second phase of therapy, each felt more respected by the other and less need to insulate him- or herself emotionally. In the final phase of therapy, I helped Fred and Mary deepen feelings of love, tenderness, and the desire for connection. Many years ago, each partner had given up on the idea of having the kind of companionship that he or she had originally wanted. I helped rekindle dormant desires in each of them, and they began devoting considerable effort to trying to meet each other's wants and needs. These efforts were important, but Mary and Fred needed more than well-intentioned efforts from each other. Each partner needed to experience genuine warmth, tenderness, fondness, affection, and sexual interest emanating from his or her mate. Each needed to know that the other was enjoying his or her company, that the other was having fun when they were together, and that the other missed him or her when they were apart. In the last phase of therapy, the focus alternated between (1) an exploration of things that each of them could do to spark feelings of love and desire in the other and (2) an exploration of ways that each partner could increase his or her own capacity to get into the mood for connection. Mary and Fred both wanted to be the sort of individuals who experience loving and desirous feelings freely and abundantly. In the final weeks of therapy, they discovered ways to consciously open their hearts to each other, allowing feelings of warmth, tenderness, affection, playfulness, sexual interest, and the desire for loving connection to emerge.

Summary

Throughout therapy, each partner was helped to realize that his or her own internal abilities and interpersonal habits significantly constrained or enhanced the degree of satisfying connection that he or she could make with his or her partner. Early in therapy, Fred and Mary each made a conscious decision to adopt the following philosophy: "If I want the love and respect of my partner, I need to develop the habits that are shared by almost all people who know how to get their partners to treat them well—and I certainly want to avoid habits that characterize people who almost always end up feeling unloved and disrespected." As a therapist, my experience is that if even one partner develops the full range of abilities needed to form a secure partnership, the other will usually follow, and a secure emotional bond will develop.

Resources

Atkinson, B. (2005). *Emotional intelligence in couples therapy: Advances from neurobiology and the science of intimate relationships.* New York, NY: W. W. Norton.

Atkinson, B. (2011a). *Developing habits for relationship success.* (Version 4.1). Geneva, IL: Couples Research Institute.

Atkinson, B. (2011b). Supplementing couples therapy with methods for rewiring emotional habits. *Family Therapy Magazine, 10*(3), 28–32.

Atkinson, B. (2010a). Rewiring emotional habits: The pragmatic/experiential method. In A. Gurman (Ed.), *Clinical casebook of couple therapy* (pp. 181–207). New York, NY: Guilford Press.

Atkinson, B. (2010b). Interview with Brent Atkinson on the brain and intimacy. In A. J. Carlson & L. Sperry (Eds.), *Recovering intimacy in love relationships: A clinician's guide* (pp. 233–247). New York, NY: Routledge.

Additional articles and resources related to pragmatic/experiential therapy for couples can be found at www.thecouplesclinic.com.

55

BRIEF SEX THERAPY

Douglas Flemons and Shelley Green

Most clients come to us with the expectation, or at least the hope, that we will be able to help them contain or cure a problem that they locate inside of themselves or someone else. We respect our clients and work hard to develop an empathic understanding of their experiential world; however, we never accept such a request at face value. Problems, from our perspective, are best conceived not as things that reside inside of people but, rather, as patterns of relationship, unfolding through time.[1] Such relationships are comprised of interweaving strands of both intrapersonal experience (thoughts, sensations, emotions, behaviors, images, perceptions) *and* interpersonal experience (verbal and nonverbal communications within a couple, a family, an extended family, a group, and so on).[2]

If problems were things, they could be isolated and tossed away like so much garbage. But because problems are relationships that weave through the experience of those contending with them, then no such isolation is possible. Relationships are always connections, so any effort to purposefully separate from a problem will only serve to create yet another connection to it. We see this often in our sex therapy work when couples come in, struggling with the aftereffects of an affair. Their desire to put it behind them, to not talk or think about it, keeps it very much alive. Similarly, clients trying to rid themselves of performance-related sexual problems discover again and again that they can't just will themselves not to feel anxiety.

If any effort to resolve a problem creates a kind of connection to it, then the art of therapy is in helping to create connections that are characterized by a comfortable, loose grip—connections that are able to fade in significance. One way we do this is to bring legitimacy to the presence of a problem, honoring how it fits into the logic of the clients' lives. When the problem stops being an enemy to be destroyed, clients can relax their efforts to rid themselves of it, thereby allowing it to diminish in significance and wander away on its own. We specialize in seeing sex-related issues, but this work fits into a more encompassing relational approach to any concern expressed by an individual, couple, or family (Flemons, 2002; Green & Flemons, 2007).

As the first session commences with Mary and Fred, and we have learned a bit about their social, family, and professional contexts, we begin to explore their hopes and desires for an intimate relationship. As we ask about this, we also attempt to learn about what they believe is getting in the way of their intimacy. We learn about the meanings that each of them ascribe to their intimate encounters as well as to the times when intimacy has not been possible. We also learn about how they have attempted to resolve this situation, as we assume that the relationship they have with the problem of "lack of intimacy" will be a particular focus of our therapeutic involvement.

In the first session, Mary begins to tell us that Fred has always had an "inexhaustible" sex drive. In the beginning of their relationship, she found this incredibly sexy and in fact bragged to her friends about his desire for her and their dynamic sexual relationship. However, over time, and especially after the birth of their child, she began to feel oppressed by the magnitude of his desire. She began accusing him of being a "sex addict," interested more in orgasms than in her. Fred, of course, took offense at this. His anger, an expression of his hurt, confirmed Mary's growing sense that he was uninterested in and incapable of emotional closeness, which led to her pulling away from him more and more. In the last several years, she has found herself rejecting almost all of Fred's requests for sex. She explains this by saying that if she "gives in," he will just want more and more, and "I will never be enough for him." She does worry now that Fred will seek sex outside their relationship; this has heightened her fears for the marriage but has done nothing to ease her anxiety that Fred will always want too much sex from her if she opens the door to any sex at all. She says she loves Fred and deeply misses the emotional intimacy they once shared, but she doesn't feel it's safe to initiate sex or to respond positively to a sex addict.

As Fred listens to this story, he becomes increasingly upset. We ask him how this makes sense to him, and he quickly replies, "It doesn't! I love Mary, and I just need to be able to show her that physically. I feel completely cut off from her, but I would never force myself on her. She used to love sex with me; now she wants nothing to do with me. She never initiates, but she gets mad at me when I try. If I stop trying, we will never have sex again, I guarantee it."

This conversation helps us to understand the dynamics that are preserving Mary and Fred's impasse. Mary's attempts to protect herself from Fred's strong sex drive have resulted in no sex at all; Fred has alternated between angry recriminations, depressed withdrawal, and vigorous efforts to rekindle their once-active sex life. In doing so, with increasing urgency, he has unknowingly confirmed Mary's belief that she will never be enough for him, further entrenching her "no-sex" position. Their efforts to control and rid themselves of the problems they have each located in the other ("he needs to get his sex addiction under control"; "she needs to thaw her frigidity") have created painful connections to the problems and to each other.

At this point in the session, our primary goal is to shift the nature of these connections by acknowledging and respecting the efforts of both Fred and Mary, making sense of, and thus legitimizing, each of their behaviors within the context of meaning they have created around their relationship. We comment to Mary on the wisdom of her desire to preserve the integrity of their intimacy by ensuring that they are never reduced to having empty or meaningless sex; we also note that while painful for both of them, her reluctance to have sex regularly with Fred has allowed Fred to feel almost constant desire for her. Although at the moment, that desire is coupled with anger, clearly the passion remains and can be a starting place for sexual and emotional intimacy when that becomes safe. We acknowledge as well Fred's willingness to openly express his ongoing desire for Mary and comment on the vulnerability he has shown by continuing to risk rejection from her. We note that while this has been painfully frustrating for him, we believe the openness of his desire and vulnerability creates a beautiful place to begin exploring what emotional intimacy would look like for them. We recognize that Mary has been concerned that he has a sex addiction, but we are curious how his sexuality will be expressed and satisfied when it isn't intermixed with anger, fear, loneliness, and sadness.

Each of them begins to soften a bit as they hear their positions respected and honored. We then ask Mary what it would be like for her to believe that Fred could be intimate without necessarily being sexual. She says that would be "unbelievable" but that if she could actually see that from him, she would feel less at risk exploring being sexual with him. We then ask Fred what he believes this would be like for him. He says that it has been so long since he has felt any emotional connection with Mary, he assumed she didn't even want that any more. He had simply continued to hope that she was at least "human" and still had a sex drive. The idea that she wanted an emotional connection with him was much better news than he expected to hear.

As the session ends, we ask Mary to consider what a sexual encounter with Fred might look like if it were based on a strong emotional connection; we ask Fred to think about how he might make space for that emotional connection to grow, as it is clearly something that he values as well.

This, of course, is a beginning, not an ending. We would anticipate seeing the couple for as many sessions as it took for them to begin noticing and negotiating their way through the changes that are initiated by our inviting relaxed connections between them and the problems they have identified.

Notes

1. See Bateson (1972) for his discussion of "dormitive principles" and Albert North Whitehead (1925/1953, p. 51) for what he called the "fallacy of misplaced concreteness"—the "error of mistaking the abstract for the concrete."
2. We never attempt to educate our clients about these ideas, as this would mean telling them how wrong they are. Our understanding is reflected in our therapeutic choices, in the ways we invite clients into alternative approaches to solving their problem.

References

Flemons, D. (2002). *Of one mind: The logic of hypnosis, the practice of therapy.* New York, NY: W. W. Norton.

Green, S., & Flemons, D. (2007). *Quickies: The handbook of brief sex therapy.* New York, NY: W. W. Norton.

56

COMPARE AND CONTRAST

Specific Couples Therapy Approaches

Anne Rambo, Charles West, AnnaLynn Schooley, and Tommie V. Boyd

We first note the tremendous influence of behavioral theory on most of these models. While not specifically a systemic theory, the ideas of behavioral theory have application to family therapy and, in particular, to couples therapy. The focus on skills training seems to be a natural fit with the pragmatic focus of this type of couples therapy. We see an influence on the skills training and behavioral analysis portions of EFCT (Chapter 50) and PET (Chapter 54), and clearly the influence is dominant in the behavioral models (Chapters 51, 52, and 53). Relational sex therapy is less influenced as it seems to remain within the systemic brief therapy tradition (IID). This didactic element is clear within EFCT. These behavioral ideas appear to have influenced all of the models except brief sex therapy, which draws from a brief therapy background instead.

There are brief therapy influences on the other models as well, however. In the third-wave behavioral approaches described in this book, one can also see similarities to Ericksonian work in the interest in states of consciousness—what is noticed and what is ignored, and how what has been ignored can be brought back into the foreground (see Chapter 28). In the behavioral approaches, and most particularly in those approaches influenced by the research of the Gottmans, one can also see similarities to SFBT (Chapter 30)—the focus on the positive, on what works for the couple, and the Ericksonian intention to avoid discussion of the negative (so as not to give it undue importance).

One can also see the influence of attachment theory, especially in EFCT (Chapter 50) and PET (Chapter 54). With the focus on experience and expression of emotion, at times their language can seem similar to psychoanalytic/experiential family models (IIA). In general, most of these couples-specific models are highly integrative, using techniques and ideas from a wide range of models as well as specific research knowledge and information about couples. This relates to the distinctions Marquez makes in her introduction about differences between systemic and couples-specific models (Chapter 49). The exception again is brief sex therapy, which remains a fit with the brief therapy tradition.

Couples therapists sought empirical validation early. EFCT is strongly evidence based and has abundant research demonstrating its effectiveness. Behavioral marital therapy is also evidence based. The Gottman method is based on marital research, although the research to date has focused primarily on marital process, not on the efficacy of the therapy. PET is still a young model, as is brief sex therapy, and evidence to date for both is of the anecdotal and client satisfaction variety.

The models in this couples-specific section differ considerably on their application of the common factors. EFCT (Chapter 50) and PET (Chapter 54) appear to try to bring about change in all three of the indicated areas—thinking, feeling, and doing. Cognitive behavioral therapy (Chapters 51 and 52) addresses both thinking and doing, as does Gottman-based marital therapy (Chapter 53). Brief sex therapy is in the brief therapy tradition, which embraces client reality and brings about change through action (IID). Sprenkle, Davis, and Lebow's (2009) list of common family therapy factors—conceptualizing systemically, interrupting the dysfunctional family pattern, and expanding the therapeutic system—could be seen to apply to some of these couples models as well. EFCT (Chapter 50) and PET (Chapter 54) conceptualize the couple over time and in the context of past family patterns; they alter the sequence with direct intervention (EFCT) or building new habits (PET); and they expand the system by joining with both husband and wife. CBT, third-wave, and Gottman-based marital therapy models, however, seem more comfortable with the behavioral individual tradition. And again, brief sex therapy stands in the brief therapy, Ericksonian tradition (IID).

Going back to our introduction to this section, it is interesting to note that (with exceptions) these models do appear to be more integrative, more pragmatic, and less purely systemic than the family therapy models presented in section two (IIA–F), just as Marquez predicted. It is interesting to consider the implications for the field of this differing approach.

Reference

Sprenkle, D., Davis, S., & Lebow, J. (2009). *Common factors in couple and family therapy: An overlooked foundation for effective practice.* New York, NY: Guilford Press.

57

A FINAL NOTE

Choosing a Model or Models

Anne Rambo, Charles West, AnnaLynn Schooley, and Tommie V. Boyd

As frequently noted, the model or models you choose to practice do not influence outcome as much as your belief in your model (Sprenkle, Davis, & Lebow, 2009). How then should a beginning therapist select a model to practice? One consideration is the nature of the therapist's clientele. There are indications that the more action-oriented models (structural/strategic, IIC, and brief, IID) are more effective with at-risk youth than other models, and those models that avoid a focus on the negative (SFBT, Chapter 30; EFCT, Chapter 50; and Gottman marital therapy, Chapter 53) are more effective with couples (Sprenkle et al., 2009). Yet greater than these trends is the influence of the relationship of the client with the therapist (nrepp.samhsa.gov/Norcross.aspx). And surely a model that is a fit with the therapist's personality, philosophy, and way of being in the world will best allow the therapist to develop an authentic relationship with his or her client. The choice of approach tells much about the therapist (Keeney, 1983); it is recommended, then, that the beginning therapist read widely and consider a variety of factors when choosing which models to study more deeply, not least his or her own personal understanding of the nature of change.

References

Keeney, B. (1983). *Aesthetics of change.* New York, NY: Guilford Press.
Sprenkle, D., Davis, S., & Lebow, J. (2009). *Common factors in couple and family therapy: An overlooked foundation for effective practice.* New York, NY: Guilford Press.

Section IV
APPLICATIONS

58

INTRODUCTION

Anne Rambo, Charles West, AnnaLynn Schooley, and Tommie V. Boyd

Having considered a wide range of family and couples therapy models, we now turn to family therapy applications, across models. This section will present brief examples of some of the up-and-coming growth areas for marriage and family therapists. These are a key reason why marriage and family therapy is listed as a top career by employment-related sources (Webster, 2010).

Reference

Webster, H. (2010, December 6). Best careers 2011: Marriage and family therapist. *U.S. News and World Report*. Retrieved from at http://money.usnews.com

59

MEDICAL FAMILY THERAPY

An Overview

Tommie V. Boyd and Yulia Watters

Engle (1977) first articulated the biopsychosocial model in the prominent journal *Science*. In addition to biological aspects of an illness, Engle invited clinicians to consider its cultural, social, and psychological elements, urging physicians to listen to patients' stories in addition to taking a thorough medical history.

Upon publication, the biopsychosocial perspective received a mixed acknowledgement from the medical milieu. Nonetheless, this perspective found its followers among physicians as well as mental health professionals. Appealing to the humanistic side of medicine, the biopsychosocial paradigm became a foundation for patient-centered and relationship-centered approaches in health care (Frankel, Quill, & McDaniel, 2003). It offered physicians an opportunity to engage in a more egalitarian practice of medicine, based on the premises of a co-constructed reality, respectful dialogue, and careful use of power.

In addition, the biopsychosocial perspective provided a theoretical framework for mental health professionals already exploring the interconnection between soma and psyche in patients and their families. It complemented other systems theories that addressed families facing health care problems and became a platform for further theoretical development. In 1978, Minuchin and Rosman worked with pediatrician Baker to address psychosomatic manifestations of asthma, diabetes, and anorexia nervosa to develop a psychosomatic family model. In 1981, Reiss, Steinglass, and their colleagues from George Washington University articulated a theory portraying an illness as an organizing principle of the family unit. In 1984, Rolland from the University of Chicago proposed a psychological typology of chronic illness. In 1988, Patterson articulated the family adjustment and adaptation response theory (FAAR), which combined the principles of stress theory and family systems theory. Doherty and Colangelo in 1984 advanced the family fundamental interpersonal relations orientation (FIRO) model, an application of Schutz's fundamental interpersonal orientations model to the treatment of families. Additionally, complementing an initial outline of the biopsychosocial model, Doherty, McDaniel, and Hepworth (1994) emphasized the systemic character of the medical family therapy approach, incorporating biological, psychological, and social elements, and also the interactive nature of their manifestation.

It is important to emphasize that further development of the medical family therapy model was characterized by the involvement of both health care professionals and mental health professionals. Thus, even though the medical family therapy approach shares systemic relational premises characterizing the field of family therapy at large, it also holds unique foundational principles characterizing this particular model. One of the basic premises is the focus on an interdisciplinary collaborative effort in the provision of patient's care. Multiple books and articles have addressed the delivery of integrative care and the establishment of different collaborative levels of care among health care and mental health professionals (Blount, 1998; Doherty & Baird, 1983; Hodgson & Marlowe, 2011; McDaniel & Campbell, 1997). Even though the detailed outline of the collaborative effort in medical family therapy is beyond the scope of this chapter, one cannot emphasize too much the importance of this premise for the tenets of the biopsychosocial approach. The website of the Collaborative Family Healthcare Association (www. cfha.net) is an illustration of an ongoing effort in this direction. As the work of a medical family therapist is envisioned in the context of such interdisciplinary collaboration, working alongside and in collaboration with medical professionals, clinical strategies reflect the medical context of medical family therapy practice.

Since the appearance of the biopsychosocial model 30 years ago and the pioneering efforts of family therapists and physicians interested in exploring the interplay of physical and emotional components in the context of a health care system, the development of medical family therapy has proceeded. Acknowledging that the basic premises of this model require acquiring specific therapeutic and interdisciplinary skills as well as specialized knowledge of the health care system and community resources, several universities now offer specialized training in medical family therapy. Ranging from a graduate certificate to a doctoral degree, the curriculum offers students an opportunity to acquire necessary clinical skills, deepen their knowledge about contemporary health care systems, and become familiar with available theoretical frameworks helpful to address health care issues. Such programs aim to assist future medical family therapists to practice in collaboration with primary care physicians, specialists' offices, and mental health settings related to health care problems (e.g., eating disorder and weight management clinics).

The biomedical model remains the predominant framework in the practice of medicine (Alonso, 2004; Suls & Rothman, 2004). Nonetheless, in comparison to 30 years ago, major medical journals, such as *New England Journal of Medicine, Lancet, Journal of the American Medical Association,* and *Annals of Internal Medicine,* contain more references to the biopsychosocial approach to patient care. In addition, biopsychosocial ideas intrigue and inspire clinicians internationally (Kates, 2008). Therefore, the medical family therapy field remains a work in progress, and it calls for advanced education, evidence-based research, enriched clinical practice, and informed policy changes (Miller, 2010).

References

Alonso, Y. (2004). The biopsychosocial model in medical research: The evolution of the health concept over the last two decades. *Patient Education and Counseling, 53*(2), 239–244.

Blount, A. (Ed.). (1998). *Integrated primary care: The future of medical and mental health collaboration.* New York, NY: W. W. Norton.

Doherty, W. J., McDaniel, S. H., & Hepworth, J. (1994). Medical family therapy: An emerging arena for family therapy. *Journal of Family Therapy, 16*(1), 31–46.

Doherty, W. J., & Baird, M. A. (1983). *Family therapy and family medicine: Toward the primary care of families.* New York, NY: Guilford Press.

Engle, G. L. (1977). The need for a new medical model: A challenge for biomedicine. *Science, 196*(4286), 129–136. doi:10.3109/13561828909043606

Frankel, R.M., Quill, T. E., & McDaniel, S. H. (Eds.). (2003). *The biopsychosocial approach: Past, present, future.* Rochester, NY: University of Rochester Press.

Hodgson, J., & Marlowe D. (2011). The role of MFT in healthcare: Models of collaboration. *Family Therapy Magazine, 10*(4), 10–14.

Kates, N. (2008). Promoting collaborative care in Canada: The Canadian collaborative mental health initiative. *Families, Systems, and Health, 26*(4), 466–473. doi: 10.1037/a0014230

McDaniel, S., & Campbell, T. L. (1997). Training health professionals to collaborate. *Families, Systems, and Health, 15*(4), 353–359. doi:10.1037/h0090138

Miller, B. F. (2010). Collaborative care needs a more active policy voice. *Families, Systems, and Health, 28*(4), 387–388. doi: 10.1037/a0021489

Suls, J., & Rothman, A. (2004). Evolution of the biopsychosocial model: Prospects and challenges for health psychology. *Health Psychology, 23*(2), 119–125. doi: 10.1037/0278–6133.23.2.119

Additional Resources

Anderson, N. B., & Armstead, C. A. (1995). Toward understanding the association of socioeconomic status and health: A new challenge for the biopsychosocial approach. *Psychosomatic Medicine, 57*(3), 213–225.

Brown, T. M. (2000, May 24). *The growth of George Engel's biopsychosocial model.* Paper presented at the meeting of Corner Society, Rochester, Minnesota. Retrieved from http://www.human-nature.com/free-associations/engel1.html

Walsh, F. (Ed.). (2009). *Spiritual resources in family therapy.* New York, NY: Guilford Press.

60

FAMILY THERAPY IN SCHOOLS

Linda Metcalf

At present, school districts nationwide are not mandated to hire family therapists, as they are guidance counselors. But this is a focus of lobbying and could change soon. In the meantime, school districts are voluntarily embracing the benefits of family therapy. As early as 2001, Insoo Kim Berg and Cynthia Franklin, Ph.D., worked with principal Victoria Baldwin to bring the strategies of SFBT to Garza High School, an alternative school by choice in Austin, Texas. Franklin has documented the success of creating a strength-based school environment in which administrators, teachers (facilitators), and students collaborate in a solution-building school.

In 2003, Working on What Works (WOWW) was developed by Insoo Kim Berg and Lee Shilts, Ph.D., as a solution-focused classroom management program that was originally implemented in New River Middle School in Fort Lauderdale, Florida. The program was designed for facilitators to coach teachers in how to utilize the strategies of SFBT. The goal was to improve the classroom environment by creating a collaborative relationship between the administration, teachers, and students, resulting in students becoming more successful in school. This model is used in schools in the United States and has spread internationally. Currently, the WOWW manual has been translated into multiple languages.

The advantages of family therapists in school settings are shown by the following case study, in which the author (Metcalf) was the therapist.

At age eight, Shawn had everyone convinced that he was different. He preferred to wear clothes to school that he had slept in the night before because it made getting up a little easier. His parents had learned that asking him to tie his shoes, brush his teeth, and pick up his backpack (all at one time) was too much to ask. His teacher had learned that Shawn's distractibility had to be controlled by her constant consequential actions. His principal had also learned that if she came down on Shawn for anything, she was sure to get a detailed and extensive list of reasons why he should not be in trouble. Exhausted, his parents brought him to family therapy that I (Metcalf) provided on campus because, in their words, "something had to give." Either he learned to control his attention deficit disorder, or he was off to boarding school.

In interviewing Shawn and his family, I learned that during the previous few years of school, things had gone well, particularly last year, when he had the teacher from "Oz." She had taught school for what probably seemed a zillion years, according to Shawn, and loved her students, no matter what they did. She loved the energy of her second grade students, so she was infatuated with Shawn, said his parents. Of course, that did not mean that Shawn did not have to perform or behave. It did mean that she had to find ways to coax him into paying attention. She took up the polite, respectful habit of whispering to Shawn, "Time to pay attention," when he began daydreaming and wandering about. Each day when school let out, she would tell him how much she enjoyed him that day. During that school year, I learned, Shawn never went to see the principal. His home life was slightly better as well, since Shawn never brought home any negative notes from school.

As a family therapist in the school setting, the information I learned from Shawn and his family was very helpful as it provided a view of a system at school and home the previous year that had worked for Shawn. I view the system at school as a family. By system, I mean each person who is involved in the student's life each day at school. In addition to family support, it is important to examine who in the system has had success. In this case, Shawn's teacher from the previous year had success, and, since I work with a solution-focused approach, this was an exception to the described problem. If I were to have just seen Shawn without his parents, I would not have learned about the teacher from Oz who had discovered how to cooperate with Shawn.

Shawn told me that his energy often got him the nickname of "tornado." I asked him what he knew about tornados, and he said they were very destructive. I asked if he knew how they developed, and he gave me a lengthy explanation about cold air and warm air. He also told me that he loved to read science books because they explained so much. I asked him if he knew whenever the tornado began to build, and he said he did. I asked him what it was like. He said it began as a funnel cloud, and sometimes it just kept growing until it reached the height of a tornado. I then asked him how many times that week it had developed into a tornado. He quickly said that it had only happened three times and that each of those times had been in the afternoon before school let out. Our dialogue went like this:

LM: Wow, so you were able to keep it in funnel cloud status for over six hours a day?

Shawn: Usually by the end of the day, the classroom is noisy and I have to sit next to Alex, and that's when the tornado grows into a real storm.

LM: If you and I were to plan for ways to keep the tornado a funnel cloud, just for the rest of this week, what would you suggest doing?

Shawn: I would change my seat and never sit next to Alex or behind him, so that I would not see him. If I could sit in front of him, that would really be good.

LM: What else?

Shawn: If my teacher would just be nice to me when the funnel cloud starts. Maybe she could whisper to me.

Together, Shawn and I wrote a letter to his teacher. I often do that as another means of informing the system of a student's plan for success. I may send a copy to the principal or school counselor as well as the teacher. If the teacher was not informed, chances are she might expect the same distractible behavior and react in a punitive manner. However, it has been my experience that teachers like being informed and being part of the solution. So, a letter such as the one that follows often provides such information along with a statement of the student's plan to be responsible.

Dear Ms. Smith,

I would like to do better in school. It would help me a lot if I could move my seat away from Alex. If I get upset or begin to get in trouble, please whisper to me, "Stop, Shawn, don't let the funnel cloud get control of you." Maybe then, when I leave school each day, you will smile at me.

Love, Shawn

When a student and I write a letter such as this, I walk the student back to class and personally hand the letter to the teacher, mentioning first that I am interested in helping her to have a class where she can be the best teacher she can be. This, I have found, is very important as it provides a goal for the teacher that is attractive. It also provides Shawn with the best chance of success as I go one step further to ask the teacher to watch how Shawn begins to control the funnel cloud.

While Shawn's teacher did not whisper to him as he requested, he did tell me when I saw him again that she had decided to "work out a deal with him" after she read the letter that he wrote to her. "She would let me lead everyone to music and computer class each day that I stayed focused on my work and she did not have to correct me more than two times in a day. That worked great because music and computer class was in the afternoon, the time when the tornado often tried to grow." Counseling children in this way, called "externalizing problems," gives them a chance to step out of the problem and create solutions where they can fight the problem themselves. When this opportunity is widened to included parents and teachers, the system that the child lives in becomes part of the solution as well. Shawn's parents learned from Shawn's experience at school that conquering the tornado in the morning meant letting Shawn wear those clean but slightly slept-in clothes. It also meant giving him one task at a time and recognizing that until that one task was done, it was frustrating to keep adding to the list.

Shawn not only did better in school, he also widened his science study to include…hurricanes. It is my hope that while he digests this knowledge of nature's most dangerous storm, he will come to realize the power he has over his own storm. And when he does, his system will certainly notice, providing everyone within his system with information to help him in the future.

61

WORKING WITH MILITARY FAMILIES

Tyon L. Hall

Following the collaborative efforts of marriage and family therapists, members of the Armed Services Committees, the Military Coalition, and members of Congress, MFTs were recently granted the opportunity to be included as one of three health initiatives within the Department of Defense. The final approval for marriage and family therapists to work in behavioral health positions at the Department of Veterans Affairs (VA) occurred in 2006. To get to this point, MFTs had to overcome many barriers including getting a federal job classification or General Schedule (GS) series and an amended U.S. code to recognize MFTs as skilled health care providers.

By overcoming these obstacles, MFTs were added to the list of health care professionals authorized to provide mental health services to military persons and their families. The Advisory Committee on the Readjustment of Veterans, the Department of Veteran Affairs Special Committee on Post-Traumatic Stress Disorder, and the Secretary of Veterans Affairs have acknowledged a need to increase services from family therapists. The need to include MFTs in the treatment of veterans is unmistakable. Sladana (2002) indicates that the treatment modalities executed by family therapists are uniquely effective in addressing the mental and emotional challenges presented by veterans. With the authorization by Congress, licensed MFTs are now providing services to veterans within the Readjustment Counseling Service (RCS) program at Vet Centers as readjustment counseling therapists.

Vet Centers were established in 1979 following the realization that veterans returning from Vietnam were having adjustment issues. Vet Centers are community-based programs under the VA and now serve combat veterans from all war eras. President Lincoln made a promise "to care for him who shall have borne the battle and for his widow, and his orphan." In accordance with the mission of the VA, Vet Centers continue to "keep the promise" by hiring MFTs to address individual and relational issues of veterans. Many of the issues vets face are relational. Therefore, the adjustment challenges of vets can be improved by the involvement and education of the family. The Department of Defense also hires MFTs directly to work with families still in military service, and many of the same issues apply.

For MFTs interested in working with a military population, either active or veteran, there are several areas in which a specialized knowledge base and experience are valuable. First of all, an understanding of military culture and its effects on the family is key. The ability to understand and treat the critical issues veterans face, such as posttraumatic stress disorder (PTSD), traumatic brain injury (TBI), military sexual trauma (MST), and bereavement, is imperative. PTSD is considered an invisible wound. Vets with PTSD may appear fine but report experiencing sleepless nights and intrusive thoughts, being constantly on guard, getting angry for no reason, and having difficulty getting emotionally close to others.

The involvement of families in addressing these issues is important for many reasons. First, the family may have challenges negotiating roles within the family upon a family member's return from active service. Second, the family may express a greater degree of stress learning to cope and understand the experience of the returning veteran. As a readjustment counseling therapist, I (Hall) provide veterans and their families an opportunity to reestablish a new normal. I offer a broad range of psychosocial services to veterans and their families. As part of a multidisciplinary team, I utilize my education and experience to assist combat veterans in their readjustment to civilian life. The job functions for this position include screening and assessment, treatment planning/goal setting, clinical counseling, providing outreach, crisis intervention, and referrals.

In our personal experience, we (Hall and colleagues) have noted that military families represent some of the most resilient families we have encountered. The military family unit is willing to gain the necessary skills and information to strengthen their family bonds. To support your service men and women as an employee of Veteran Affairs Vet Centers, more information can be found at www.vetcenter.va.gov or www.vacareers.va.gov. For information on positions for MFTs with the active military, check out www.usajobs.gov.

Reference

Sladana, D. (2002). Family interventions in treatment of post-traumatic stress disorders. *Journal of Projective Psychology and Mental Health, 9,* 57–61.

Additional Resources

American Association for Marriage and Family Therapy. (n.d.). *Veteran's access to family therapists.* Retrieved from http://www.aamft.org/imis15/Content/Advocacy/VA_Fact_Sheet.aspx

Armstrong, K., Best, S., & Domenici, P. (2006). *Courage after fire: Coping strategies for troops returning from Iraq and Afghanistan and their families.* Berkeley, CA: Ulysses Press.

Cantrell, B., & Dean, C. (2005). *Down range: To Iraq and back.* Seattle, WA: WordSmith Publishing.

Kay, E. (2002). *Heroes at home: Help and hope for America's military families.* Minneapolis, MN: Bethany House.

Matsakis, A. (1998). *Trust after trauma: A guide to relationships for survivors and those who love them.* Oakland, CA: New Harbinger.

Seahorn, J., & Seahorn, E. A. (2008). *Tears of a warrior.* Fort Collins, CO: Team Pursuits.

U.S. Department of Veterans Affairs. *VA careers.* http://www.vacareers.va.gov

U.S. Department of Veterans Affairs. *Vet center.* http://www.vetcenter.va.gov

U.S. Department of Veterans Affairs. *National center for PTSD.* http://www.ptsd.va.gov

U.S. Department of Veterans Affairs. *Understanding traumatic brain injury (TBI).* http://www.polytrauma.va.gov/understanding-tbi

62

FAMILY THERAPY AND FAMILY BUSINESS

Pat Cole

If family therapists want to expand their practice, one way is to use their therapy skills to work with family businesses. These businesses are ones in which a family has majority control or ownership and two or more family members work or have worked together. Some examples include the parent-child relationship of Playboy Enterprises with Hugh and Christy Hefner or Mrs. Fields Cookies, which was started by a husband-and-wife team. Sibling and cousin teams also make up family businesses. These businesses do not have to be large. Many small businesses such as your neighborhood dry cleaners or car dealership may be family owned and operated, too. What they all have in common is a dual relationship of combining family relationships with working relationships.

The juggling of a dual relationship such as father/boss, daughter/employee, brother/coworker, or wife/partner may become confusing. For example, in a business family, the problem may be that the owner's daughter does not take orders from her boss, who happens to be her father. A family therapist would be able to help this family recognize the dual relationship confusion that happens when a daughter/employee works with her father/boss. When he complains that a report that she was to do a week ago is still not ready, he sees himself as a boss asking something from an employee. She may see this demand as a father criticizing his daughter for being a procrastinator—just as he did when she was a child. She is placing their relationship in a family context, and he in a work context.

Therefore, it makes sense that family therapists, with their practice wisdom, would be comfortable working with this type of problem. From their systems training, they know how to untangle relationships that are positioned in different contexts and could help these clients understand the relationship confusion. This is just one of many examples of business family problems that a systems trained therapist could handle.

I have been working with these families since 1989 and have seen more family therapists with family business members as clients. From my experience, most of the family members who contact me are women. I believe this happens because more female family members have taken leadership positions within these companies and do not view contacting a therapist as a weakness. Instead, they understand that problematic family relationships affect the business bottom line.

How knowledgeable a family therapist wants to become about business issues is an individual choice. One can remain a family therapist who is known for his or her family relationship expertise. In this position, accountants, attorneys, management consultants, and others working with these families on their business problems will call on such a therapist to partner with them, or they will refer a family or a family member to a therapist for separate work.

If therapists want to expand their business knowledge, they can become more of family business consultants who are recognized for working with both family and business problems. Sometimes this happens naturally as one teams with other business professionals and familiarizes oneself with business issues. For more business education, family therapists may take special courses offered by professional organizations or family business centers, which are often located at universities throughout the United States as well as other countries. Regardless of the choice of whether to remain a family therapist who works with business family relationships or to evolve into a family business consultant who works with both family- and business-related problems, the opportunity is there for those who want to expand their therapy practice.

Family Firm Institute is an organization for those interested in working with family businesses. The members are professionals such as therapists, accountants, attorneys, financial consultants, and management consultants. The organization is a good resource for workshops and courses designed for family business consultants. See ffi@ffi.org or http://ffi.org.

Resources

Cole, P. M. (1992). Family systems business: A merger at last. *Family Therapy News, 23*(2), 29.

Cole, P. M. (1997). Meetings are therapeutic in family business consultation. *Family Therapy News, 28*(5), 27.

Cole, P. M. (1997). Women in family business. *Family Business Review, 10*(4), 353–371.

Cole, P. M. (2000, October). Understanding family business relationships: Preserving the family in family business. *Family Journal, 8*(4), 351–359.

Cole, P. M., & Johnson, K. (2007). An exploration of successful copreneurial relationships post divorce. *Family Business Review Journal, 20*(3), 185–198.

Cole, P. M., & Johnson, K. (2011). What's love got to do with it: Marriage and divorce in family business. In A. Carsrud, & M. Brannback (Eds.), *Understanding family business: Neglected topics and underutilized theories.* Springer International Entrepreneurship Series. New York, NY: Springer.

Cole, P. M., & Johnson, K. (in review). A perfect fit: Connecting family business with family therapy. *Journal of Marital and Family Therapy.*

Flemons, D. G., & Cole, P. M. (1992). Connecting and separating family and business: A relational approach to consultation. *Family Business Review, 5*(3), 257–269.

Flemons, D. G., & Cole, P. M. (1994). Playing with contextual complexity: Relational consultation to family businesses. *Transitioning from individual to family counseling monograph.* Alexandria, VA: American Counseling Association Press.

Hilburt-Davis, J., & Dyer, W. G. (2003). *Consulting to family businesses: A practical guide to contracting, assessment, and implementation.* San Francisco, CA: Jossey-Bass/Pfeiffer.

Jaffe, D. (1990). *Working with the ones you love: Conflict resolution and problem solving strategies for successful family business.* Berkeley, CA: Conran Press.

Kaslow, F. (1993). The lore and lure of family business. *American Journal of Family Therapy, 21*(1), 3.

63

HORSES AND FAMILIES

Bringing Equine-Assisted Approaches to Family Therapy

Shelley Green

One of the more unique clinical practices to emerge in the last decade has been the inclusion of horses as a tool in working with couples, families, groups, and individuals. Typically referred to as equine-assisted psychotherapy (EAP), the practice has gained recognition and acceptance both nationally and internationally as an increasing number of clinicians (and horse lovers) have harnessed the natural traits of the horse to complement and enrich their clinical practices. A wide range of diverse approaches have been developed, and it's important to distinguish between therapeutic riding programs (often used to enhance physical stamina and coordination of individuals with physical challenges) and the practice of EAP, which most commonly does not include riding, horsemanship instruction, or mounted activities.

EAP is an experiential clinical modality that incorporates the horse as an integral part of the therapy session. As described by the Equine Assisted Growth and Learning Association (EAGALA, see www.eagala.org), EAP is a solution-oriented approach that assumes clients have the ability to find their own solutions to their problems. EAP has been used to treat many clinical concerns, including behavioral issues, depression, anxiety, substance abuse, eating disorders, and domestic violence. Outcome literature has not kept pace with the proliferation of programs and models in the equine-assisted community; however, anecdotal and clinical case study reports indicate significant changes in clients who have experienced this unique approach.

While animal-assisted therapy (AAT) has been a growing field for many years, utilizing dogs, cats, pigs, rabbits, and other animal assistants, EAP practitioners are passionate about the unique qualities of the horse as a resource within the therapy session. Because horses are prey animals, they are immediately sensitive and attuned to any changes in their environment. They also respond immediately and directly—through sometimes through quite powerful body language—providing clear messages in response to human communication. They are large, potentially intimidating animals, but they can also be calm and responsive, allowing clients to experiment with different types of behavior and gain immediate feedback. When clients are dealing with intense emotions and attempting to make significant changes in their lives, interactions with horses can pave the way to trying out new behaviors and creating solutions to long-standing difficulties.

In a typical EAP session, a licensed mental health provider works alongside an equine specialist and one or more horses. The therapist asks the client(s) to complete an experiential activity with the horses; activities are designed to allow the clients to experience metaphorically something they may be struggling with outside the arena. For example, a family struggling with conflict between parents and children may be asked to create an obstacle in the ring and find a way—together—to encourage the horses to go over or through the obstacle. The clinician observes family processes and interactions, noting when the family may become stuck, struggle to determine who is in charge, or find ways to work together. Simultaneously, the equine specialist carefully observes the horses' behavior, attending to herd dynamics as well as equine responses to human behaviors. These clinical and equine observations then inform the processing of the session, as the team learns from the family what seemed to work for them, what they tried when they were stuck, and what may have been familiar for them when compared with their daily challenges.

Because the sessions take place in a relaxed, natural environment, away from an office setting that can at times seem intimidating or emotionally stressful, clients may be able to make connections between what happens in the ring and what happens at home with less content-based discussion of the presenting problem. The takeaway from the session is not defined by the therapist; rather, the clients leave the session with experiential learning that may translate into immediate changes in their relationships.

The family therapy program at Nova Southeastern University has partnered with Stable Foundations, an independent, equine-assisted psychotherapy program, to deliver clinical services, supervision, training, and continuing education offerings in equine-assisted family therapy practices. Through our work, we have found that horses can and often do help clients make significant changes in their lives through interacting with the horses and finding what works. This fits well within a systemic framework that privileges the clients' understandings, resources, and strengths. Through observing clients' struggles to complete their tasks with the horses, therapists may notice persistence, determination, resilience, and creativity that may not have been apparent in more traditional clinical sessions.

Additionally, we have found the horses to be an invaluable tool in training and supervising therapists. Through a series of carefully designed exercises, we encourage therapists to explore who they are as therapists and what they bring into the room with them each time they meet a new client. Unlike in a conventional supervision session, we are not focused on content, therapeutic model, or technique.

Rather, using the horses as the clients, therapists explore their typical ways of assessing and developing connections, their ways of managing "stuckness," as well as their approach to change. We have found that therapists learn a great deal about who they are as therapists and who they would like to become.

There are numerous resources for clinicians seeking to learn about equine-assisted approaches to clinical work. As this field continues to develop, it can provide a rich and fertile field for applying brief, systemic methods to a wide range of presenting problems. Family therapists have the skills, training, and theoretical framework to blend beautifully with the herd.

Resources

Bowers, M., & MacDonald, P. (2001). The effectiveness of equine-facilitated psychotherapy with at-risk adolescents. *Journal of Psychology and Behavioral Sciences, 15,* 62–76.

Brooks, S. (2006). Animal-assisted psychotherapy and equine-assisted psychotherapy. In N. Webb (Ed.), *Working with traumatized youth in child welfare.* New York, NY: Guilford Press.

Chandler, C. (2012). *Animal assisted therapy in counseling.* London, England: Routledge.

Donaghy, G. (2006). Equine assisted therapy. *Journal of Mental Health Nursing, 26*(4).

Equine Assisted Growth and Learning Association. (2009). Fundamentals of EAGALA model practice. *Equine Assisted Growth and Learning Association, 6*(2), 140.

Equine Assisted Growth and Learning Association. http://www.eagala.org

Ewing, C., MacDonald, P., Taylor, M., & Bowers, J. (2007). Equine-facilitated learning for youths with severe emotional disorders: A quantitative and qualitative study. *Child Youth Care Forum, 36,* 59–72.

Frewin, K., & Gardiner, B. (2005). New sage or old? A review of equine assisted psychotherapy. *Australian Journal of Counseling Psychology, 6,* 13–17.

Horses and Humans Research Foundation. http://www.horsesandhumans.org

Karol, J. (2007). Applying a traditional individual psychotherapy model to equine-facilitated psychotherapy (EFP): Theory and method. *Clinical Child Psychology and Psychiatry, 12,* 77–90.

Lentini, J., & Knox, M. (2009). A qualitative and quantitative review of equine facilitated psychotherapy (EFP) with children and adolescents. *Open Complementary Medicine Journal, 1,* 51–57.

Meinersmann, K., Bradberry, J., & Bright Roberts, F. (2008). Equine-facilitated psychotherapy with adult female survivors of abuse. *Journal of Psychosocial Nursing, 46*(12), 36–42.

Pichot, T., & Coulter, M. (2006). *Animal-assisted brief therapy: A solution-focused approach.* New York, NY: Routledge.

Professional Association of Therapeutic Horsemanship International (PATH Intl.). http://www.pathintl.org

Solomon, M. (2010, Fall). Equine therapy: NSU's Graduate School of Humanities and Social Sciences uses horse sense in family therapy. *Horizons Magazine.*

Stable Foundations Equine Assisted Family Therapy. http://www.stablefoundations.net

Trotter, K., Chandler, C., Goodwin, D., & Casey, J. (2008). A comparative study of the efficacy of group equine assisted counseling with at-risk children and adolescents. *Journal of Creativity in Mental Health, 3*(3), 254–284.

64

FAMILY THERAPY AND CORPORATE AMERICA

Jodi Aronson Prohofsky

When I finished my doctoral program, my plan was to storm the academic world and teach the next generation of family therapists. If you asked me then if I would spend the next 20 years of my professional career in corporate America, I would have emphatically answered no. I had no penchant for business, and I was not trained for it—at least that is what I thought.

I enjoyed my family therapy training. I felt like I had come home to a way of thinking and interacting with individuals that empowered them to solve their own problems by changing their frame of references (Keeney, 1982). I defended my dissertation in August and was confirmed in September 1992 and therefore missed the opportunity to obtain an academic appointment for the very next school year. However, the timing proved to be an opportunity I would not fully appreciate for some time.

A friend and former classmate called me one day and told me that his practice was looking for a family therapist. Shortly after starting in the practice, I learned that I was working for an insurance company. Clearly I had not done my homework—I was so glad to have been handed a job and to work with people that I liked personally and respected professionally. However, I was not sure I could work for one of the insurance companies that I had come to believe was killing professional autonomy and that had not truly embraced family therapy as an effective and efficient form of treatment. I am not sure of the day it happened, but one day I challenged my thinking and realized that I could run away from the problem or I could try to be part of the solution. I was now an insider and had the energy to make a difference.

First, I began working to obtain an understanding from all key stakeholders on the definition of the business challenges, or "the problem" (de Shazer, 1982). Then I assessed if the problem was the same for everyone (Watzlawick, Weakland, & Fisch, 1974) and who were my customers for change. Working through the story, finding reframes, helping others define the solutions, and maintaining my maneuverability in order to remove barriers to success were key to achieving the outcomes needed for a successful business model.

I invited providers in my network to manage themselves. We organized trainings, showed them how our computer systems worked, explained why we did what we did, and taught them the economics and business model. This empowered them to fit into the ecosystem in a productive way. It allowed them to be part of the solution. The partnerships got stronger, the clinical outcomes got better, and the member satisfaction was at an all-time high.

I was offered a higher level job in the company and moved to Tampa to run the behavioral operations for Florida, Georgia, Louisiana, Tennessee, Alabama, and Mississippi. I had an extremely talented team who were as eager and passionate as I was to change the system for the better. We worked very hard to make sure that we didn't just take a solution that worked for one market and try to apply it to all. We interviewed key stakeholders in every market and morphed the solution somewhat to meet the needs of the constituency. We introduced a self-managed program for providers and found even more ways to streamline and obtain better clinical outcomes. This even lead to my publishing two books on the subject (Aronson, 1996, 1997).

Now I run the behavioral clinical operations for a large managed care company (initially over 11 million members) and work with all types of employers to help them solve behavioral health problems and manage their benefits. For me, it is a great puzzle—opportunity after opportunity to find the right solution at the right time and continue to help improve the system. Our membership has grown from 11 million to 18 million since I took the job.

Over the following eight years, I have had the opportunity many times over to practice the same skills—those family therapy skills that I am now applying to everyday business. I was able to grow the scope of my own responsibilities and take on leadership for various parts of the business such as medical case management, disease management, lifestyle management programs (i.e., smoking cessations, weight management, and stress management), and medical utilization review, in addition to the behavioral components. Each step of the way, as I built new teams, incorporated different staff talents, and worked to find greater efficiencies and effectiveness, I applied the same skills. I never assumed that things should stay the way they were just because they had always been that way; I always believed that you can expand on people's core talents so that they can take on more and think more systemically. I always believed that I was an agent of change but that I did not have all of the answers toward every solution. I use my family therapy skills every day as I bring people together to search for a common goal/answer and help everyone achieve that goal.

References

Aronson, J. (1996). *Inside managed care: Family therapy in a changing environment.* New York, NY: Routledge.

Aronson, J. (1997). *The dictionary of managed care: A is for access.* New York, NY:.Routledge.

De Shazer, S. (1982). *Patterns of brief family therapy: An ecosystemic approach.* New York, NY: Guilford Press.

Keeney, B. P. (1982). What is an epistemology of family therapy? *Family Process, 21*(2), 153–168.

Watzlawick, P., Weakland, J., & Fisch, R. (1974). *Change: Principles of problem formation and problem resolution.* New York, NY: Norton.

Additional Resource

Bateson, G. (1972). *Steps to an ecology of mind: A revolutionary approach to man's understanding of himself.* Chicago, IL: University of Chicago Press.

65

INTERNATIONAL FAMILY THERAPY

John K. Miller and Margarita Tarragona

> May you live in interesting times.
>
> —Confucius, 350 BC

In John Miller's practice, he travels back and forth between the United States, China, and Cambodia, taking doctoral students with him and participating in training activities in all three countries (Miller & Fang, in press). In Margarita Tarragona's practice, she participates in international family therapy in a different way: she participates in research at the Universidad Iberoamericana having to do with Mexican migrants in the United States and their family members in Mexico. In her therapy practice, she often sees families in which one member is temporarily, or maybe permanently, living in a different country. Both these experiences speak to our shrinking world, in which we are all becoming members of one global community.

Gonzalo Bacigalupe (2011) discusses how information communication technologies (ICTs) are a fundamental feature of life today and have permanently altered the connectedness of international communities. Cheap and accessible means of communication, such as cellular phones, e-mail, Skype, and social media websites, allow people to stay in contact with the families they left behind and maintain those relationships. Such technologies also increase the interest in collaboration worldwide and the ability to collaborate on training and psychotherapy across distances.

Given our increasing interconnectedness, "cultural competence" has become the new catch-word and skill set to learn in the practice of couples and family therapy—or any kind of therapy, for that matter. Cultural competence in this sense demands that we always consider the culture when we intervene with individuals and families. How will our interventions fit with the culture? How will we honor and recognize clients as we address clients from cultures that are different from our own? And how can our knowledge of cultures different from our own enhance and better the work we do with clients from our cultures?

In many situations we have benefitted from collaborative efforts to develop treatments for the families we work with. At times this has involved importing ways of doing and thinking from other countries. This has advantages to both as we do not have a need to reinvent the wheel each time for each culture. There is some transferable knowledge, and we can build upon our mistakes and discoveries. Yet as we progress, it becomes clear that we need to make sure this interaction is a *two-way street,* going both ways. The world will soon enjoy new treatments and therapists that have their roots in their country of origin. Each culture has its own unique perspective and valuable contribution to global understandings in psychotherapy.

It is important to consider also the ongoing blending of cultures. In this regard, we (especially Tarragona) have found the work of Celia Falicov particularly useful. Falicov talks about "transnational families" when she refers to the economic new Latino, Afro-Caribbean, and Asian immigrants who have arrived to the United States since 1965 (Falicov, 2007).[1] Their experience is different from the previous generations of European immigrants because of globalization. Earlier immigrants often practically severed their contact with their countries of origin and their loved ones there, while immigrants today are able to keep their ties with their families, thanks to modern communication technologies. These active family relationships that persist over geographical distance are complex, and they may constitute a virtual family that keeps a sense of identity even if they do not have the redundancy of everyday interactions that generally constitutes the repetitive patterns of family interactions. Falicov (2007) puts it beautifully when she says that in the past, immigrants lived with a broken heart, while today they live with two hearts.

Falicov encourages therapists who work with transnational families to include issues of cultural diversity in their conversations, to honor cultural differences, to have curiosity and respect, to question normative theories, and to find cultural solutions. She also takes a social justice approach in therapy, in which clients may resist oppression in relationships and cultural identities and therapists support clients' accountability and empowerment.

This is echoed in the work of Ignacio Martín-Baró, the social psychologist and scholar who studied in the United States and devoted much of his work to helping the people of Central America. Baró has been a particular inspiration to Miller. Baró insisted that psychology should be developed in relation to the contextual social and historical aspirations and needs of the people it addressed (Aron & Corne, 1996). He advocated that psychology students should view human behavior in the particular contexts where it happened. In his writings and lectures, he rejected the comfortable yet false idea of impartial psychology. Instead, our psychology is greatly influenced by our biases and values, and likewise what we call "normal" and "abnormal" has a great impact on society. As we continue to engage in a more global practice of couples and family therapy, prejudice and bias, or at times simply misunderstandings, are likely to occur. It is the challenge of this next generation to continue to address these issues in a way that promotes healing change, raising awareness, and promoting mutual understanding.

Note

1. Even though Falicov talks primarily about immigrants to the United States, we believe that most of her ideas are applicable to any migration in the world today.

References

Aron, A., & Corne, S. (Eds.). (1996). *Writings for a liberation psychology: Ignacio Martín-Baró*. Cambridge, MA: Harvard University Press.

Bacigalupe, G. (2011). Virtualizing intimacy: Information communication technologies and transnational families in therapy. *Family Process, 50*(1), 12–26.

Falicov, C. J. (2007). Working with transnational immigrants: Expanding meanings of family, community, and culture. *Family Process, 46*, 157–171.

Miller, J. K., & Fang, X. (in press). Marriage and family therapy in the Peoples Republic of China: Current issues and challenges. *Journal of Family Psychotherapy.*

66

FAMILY THERAPY AND COLLABORATIVE FAMILY LAW

Randy J. Heller

As divorce rates continue to rise, there is an increasing focus on minimizing conflict between the husband and wife throughout the process of separation, divorce, and beyond. Research findings suggest children will fare better if divorce is handled in the most amicable way, if the costs are not financially devastating, and if the parents can maintain a positive relationship and develop a viable plan for coparenting. In this way, new and different possibilities can materialize for restructuring the family and moving forward.

In 1990, Minnesota attorney Stuart Webb (2008) coined a term for a process of alternative dispute resolution called collaborative family law (CFL), which consisted of attorneys working with couples in four-way settlement conferences to resolve the dissolution of their marriage in an amicable way without going to court. Almost simultaneously, California attorney Pauline Tesler pioneered this movement in the San Francisco Bay area. Together with Peggy Thompson and her husband, Rod Nurse (both family psychologists), these professionals joined with other attorneys and mental health and financial professionals to develop a movement toward an interdisciplinary practice of CFL. In interdisciplinary CFL, professionals from multiple disciplines work together as a team, sharing their expertise to guide divorcing couples toward peaceful resolution of their issues and the restructuring of their families. To date, thousands of lawyers and mental health and financial professionals have been trained and practice interdisciplinary CFL across the United States, Canada, England, Ireland, Israel, Netherlands, Austria, and Australia.

In interdisciplinary CFL, mental health professionals (MHPs) work in a multitude of roles to support the families as well as the team of professionals. They may work as divorce coaches, whereby they work individually with one member of the couple and then together in joint meetings with the other spouse and his or her coach to develop the communication and problem-solving skills needed to make decisions about issues efficiently and effectively in settlement meetings. The coaches also consult with the team on the best ways to work with these couples. They may also work as child specialists, who work with the children and bring their voice to the parents and the team in these conferences, or neutral facilitators, working with the couple and the team of professionals from the beginning until the end of the process setting the context and promoting respectful, peaceful negotiation and problem solving. The MHP will oftentimes work with the parents, developing a plan for them to share time and coparent their children, and may continue to work with the families beyond settlement as they transition into their lives after the divorce is final. Whichever role they are in, the collaborative mental health professionals are needed to bring their discipline-specific knowledge, skills, and attitudes to the process and integrate them with the knowledge, skills, and attitudes of the other professionals on the team to promote the most effective, efficient means of communicating, interacting, and problem solving between the divorcing spouses (Heller, 2011).

The proponents of interdisciplinary collaborative family law suggest that MHPs who are trained in understanding both the dynamics of relationships and the interactions between multiple systems simultaneously are well equipped to facilitate communications throughout the process (Nurse & Thompson, 2006; Tesler, 2008; Tesler & Thompson, 2006; Webb, 2008). Marriage and family therapists are trained in just this way.

Collaboration Seen Through a Systemic Lens

Ideas of mutual influence, interconnectedness, and relationships are found throughout the family therapy literature. Interdisciplinary collaborative family law and systems theory share the same philosophy. It is based on the ideas of interconnectedness and relationship (Bateson, 1972; Webb, 2008); the notion that the sum of the parts is greater than the whole (Bateson, 1972); and the idea that if we listen to and utilize multiple perspectives, and build on the strengths and the expertise inherent in all the various parts of the team, we can influence each other toward the greater good (Rogers, Szasz, Rollo, & Satir, 1985; Tesler, 2008; Webb, 2008). In the development of this process and through her teaching, Tesler espouses these same ideas (P. Tesler, personal communication, July 2010).

Interdisciplinary collaborative family law is all about envisioning possibilities (de Shazer, 1982; O'Hanlon & Beadle, 1997; Tesler, 2008; Webb, 2008). It combines beliefs about the client as the expert, lack of judgment, and unconditional positive regard (Rogers et al., 1985; Tesler, 2008; Webb, 2008). This process takes into consideration the reciprocal interactions of family members, the significance of multigenerational family patterns, and the implications of triangulating a third party into a dyad to regulate and deflect the anxiety in the system (Kerr & Bowen, 1988, Tesler, 2008; Webb, 2008). It understands the benefits of attending to interactional cycles and helping people creatively find a way to do something different (Tesler, 2008; Watzlawick, Weakland, & Fisch, 1974; Webb, 2008).

Interdisciplinary collaborative family law provides empathy, compassion, and hope while focusing on the present, the future, and the discovery of solutions (de Shazer, 1982; O'Hanlon & Beadle, 1997, Tesler, 2008; Webb, 2008). It attends to the significance of the co-construction of language to discover a more viable reality with the understanding that as problems can be organized through language, they also can be dissolved through language (Anderson & Goolishian, 1988; Gergen, 2009; Monk & Solomon, 2008). Interdisciplinary collaborative family law sets the context for transforming relationships between and among people and their problems (Green & Flemons, 2004; Tesler & Thompson, 2006) by offering different ways for people to think about and manage the challenges they face.

Licensed MFTs must have specialized training to participate in this process. Basic training typically consists of a minimum of two days of didactic and experiential interdisciplinary workshops facilitated by professionals from all three disciplines. Most states are developing and adopting protocols of practice for professionals in this process that identify necessary background and education, training requirements, and practice guidelines for each group of professionals. Local practice and study groups are in place for participants to meet regularly and brainstorm about matters relevant to continued education and professional development. The future of interdisciplinary CFL for MFTs and families is now!

References

Anderson, H., & Goolishian, H. (1988). Human systems as linguistic systems: Preliminary and evolving ideas about the implications for clinical theory. *Family Process, 27*(4), 371–393.

Bateson, G. (1972). *Steps to ecology of mind.* Chicago, IL: University of Chicago Press.

de Shazer, S. (1982). *Patterns of brief family therapy: An ecosystemic approach.* New York, NY: Guilford Press.

Gergen, K. J. (2009). *Relational being beyond self and community.* Oxford, London: Oxford University Press.

Green, S., & Flemons, D. (2007). Just between us: A relational approach to sex therapy. In S. Green & D. Flemons (Eds.), *Quickies: The handbook of brief sex therapy* (pp. 126–150). New York, NY: W. W. Norton.

Heller, R. J. (2011). *Exploring competency and the rule of the mental health professional in interdisciplinary collaborative family law: What do "they" do?* Unpublished doctoral dissertation, Nova Scotia Southeastern University, Fort Lauderdale, FL.

Kerr, M. E., & Bowen, M. (1988). *Family evaluation: An approach based on Bowen theory.* New York, NY: Norton.

Monk, G., & Solomon, L. (2008). *Proceedings from the IACP Forum 2008: What language do you speak? Strengthening the lawyer–mental health professional relationship.* New Orleans, LA: International Academy of Collaborative Professionals.

Nurse, R., & Thompson, P. (2006). Educating family psychologists: Toward competent practice. *Family Psychologist, 22*(3), 26–27.

O'Hanlon, B., & Beadle, S. (1997). *A guide to possibility land: Fifty-one methods for doing brief respectful therapy.* New York, NY: W. W. Norton.

Rogers, C., Szasz, T., Rollo, M., & Satir, V. (1985). *The evolution of psychotherapy.* Presented as part of the proceedings of the Evolution of Psychotherapy Conference, Phoenix, AZ, December, 13, 1985.

Tesler, P. (2008). Collaborative family law: The new lawyer and deep resolution of divorce related conflicts. *Journal of Dispute Resolution, 2008,* 83–130.

Tesler, P., & Thompson, P. (2006). *Collaborative divorce: The revolutionary new way to restructure your family, resolve legal issues, and move on with your life.* New York, NY: Regan Books.

Watzlawick, P., Weakland, J. H., & Fisch, R. (1974). *Change: Principles of problem formation and problem resolution.* New York, NY: Norton.

Webb, S. (2008). Collaborative law: A practitioner's perspective on its history and current practice. *American Academy of Matrimonial Law, 21,* 155–169.

Additional Resources

International Academy of Collaborative Professionals. http://www.collaborative practice.com

Lawson, D. M., & Prevatt, F. F. (1999). *Casebook in family therapy.* Belmont, TN: Wadsworth Publishing Company.

Tesler, P. (2009). Goodbye homo economics: Cognitive dissonance, brain science, and highly effective collaborative practice. *Hofstra Law Review, 38*(2), 635–685.

Webb, S., & Ousky, R. (2006). *The collaborative way to divorce: The revolutionary method that results in less stress, lower costs, and happier kids—without going to court.* New York, NY: Hudson Street Press.

INDEX

Made in United States
Orlando, FL
05 January 2023

28154012R00173